For Bernadette,
who spent countless hours making this better

Acknowledgements

For many of the people involved in it, the story of what really happened at Stratford during its crisis is an extremely painful subject. But I found that almost all the people I needed to talk to were surprisingly open and generous about sharing their memories and records with me. Without their co-operation, this book obviously would not have been written.

I am grateful, too, to *Saturday Night,* which got me into this project by inviting me to write a magazine article about the Stratford controversy. The article, which appeared in the June, 1981, issue of the magazine, led directly to the book.

The book was written with the generous assistance of an Ontario Arts Council grant and a Canada Council Explorations grant.

Among those who read pieces of the manuscript and offered valuable suggestions are Robert Fulford, Phyllis Grosskurth, James Lorimer, Barbara Moon, Christina Newman, Gary Ross, and Richard Sutin.

Martin Lynch, the editor's editor, read page proofs and saved me from countless gaffes and stylistic offences.

Constance Craig prepared the index.

Contents

In this world the worst part is—everyone has his reasons.

Jean Renoir, *The Rules of the Game*

CHAPTER ONE

Once More
unto the Breach

Right from the start the story of the Stratford Festival had been at least partly a gleeful farce about a group of rustics, not unlike those in *A Midsummer Night's Dream,* who had stumbled onto something big. It was part of the comedy that Tom Patterson, the man who inspired Canada's most prestigious cultural institution, had seen only one professional play in his life and was less interested in the aesthetics of Elizabethan theatre than in finding economic salvation for a town that was losing its chief industry – a repair centre for railway steam engines. When Patterson sought out Tyrone Guthrie to head the Festival, it was part of the comedy that he didn't really know who Guthrie was until he went to the library and checked *Who's Who in the Theatre.*

When Guthrie agreed, on God knows what wild impulse, to come to this sleepy southwestern Ontario town, with its patina of imitation-English reserve, he became another player in the long tragicomedy of Canadian colonization. It was a story ingrained in our history, enshrined in our school system. Canadians may have been tuned in to American mass culture, but when it came to the official high culture, the British models went unchallenged. As a matter of course, British adjudicators were brought to Canada annually for decades to judge our child musicians and our amateur theatre groups. Guthrie became the latest cultural overlord in a long line that stretched all the way from Lord Durham to John Grierson, founder of the National Film Board, and Peter Dwyer, architect of the Canada Council. (Guthrie was Irish, and a bit of an outsider in England. That was also true of Grierson, a Scot. But Canadians perceived both of them as part of British cultural authority.) This saga was perfectly satirized by the hilarious interlude

7

in *The Apprenticeship of Duddy Kravitz* about the fraud from England who, posing as a great artist of the cinema, is hired by Duddy to film affluent bar mitzvahs.

Guthrie was no poseur; he was the man who would be king. After a scouting trip, he announced he would return the next year. In 1953, he came back with Alec Guinness and Tanya Moiseiwitsch, the designer, to present *Richard III* and *All's Well That Ends Well* in a tent supplied by a man from Chicago whose regular clients included circuses and evangelists. The raising of the tent became a symbolic gesture, prayed for and doubted, and there were dark days when the money seemed to have run out and the dream to have been smashed. The bold open stage, designed by Moiseiwitsch, jutting out into the audience like an Elizabethan stage, made its own promise, and on the first night in the tent, the audience sensed that Canada had made a great breakthrough, and refused to stop cheering. Backstage, Guthrie told his actors, "We got away with it." He was gone within a couple of years, having persuaded a protégé, Michael Langham, to take over.

In 1957 the Festival Theatre, built by a Stratford contractor who became a fixture on the Festival Board, replaced the tent. The first theatre in four centuries built in the style of an Elizabethan playhouse, with the stage spilling right out into the audience, it had a revolutionary impact.

Langham stayed twelve years – too long, some said – surviving a shaky period in the late 1950s to emerge as the widely hailed master of classical productions on an open stage. Then, for the first time in its history, Canadians were given artistic control. After Langham's departure in 1967, there were two uneasy seasons when Jean Gascon and John Hirsch (Langham's two lieutenants) held the reins jointly, with William Wylie as the administrative strong man in the triumvirate. Hirsch withdrew, under something of a cloud, in 1969, and Wylie died unexpectedly in 1972, leaving Gascon to rule alone.

By the next year, it was clearly time for him to leave, and there was no heir apparent. The chairman of the Stratford Board's search committee was Donald McGeachy, a former Board president, and other members of the search committee were Russell Payton, John Killer, Professor Berners Jackson, Dr. Ian Lindsay, and Barbara Ivey. The committee knew there was a strong case for choosing a Canadian, but they couldn't agree on a candidate. They sought advice from Jean Roberts, then in charge of English-language theatre at the National Arts Centre, but after going through the list of twenty-nine names she provided, they ruled them all out.

It wasn't easy finding Canadians who had experience with a theatrical organization as large as Stratford, or even close, because in Canada Stratford was one of a kind. Being successful as the artistic director of a fringe theatre in Toronto or a regional theatre in Saskatchewan didn't give you the experience needed to run Stratford. The job demanded someone steeped in the classical repertory tradition and experienced with a thrust stage. There was no obvious way for a Canadian to acquire the right kind of training without leaving Canada.

Among the Canadians who were approached were William Hutt, a veteran member of the Festival's acting company, and Michael Bawtree, who had been literary manager and had directed a couple of productions. Bawtree wavered, and in the end the job wasn't offered to him. Hutt was only temporarily disappointed about being passed over. The search committee also approached two Canadian theatrical figures well established in New York—Robert Whitehead, the producer, and Hume Cronyn, the actor-entre-preneur—but neither was interested. Cronyn suggested a few candidates in the United States, but the search committee wasn't seriously interested in any of them.

There was one conspicuously obvious candidate they had decided not to approach: John Hirsch. Here was a vigorous, talented Canadian director who had an international reputation and who had worked at Stratford. But there were Board members and members of the search committee who still had rueful memories of Hirsch's bitter departure from Stratford in 1969, after his two-year stay as a partner of Gascon. It wasn't just that Hirsch and Gascon had quarrelled. It wasn't just that Stratford's winter season at the National Arts Centre (which was Hirsch's baby) had died of inadequate funding. It wasn't even just that Hirsch's show The Satyricon had gone way over budget and scandalized the town with its exuberant bad taste. The real sore point was that Hirsch had been openly critical of the Stratford Board, regarding it as an impediment that came between him and the creative process. Four years later there were still Board members who felt sure Hirsch could never be happy saddled with a huge bureaucracy like Stratford's.

And so once again Stratford looked to England for its artistic director. Almost from the day Tom Patterson made his pitch for a summer Shakespeare festival to the Stratford City Council in 1952, there had developed a tradition of searching for the tyrannical genius from England who could make something magical happen. This became known, in Hirsch's sarcastic phrase, as the "send for the colonial governor" syndrome. The Stratford Board was dominated by people who understood that the artistic director of Stratford must be a first-class figure, and who usually assumed that "first-class" and "British" were synonymous. This had been the thinking at Stratford all along – when Tom Patterson tried to get in touch with Laurence Olivier, when Tyrone Guthrie was brought straight from the Old Vic to launch an unlikely summer Shakespeare festival in a tent beside a river in a small Canadian town, when Michael Langham was persuaded to succeed his mentor.

Like many other towns and cities in Ontario, Stratford had always been a kind of provincial outpost of British society, and its white Anglo-Saxon Protestant population had never been challenged by the waves of immigrants who transformed Toronto after World War II. In Patterson's mind, one of the main reasons for Stratford's economic malaise was the strike of 1934, in which Communists organized, among others, chicken pluckers, and the government called in the troops. Some people, including Patterson, thought that this bizarre chapter of Canadian labour history gave Stratford a black eye and scared off potential industry. (The Stratford Festival wasn't the only scheme dreamed up to save the town; another plan was to start an international hockey school, since Stratford had contributed Howie Morenz, "the Stratford Streak," to the National Hockey League.) But the strike, if anything, made the townspeople more conservative than ever. In Stratford, a radical was someone who thought it might not be absolutely necessary to have the Lord's Prayer recited daily in the schools, or who thought it might be all right for people to be allowed to drink wine in restaurants. The town clung to its rustic innocence, even in the midst of a Festival that was earning an international reputation.

In the beginning, the Stratford Board was a group of highly dedicated local people who had to their credit the stupendous feat of getting a major institution launched against overwhelming odds. Indeed, they were almost too successful for their own good. The Stratford Festival captured the imagination of the entire country and became a model of excellence for Canadian culture. Inevitably there was going to be friction between those who saw it as a local event that must never lose sight of its original purpose – to create a new life for the town of Stratford – and those who believed that it must be nothing less than Canada's national theatre. As the Festival grew, the Board had to expand to include people from Toronto and Montreal with links to the corporate establishment so crucial to major funding in the arts. This created a city-mouse, country-mouse dichotomy within the Board; no matter how harmonious the proceedings appeared to be, people were always counting heads and keeping score.

In every arts organization there is always a natural tension between the board and the professional artists, but at Stratford this was complicated by additional layers of rivalry – between the town and the worldly city ready to gobble up the town's proudest creation, between the theatre itself and the other arts. In Toronto, every arts board had a designated place in the society, and there wasn't really a theatre board that counted in establishment society the way the National Ballet Board or the Toronto Symphony Board or the Art Gallery of Ontario Board counted. For the most part, the culture of Upper Canada was created by prosperous WASPs, and for the most part the theatre didn't have the same respectability as opera, ballet, and the visual arts. The Stratford Festival emerged as something of a freak, and it filled a conspicuous vacuum.

It was Ronald Bryden who in 1973 brought the name of Robin Phillips to the attention of the Stratford search committee. Bryden, who was then the literary manager for the Royal Shakespeare Company, would soon be leaving England (after twenty years) to return to Canada to become a drama professor at the University of Toronto. Born in the West Indies, Bryden had lived in Toronto as a boy and attended school there; then he had gone to England as a scholarship student at Cambridge. He had stayed on in England through the 1950s and 1960s, eventually inheriting Kenneth Tynan's old job as drama critic of the *Observer*. (His immediate predecessor was Penelope Gilliatt.) The *Observer* job, which he held from 1966 to 1971, made Bryden an important figure in the London theatre, and just as the National Theatre had plucked Tynan to be its literary manager, so in 1971 Trevor Nunn of the Royal Shakespeare Company landed Bryden as his literary manager.

The early 1970s were glorious days for the two big repertory companies of Britain, and with generous public subsidies, the

11

National and the RSC kept a spectacular competition going. New work was one of the keys to prestige and the public's loyalty, and among the plays Bryden discovered, or rediscovered, for the RSC were *Sherlock Holmes, Travesties,* and *Wild Oats.* In 1967 Bryden had begun coming back to Canada each July for an annual Stratford seminar organized by Berners Jackson, a McMaster University English professor. During the winter of 1972–73, Jackson, who had by then become a member of the Stratford Board, called Bryden to ask him to provide lists and assessments of possible successors to Jean Gascon.

Bryden flew in from London and spent three days with the search committee in January, 1973. Bryden told them it would be marvellous if they could get John Barton or one of the other famous English directors, but then provided a list of people they would be more likely to be able to get. Besides Phillips, the British names on the list included David Jones (an associate artist of the Royal Shakespeare Company) and David William, who was eliminated because of his disastrous production of *Othello* during Stratford's 1973 season. One who was actually offered the job and turned it down was Michael Blakemore, the Australian director, who had been working regularly at the National during the Olivier era (though he was about to be squeezed out by the Peter Hall regime). Blakemore said he might like to be asked again later.

* * *

Robin Phillips was ready when the call came from Canada in the summer of 1973. At the age of 31, he was starting to outgrow his role as the boy genius of the English theatre, and there were signs that he would never be a member of the club. There had already been rows with the theatre establishment: on the eve of his opening at Stratford-upon-Avon, his production of *The Two Gentlemen of Verona* had almost been cancelled, and in 1972, to the surprise of many, Phillips had been passed over for the post of artistic director at Chichester, the thrust-stage theatre (its design much influenced by Stratford, Canada) where he had scored some of his early triumphs. Phillips had just spent a year at a converted music-hall theatre in Greenwich, on the outskirts of London, and had formed his own company there, but his future in England was murky, and he had been telling friends that he wanted his own theatre and would even be willing to go to Australia or Canada to get it.

Robin Phillips wasn't quite like anybody else in the British theatre. His background was working class and country boy, and he was never perceived as part of the revolution that swept the drawing-room aristocrats off the London stage, replacing them with rude upstarts like John Osborne's raging hero, Jimmy Porter, in *Look Back in Anger*. He wasn't defiantly punkish like John Dexter, and he didn't see the world in the same terms as Peter Hall and Trevor Nunn, whose fathers were both stationmasters in East Anglia. Robin Phillips was immaculately presented; his speech and dress suggested a character from a Noel Coward play. Who would have guessed that his father was a gardener and his mother a housekeeper? They lived in Sussex, looking after a house owned by Stewart Granger, the English film star. They managed the estate and lived in a lodge house on the grounds. When the Granger marriage broke up, another family came to live in the house, but the Phillips family stayed on.

At Midhurst Grammar School, Robin appeared in a production of Shaw's *Androcles and the Lion*. There was a time in his life when he thought he wanted to become a minister, and an element of zeal became a part of his personality. He was destined to find his true congregation in the theatre rather than the church. No matter how far he strayed from the clerical path, there would always be a trace in Robin Phillips of the fresh-faced, impeccably groomed choirboy.

Robin was no scholar, and he left school as soon as the law allowed. Just after his fifteenth birthday, he went to work at Nathan's, the London theatre costume supply house. (He hid among the costumes to spy on Marilyn Monroe when she came to Nathan's to be outfitted for her London-made movie *The Prince and the Showgirl*.) By pretending to be older than he was, he got into the Bristol Old Vic School, where he became a backstage trainee with a special interest in wigs.

He was one of only two students from the school who won places with the Bristol Old Vic company, and it was there that his reputation as a boy wonder began. He was determined to learn everything about the theatre, which is why throughout his career he has been able to astonish colleagues with his knack for everything from fixing bad costumes to polishing tables. It was at Bristol that he met Daphne Dare, the designer, beginning a long, creative partnership. In his second year with the company, Phillips was made associate director, but for the next few years he was to make his mark as an actor rather than as a director.

Robin Phillips made his acting debut at Bristol in June, 1959, playing Mr. Puff in *The Critic*. He also appeared in *Romeo and Juliet* (as Romeo), *The Seagull* (as Konstantin), and *A Taste of Honey*. Under the direction of John Dexter, he appeared in *South* at the Lyric Hammersmith in 1961, then landed in Laurence Olivier's company for the first season at Chichester in the summer of 1962. Joan Plowright, one of the senior members of the original company (which also included Michael Redgrave and John Neville), remembers Phillips as an extraordinary young creature – an Oscar Wilde figure with gorgeous curls – who once came to her dressing-room to present her with an exquisite ivory miniature he had carved in the likeness of the character she was playing.

As a performer, Robin Phillips had a peculiar *ingénu* quality. Strikingly delicate, he was good-looking in a way that went beyond convention. He was boyishly beautiful and vulnerable – a Byronic urchin figure. That's why he nabbed the leading role in the 1968 movie based on Evelyn Waugh's *Decline and Fall* from another actor who was confident of getting it; that's why Ted Kotcheff cast him in one of the title roles in *Two Gentlemen Sharing;* and that's why he was chosen to play the title role in the 1970 all-star film version of *David Copperfield*.

Phillips continued to work as an actor even after establishing himself as a director, but he knew that sooner or later he would have to make a choice, and that he would opt for directing. After all, he couldn't be an *ingénu* for ever, and he knew he didn't have the vocal power to be a great actor. As a young performer sneaking into directing, he first worked with the Royal Shakespeare Company as an assistant to John Schlesinger on *Timon of Athens* and Peter Hall on *Hamlet,* then became, for a short time, associate director of the Northcott Theatre at Exeter. His breakthrough hits were Albee's *Tiny Alice*, with David Warner and Irene Worth, at the Aldwych and a West End production of *Abelard and Heloise,* starring Diana Rigg, which was popular enough to earn an American tour. Phillips had developed a reputation for stylishness; he was fond of black-and-white sets on gleaming linoleum.

Some young actors said he was the best director they had ever worked with, but he was intensely disliked by those who considered his style smart in a shallow way. It was this tendency that got him into trouble at Stratford-upon-Avon in 1970. His ideas were too outrageous for the powers that be; he wasn't merely breaking with tradition, he was offending purists. Late one night, overworked and exhausted, he told his friend Zoe Dominic, the photographer, that he was going to a show-down meeting. She told him, "There's no way you can win any sort of argument in the state you're in tonight." Phillips replied, "You don't know what nervous resources I have." Sure enough, he did win his point. The production not only opened but was a great success, and transferred at the end of the year to the Aldwych, the London home of the RSC.

Returning to Chichester in 1971, Phillips directed a controversial production of Shaw's *Caesar and Cleopatra* which featured hula hoops, bouncing balls, and John Gielgud making his entrance on a slide. His production of *Dear Antoine* starred Edith Evans, and he had another big critical success with an RSC production of *Miss Julie,* which was later filmed. In his last season at Chichester, in 1972, Phillips directed *The Beggar's Opera* (John Neville played Macheath) and acted in *The Doctor's Dilemma.* Phillips was considered a hot candidate to succeed Sir John Clements as artistic director at Chichester, but the board chose Keith Michell.

It was at this point that Phillips went to Greenwich to form an unlikely partnership with Ewan Hooper, a man who was as austere and reserved as Phillips was flamboyant and dynamic. Hooper had been thinking of forming a company to fill the theatre at Greenwich, which was operated under the authority of the local council, and Phillips was just the man to lead a company. Calling his new troupe the Company Theatre, Phillips startled everybody by drawing a number of big names to this small local theatre operating on a shoe-string. Among those who agreed to work at Greenwich for next to nothing were Mia Farrow and Joan Plowright. The night before his first show opened, Phillips and Daphne Dare, who was brought in to do the design, stayed up most of the night scrubbing the ladies' loo. But there were continuing conflicts between the Phillips troupe and the staff of Hooper's theatre. At one point when the tension reached a fever pitch, Plowright and her husband, Laurence Olivier, turned over their London flat as neutral ground for a summit meeting.

The loss of the top job at Chichester had been a serious blow to Phillips' ambition, and Greenwich wasn't the right spot for him. Like Guthrie at the moment that Tom Patterson called from Dora Mavor Moore's house in Toronto in 1952, Robin Phillips was in a mood to take a big gamble. No wonder the Stratford people were drawn to him. Phillips was a hot property, he was high-powered, and he was available. He was no intellectual, but he was a smart operator, with fantastic energy and ambition, and a dazzling understanding of every practical aspect of theatre. Bryden regarded him as someone to bet on, and told the search committee, "Don't expect another Michael Langham. He has more in common with Noel Coward. He doesn't have the depth of Langham; on the other hand, he does have the flair of Peter Brook."

Phillips was not immediately offered the job in Canada. He was asked to pay a flying visit, look the place over, and give the Board his assessment. The first time he stepped into the famous auditorium, he was overwhelmed by the excitement of the space. Maybe the theatre was built slightly larger than it should have been, and maybe the 220-degree arc was too extreme, but the Festival Theatre is still sensational. Because of his Chichester work, Phillips knew something about the challenges and dangers of a thrust stage: to work successfully on this kind of stage, a director has to throw out the rules and habits learned on conventional proscenium-arch stages. Everyone in the audience sees the play from a different angle, and the actors have to keep moving so that no one speech gets directed to one part of the audience to the exclusion of everyone else. The moment Berners Jackson opened the door for him, Phillips exclaimed, "Wow."

The first production Phillips saw was *She Stoops to Conquer*, and when he was asked for his view of it, he gave a precise answer, putting his finger on just what was wrong and explaining how it could be fixed. But when Russell Payton asked, "What do you see as your place here?" Phillips shocked everyone on the committee by replying, "I don't." He saw Stratford as a nice secure tourist attraction, and he said there was no need to bring in someone who would want to revolutionize it. Phillips said he wanted to go somewhere only if there was a specific need for him.

That remark only made the Stratford search committee more eager to get him. They wanted a fresh start and felt it was imperative to find someone who could not only work confidently on the open stage at the Festival Theatre but also find a separate identity for the Avon Theatre. The Avon had been redesigned at great cost in 1968, but the light operas that were originally planned for it had been scrapped, and Gascon's experiments with avant-garde European plays like *The Architect and the Emperor* had been disastrous at the box office. After Phillips made his provocative remark, Barbara Ivey took off like a rocket. She gave a long, impassioned reply to Phillips, explaining that Stratford did need to change, that the Board wanted to find new excitement and new directions, that the place mustn't turn into a museum, that Stratford needed someone exactly like Robin Phillips. She said the place was in a rut; it was too old-line. It needed new blood, the kind of things that Phillips could do.

From that moment on, there was an immediate rapport between Phillips and Mrs. Ivey. This was the beginning of a special alliance. Barbara Ivey had married into one of the wealthiest, most prominent families in London, Ontario, and she was one of the few women on the Board. She could pride herself on having a greater understanding of the arts than some of her colleagues on the Board – local businessmen who got involved in the theatre because it was a prestigious form of community service, like volunteer work for the Kiwanis Club or the YMCA. Phillips may have been wary of the Stratford Board, but he could see that Barbara Ivey was different – a Medici patron in the colonial wilderness. Phillips took to Mrs. Ivey instantly, recognizing an ally who would be invaluable if he were to take Stratford on.

It took a couple of months before the search committee got back to Phillips and offered him the job. Once more he came to Stratford, this time with Joseph Mandel, his long-time friend, and James Sharkey, his agent. They went to see a very bad production of *Othello,* and Sharkey was so discouraged he wanted to get on the next plane to London, but Phillips could see exactly what was wrong and what should be done about it. Phillips waited in another office at the Festival Theatre while Sharkey and Mandel tried to hammer out a contract with the Board in the VIP room. After some haggling, Sharkey went upstairs to discuss the problem with Phillips. When he came down, Sharkey said, "Robin wants the job" – and that was the end of the haggling.

CHAPTER TWO

The Rebels

Within the Canadian theatre community, reaction to the news of Robin Phillips' appointment was predominantly hostile, and this brought into focus something that should have been obvious all along: the Stratford Festival was, to a spectacular degree, out of touch with what was happening in Canada. The mood everywhere was bullish, reflecting a new self-confidence. In the arts especially there was a great deal of national muscle flexing going on. The Stratford Festival was located in a quiet, conservative town. Stratford's vision of Canada and its place in the world had hardly budged since 1953. But the rest of the country was now marching to a very different drummer. *My Fur Lady,* the 1957 McGill college revue, had given the final satiric kiss-off to the image of the Canadian as a bland, nice, indecisive simpleton.

That same year the government, finally acting on the recommendations of the 1951 Massey Report on the state of the arts in Canada, had set up the Canada Council, which offered a new deal to writers, artists, and performers. The Council demonstrated that it really was possible to nurture, through government subsidy, a genuine Canadian culture. In the 1960s, English-speaking Canada was throwing off the yoke of both British and American influence at almost exactly the time that Quebec was declaring its own distinctiveness. Canada's ties with Britain had become weaker as the Empire turned into the Commonwealth and the Commonwealth threatened to blow away. And the notion of English Canada as just a fringe area of the friendly American giant received decisive blows from Walter Gordon's brand of economic nationalism – which established the imperative of buying the country back from the Americans – and from the Vietnam war – which dramatically defined an American destiny that Canada wanted no part of, and which enlivened Canada by sending an energetic contingent of draft dodgers, the Huck Finns of their age, north of the border for sanctuary. This was the climate in which Canadian universities suddenly found themselves under pressure to stop hiring American Ph.D.s and start hiring Canadians, and the Canadian Radio-Television Commission began ordering TV stations to limit their imported programs, and shoe-string theatre companies with radical ideas started taking root in abandoned church basements. It was a heady era, capped by that great extravaganza of national celebration, Expo 67. Canadians were no longer willing to wander through the world apologizing for their inadequacy.

But at Stratford the colonial charade had gone on and on, with empty, rhetorical productions aspiring to some English or European standard, the point of which had long since vanished. And now the Board of Governors, cut off from the juices flowing through the universities and the arts communities, was showing its indifference to the new Canadian sensibility by going to England to find a new artistic director – as if nothing had changed since 1953. The recruitment of Robin Phillips was the latest chapter in a long, ongoing story, and the storm that lay ahead was a confrontation between those who were content to let this story go on repeating itself and those who were enraged by it and determined to put an end to it.

Few people felt more strongly about this issue than John Hirsch, who had been carrying on a love-hate relationship with Stratford almost from the moment he first went there in 1965. When Hirsch was brought to Stratford by Michael Langham, he was already the established boy wonder of Canadian theatre. He had come to Winnipeg from Hungary as a scrawny teen-age war refugee, speaking no English. Within a decade of his arrival, he had created a professional theatre with his own stamp which would stand as a model for regional theatres all over the continent.

The theatre was in John Hirsch's blood. One of his ancestors travelled around Europe with five actors in a cart, performing German plays. Hirsch's mother was not only interested in theatre but spoke five languages and played the piano. Her family were assimilated Jews who lived in Budapest, having moved there from Vienna. They made their money in liquor factories. Hirsch's father had a country family in the grain business. One of Hirsch's relatives was a composer of operettas, and he began attending musical comedies when he was very young. When John Hirsch was three, a friend of Hirsch's mother brought Nijinsky and his wife to the Hirsch house, and John danced to the music of "Who's Afraid of the Big Bad Wolf?" while Nijinsky watched. Years later Hirsch remembered Nijinsky as a bald, fat man, totally immobile, wearing a long black coat and a hat in mid-July.

In 1944 the Germans took over their wartime ally Hungary, and what Hirsch's parents had said could never happen in Hungary did happen. His parents were taken to Auschwitz. His eight-year-old brother died in the gas ovens. His mother died at Auschwitz. His father was shot in an Austrian labour camp just before it was liberated by the Russians in 1945. John Hirsch, then fourteen years old, was saved from the Nazis by a maid who took him to the Budapest ghetto. At the end of the war he wandered around Europe alone for a year and half. He wound up in Paris, making the rounds from soup kitchen to soup kitchen and consulate to consulate. He was too young to emigrate to Brazil. The United States rejected him as underweight. But the Canadian Embassy took his blood three times within a week and judged it good.

The Canadian Jewish Congress brought him to Winnipeg in 1947 and placed him in the North End with a working-class family named Shack. His new father was an inspector for the Manitoba Hydro system. His new mother was a proud socialist who in 1919 had carried her own soap-box and spoken in front of City Hall to the rebels in the Winnipeg Strike. Hirsch saw in her "Tolstoy without the beard" and loved her for her contradictions. Pauline Shack was an agnostic who kept a kosher kitchen, a vegetarian famous for her stuffed chicken, and a pioneer socialist who turned against the New Democrats when they got elected, on the grounds that nobody could be trusted with power. Sybil Shack, his new sister, was a teacher and later a principal. Hirsch started out doing odd jobs; he was an office boy and then a gardener. But Sybil arranged for some tests at the University of Manitoba, and the man who did the testing called her to say, "Sybil, you have a genius on your hands." So Hirsch went back to school, graduating in 1952 with the highest marks given in English by the university that year. Among the people he met there was James Reaney, who arrived from Stratford and carried around with him the plays and poems he was writing.

Television hadn't come to Winnipeg, and air travel was still considered exotic. The isolation as well as the cold and the flatness made Winnipeg seem special. The young intelligentsia would gather at Child's restaurant, where they talked about T.S. Eliot, the Bloomsbury Group, the Old Vic, and their plans to escape from Winnipeg and move to London. John Hirsch didn't want to move. He loved the space and the peace. And he had a fierce need to put down roots.

Hirsch had always wanted to be in the theatre, but now he lived in a city where there was no professional theatre activity. Four times a year, the amateur Little Theatre put on a play—often something by Shaw, Priestley, or Coward—for two nights. Hirsch managed to persuade a group of prosperous women to give him and a few colleagues three hundred dollars to start a puppet theatre, and out of that grew the Touring Children's Theatre, sponsored by the Winnipeg Junior League. When the CBC opened a Winnipeg station, Hirsch became a TV producer. He spent a winter in England observing acting classes at London's Central School of Drama. Next came Rainbow Stage, an outdoor musical theatre in Kildonan Park. The city had built a bandshell with the intention of using it for ethnic folk performances, but the venture died. In its place, James Duncan launched an open-air musical theatre in 1955. Duncan hired Hirsch to direct shows in 1956, and by 1957, Hirsch was functioning as artistic director. Finally Hirsch was ready to start a full-fledged professional theatre. In 1957 Hirsch and Tom Hendry founded Theatre Seventy-Seven in a run-down movie house seventy-seven steps from Portage and Main. The next year Theatre Seventy-Seven merged with the Little Theatre to form the Manitoba Theatre Centre. Among those who helped get it going were Tyrone Guthrie, who arrived from Stratford to lend support, and Peter Dwyer, the head of the new Canada Council, who came through with some crucial funding.

Hirsch was by this time known for his temper. Tempestuous and difficult to get along with, he was also a source of creative energy, whipping up excitement wherever he went. Under his leadership, the Theatre Centre became one of Winnipeg's most dynamic cultural institutions, as important a part of community life as the fortunes of the Blue Bombers football team or the biggest snowfall of the winter. People went to see whatever was playing there, whether it was *The Hostage* or *The Boyfriend* or *Mother Courage* or *Lulu Street,* a play about the 1919 General Strike by Winnipeg's own Ann Henry.

Hirsch was so successful that Winnipeg had become too comfortable by the mid-1960s. He had the soul of a gipsy, and it was time to move on. He needed to test himself in the larger world. He went to Stratford at Langham's invitation, directing *The Cherry Orchard* on the Festival stage in 1965. That was followed by *Henry VI* in 1966 and two productions in 1967 – an unorthodox *Richard III* with Alan Bates and one of Stratford's rare original Canadian plays, Reaney's *Colours in the Dark.* In 1968, the year Gascon and Hirsch took over from Langham, Hirsch directed *A Midsummer Night's Dream* and *The Three Musketeers.* In 1969, his last year, Hirsch directed *Hamlet* and the notorious *Satyricon.*

"I never felt at home in Stratford," Hirsch wrote in a memoir a decade later, "partly because it was not like Winnipeg. For me, Canada still means Winnipeg. I felt like a stranger in Stratford." In Winnipeg, Hirsch had responded to the eclectic ethnic mishmash of the celebrated North End. In Stratford he felt hemmed in. Everybody in town seemed to be a reserved middle-class WASP. And those who weren't, including Americans and Jews, seemed to feel pressured to behave like imitation Englishmen. Hirsch missed the eccentric characters, the diversity, the invigorating craziness of Winnipeg. The WASP establishment of Winnipeg had somehow been more welcoming to an outsider, maybe because in western Canada not even the establishment had been there more than a few generations, and no one felt firmly entrenched. It seemed more natural to find an influential Jew on an arts board in Winnipeg than it did in the East. In Stratford, Hirsch felt that his Jewishness and his European temperament made him a freak. And he was torn: Guthrie and Langham were his mentors, yet in some sense they represented the British colonial yoke he was so eager to throw off. Nathan Cohen, the legendary *Toronto Star* drama critic, was intensely scornful of Stratford, which he regarded as a disastrous blow to his own dream of a genuine Canadian dramatic flowering. Cohen had lauded Hirsch's work in Winnipeg, but he deplored Hirsch's move to Stratford. On one occasion, Cohen took Hirsch aside and said he was going to make it his business to get Hirsch out of Stratford. "But why, Nathan?" Hirsch asked. "Because," thundered Cohen, "it's so goyish."

Hirsch decided that he would have to leave Canada and go to New York to make a name for himself. He worked at Lincoln Center for several years, directing *Yerma, Galileo, Saint Joan, The Time of Your Life, Beggar on Horseback, The Playboy of the Western World,* and *Antigone.* During his New York period he also directed the Broadway production of *We Bombed in New Haven* and won an Obie for his production of *AC/DC* at the Chelsea Theater Center in Brooklyn.

By 1973, Hirsch was ready to come back to Canada, and he found it insulting that the Stratford search committee didn't even call him. Not that he was out of work: the CBC was asking him to take on a huge job as head of television drama, which Hirsch had decided to accept, starting in mid-1974. And he was deeply involved in a theatre project with which he felt an extraordinary personal connection – a production of the Yiddish classic *The Dybbuk,* newly adapted by Hirsch, which opened at the Manitoba Theatre Centre early in 1974 and was so successful that Hirsch was invited to restage it for the St. Lawrence Centre in Toronto and the Mark Taper Forum in Los Angeles. The theme of the play is possession (a young bride's body is possessed by the soul of a dead boy who feels she was rightfully his). *The Dybbuk* is a parable about cosmic justice and order, about the pact the living have with the dead. Hirsch took this suggestive material, steeped in Jewish mysticism, and fashioned something of surpassing power and richness out of it. Scene after scene was infused with mythic and ritualistic intensity, creating a kind of spell. Watching it, one could feel that John Hirsch had poured his entire life into this one production, finding the links between religion and theatre, between the old world and the new. *The Dybbuk* was his tribute to the vanished world that propelled him, and it was a beautiful embrace.

Hirsch was, by 1973, regarded in the Canadian theatre community as something of an elder statesman, and it was as part of a group that he expressed his anger at Stratford's decision to bring in a new artistic director from England. When the Stratford Festival announced the Phillips appointment, a group of Canadian theatre directors cast themselves in the role of rebels in a Shakespeare history epic. They wrote to the Board of Governors, expressing their dismay and asking for a formal meeting. When that meeting was held, on a Sunday afternoon in April, 1974, in the Toronto offices of the Ontario Arts Council, the directors presented their manifesto, first to the Board and then to the press. They had asked Robertson Davies to draft it for them, because they knew that Davies was not only a Guthrie disciple, the author of a book about Stratford, a former Board member, and an unimpeachably respectable cultural authority, but also a Canadian cultural nationalist who felt Stratford had gone astray. Davies toned down the brief and tried to make it more diplomatic; he told the directors that it wouldn't get them anywhere to say, in effect, that they had a right to run Stratford just because they lived in Canada. Here is what they said instead:

We have asked for this meeting because of our concern for the future of the theatre in Canada, and our conviction that the Stratford Festival must play a dominant role in that future. In the broadest terms, we ask what your long-range plan is for the Festival, and what steps you hope to take to integrate it with Canadian theatre.

When Stratford was founded it began a new era in Canadian theatre, and we have benefitted from its enterprise and courage. Now, it appears that the theatre we represent is taking one direction, and Stratford another. During the past twenty-five years theatre in Canada has advanced in a direction that Stratford does not reflect. Canadian theatre is now working consistently to present world theatre in Canadian terms, to reveal a truly Canadian sensibility, and to advance, under the best circumstances at its command, Canadian plays, and the work of theatre artists in every field. The time has come when we have a right to expect leadership from your theatre, which is the national theatre of our country whether it accepts that title and the accompanying burdens or whether it does not. Your theatre receives the largest public subsidy of any theatre in Canada, and we think the time has come for some public statement as to its function, and its plans for fulfilling that function.

We fear that Stratford's seeming lack of a coherent long-term policy will bring about a divergence of aims and ideals which can only work against the development of a truly Canadian theatre and thus, in larger terms, against the development of a Canadian culture. We do not want to see two theatres in Canada – ours, and yours – one firmly national and the other imitatively international.

We are not so naïve as to think that Canadian culture can

develop without playing its part in the culture of the western world in our time, nor are we so nationalistic as to wish to exclude from Canadian theatre anything that can nourish and enlarge it. But we are convinced that a Canadian sensibility is now a fact in the theatre as in the other arts, and we are anxious to serve it and strengthen it in a realistic way.

May we therefore offer for discussion the following points which seem to us to outline what Canada might expect from its national theatre, and assert that the theatres we represent have tried to embody some of them, acknowledging that none of our theatres has been able to encompass them all:

(1) That a national theatre should interpret the classics of world theatre, and explore the literature of world theatre in the light of a Canadian sensibility, which would imply that it would also,

(2) Use the best theatrical talent of the country to give something more than perfunctory attention to plays of Canadian origin that need the resources of the best equipped and most highly subsidized theatre in the country.

(3) That it should exploit the human resources of Canadian theatre by giving mature and experienced Canadian directors, designers, and actors an opportunity to extend their talents within this country, and should bring back artists who have gained experience abroad.

(4) That it should nurture growing theatre talent by providing it with the opportunity of working with the most mature and experienced theatre talent in Canada.

(5) That it should enrich our theatrical life by bringing the finest world theatre artists to Stratford from time to time as guests and exemplars, but not as permanent appointees.

(6) That it should represent the best that is Canadian in the theatre for audiences here and throughout the world.

A national theatre is a national resource of incalculable influence and significance. We feel that Stratford should take its responsibilities as a *de facto* national theatre more seriously than it has done in the past; specifically we suggest that your Board be less heavily weighted with members whose realm of expertise is finance, and should include patrons and practitioners of the arts and a greater representation from the world of scholarship. We suggest that the Board, rather than its artistic direction, be ultimately answerable to Canada for what is done in its national theatre.

We urge you to reconsider your position with which our own is inextricably linked. It is because of this link that we appeal to you now in a spirit in which co-operation and criticism are necessarily mingled, but in which the will toward co-operation is certainly dominant.

This manifesto was signed by Bill Glassco, John Hirsch, Martin Kinch, George Luscombe, Leon Major, Henry Tarvainen and Keith Turnbull – all of whom worked in Toronto. (There was some communication between these seven and certain directors elsewhere in Canada, but those outside Toronto neither signed the manifesto nor attended the meeting with the Board.)

Urjo Kareda, the *Toronto Star* drama critic, commented: "The Stratford Festival has long been a target for criticism because of its wilful disregard of Canadian theatre. Thus, the directors' statement is an organized though by no means pioneering outcry against the scandal. Stratford hasn't toured in Canada, it hasn't shown much interest in Canadian plays, it hasn't developed Canadian directors, it uses only a limited supply (in numbers, and often in ability) of Canadian actors, and it has almost never used Canadian designers. In recent years, the responsibility for this must be applied jointly to the Board and to the current artistic director, Jean Gascon, who is Canadian in nationality though not outstandingly in viewpoint. The irony, of course, may be that the Canadian Gascon is being replaced by the English Phillips, who seems, from all advance reports, insistent on undoing much of the indifference of the previous regime."

Keith Turnbull's report on the meeting to other interested directors unable to attend indicates an extremely gloomy assessment of the proceedings:

The barriers of understanding on all but the most obvious and naïve levels were enormous, and more often than not absurd. Not one of the Board members seemed capable of getting beyond the fact that they felt that the aims and functions were completely reflected in what they are doing at present and in the recent past and that the prospects for the future were in doing it all a bit better.

The recurrent theme was how valuable this "dialogue" was in spite of the fact that they found everything we were saying totally incomprehensible at best and we found everything they were saying all too clear. It was even suggested that a permanent platform for discussion be established on a regular basis irrespective of the fact that nothing was accomplished on the first attempt.

However the "isn't this wonderful we're getting together and listening to the profession" guise was quickly dropped when they discovered that as had been clearly stated at the beginning of the meeting we still intended to give our initial statement to the press. We were all somewhat dumbfounded by the violence of their reaction to this suggestion as I think we all felt the statement to be as considered, sympathetic, and middle of the road as one could be....

Anyway the moral of the whole story seems to be that there are more constructive ways of spending a Sunday afternoon in April than talking to a Board. At best the event may have been valuable in getting a monolithic body to move an inch towards realizing that there is a real problem – no more.

Robin Phillips was shaken by the controversy, the the focus of his unhappiness became the way media coverage of the manifesto was handled. Mary Webb, the Festival's publicist, got a call from Phillips the day the seven directors issued their manifesto to the Board and the press. Phillips wanted to make an immediate announcement of his plans for major changes – including a redesign of the Avon stage, alterations in the Festival stage, the formation of a Youth Company, a national tour, and commitments to develop Canadian talent. Phillips felt that an announcement of his plans would be an effective rebuttal to the criticisms contained in the manifesto, and that the publicity could be made to work positively for Stratford. But Mary Webb told him it wasn't the right time to make an announcement; on a Sunday night it would be hard to track down any of the important cultural reporters, and she didn't want to blow a big announcement by letting it out to whoever happened to be manning the Canadian Press office on off-peak hours. Webb told Phillips to wait until all the details were set and then hold a press conference to which all the major cultural journalists would be invited.

Phillips was shocked. He found it hard to believe that a publicist was saying no to him. He got so upset about it that he began calling Board members to say he was going to resign. Phillips' point was that he couldn't run Stratford unless he controlled all the important details, including publicity. Eventually Phillips was talked out of resigning, and his plans were announced at a press conference a few weeks later. John Killer, a Stratford insurance salesman who was then president of the Board, called Mary Webb and told her, "I'm sorry about this, but from now on, if Robin wants a press release, we have to do it, even if it's three o'clock in the morning." Webb resigned within a year, before the opening of Phillips' first season. The pattern was set for the next six years: the Board had weathered Robin Phillips' first threatened resignation; Phillips had won an important concession and had consolidated his power.

* * *

Before mounting his first season at Stratford, Robin Phillips spent a year observing and acclimatizing himself. He spent 1974 (Gascon's farewell year) watching Stratford from the inside and became an expert on who was capable of doing what. He also travelled all over Canada getting to know the country's theatre, evaluating talent, talking to people. Phillips was a charming politician, and he had a huge obstacle to overcome: the resentment that Canadian nationalists, especially those in the arts, felt about his appointment. He had come to Canada prepared for a challenge, but not prepared for the wave of protest against his presence. Phillips had been so disconcerted by the fuss that he had wondered aloud whether he should go back to England. But he found a way of using the controversy to score points: he would say that he sympathized with the nationalist cause, and that he was going to make sure it wouldn't be necessary for Stratford to go outside the country again when his era was over.

Officials of Canadian Actors' Equity believed they had won a concession from the Board: an assurance that this was the last time this would happen. Phillips would say that eventually his work at Stratford would be perceived as a necessary transitional phase in achieving the goals of the nationalists. He backed up these statements by recruiting Urjo Kareda, the *Toronto Star*'s brilliant young drama critic, to be Stratford's literary manager, and by persuading various distinguished theatre people to accept the honorary position of associate directors. (The theory was this would give Phillips a wealth of Canadian theatrical experience as a resource on which he could draw.) He also invited Bill Glassco, one of the Toronto fringe directors who signed the manifesto, to direct a small production at the Third Stage of the contemporary American play *Kennedy's Children* during Phillips' first season.

Phillips was starting out in Canada just at the time when the whole question of outsiders had become a touchy issue. When John Fraser of the *Globe and Mail* told Rudolf Nureyev, in the pages of the Sunday *New York Times*, that the National Ballet of Canada would be much better off if Nureyev left, the article set off an international incident. Fraser managed to get told off by Martha Graham and Clive Barnes, among others, but what he wrote wasn't out of step with how people felt in Canada. The mood had become truculent – almost absurdly truculent. It was in this climate that John Hirsch, in his new job as head of CBC drama, had to postpone a TV play about Canadian suffragette Nellie McClung because the Association of Canadian Television and Radio Artists (ACTRA) refused to allow Kathleen Widdoes, an American actress, to play the part. (The project went ahead later with Kate Reid in the role.) It was in this climate, too, that after the *Toronto Star* brought in a drama critic, Gina Mallet, from *Time* in New York, the small theatres of Toronto organized a public protest, claiming that Mallet (who was filling the job Kareda had taken over from Nathan Cohen) didn't have the required background in Canadian theatre to give her criticism credibility.

The suspicious reception Phillips received was not an isolated phenomenon. During the same period, Hilton Kramer, art editor of the *New York Times*, confessed in print that he was appalled by the new chauvinism he found in Toronto, where people seemed to think that museums should buy Canadian paintings only. What would have happened, he wondered, if the great American museums had ignored European paintings and purchased American work exclusively? But if parochialism was now a danger in Canadian culture, it had to be seen against the background of a country where a sense of colonial inferiority was so deeply ingrained that for decades it was unconsciously assumed that nothing had any value unless it was brought in from somewhere else. The consequences of that mentality could still be seen in the film industry, where despite huge government subsidies there were still mainly two types of Canadian movies – the underground Canadian movie, which generally had no chance at all of being shown in theatres or on television, and the imitation American Canadian movie, which generally could be called a success if it was terrible in ways that

29

made it impossible to say for sure that it wasn't produced in Hollywood. It had taken a long time to end the special privileges that *Time* enjoyed in Canada at the expense of Canadian publications. Canadians had become so self-conscious about these struggles that it was understandable if people sometimes failed to draw the distinction between outsiders who came to exploit Canada and outsiders who came to contribute something that Canada really needed. In this environment Robin Phillips had to be exceedingly careful not to step on any toes.

CHAPTER THREE

Robin's Nest

Almost from the moment he arrived, Robin Phillips began reshaping Stratford. There was no detail of the Festival's operation in which he was not interested – up to and including the crests on the uniforms worn by the ushers. When the Avon Theatre was redesigned, Phillips climbed up to paint a gold leaf on the ceiling. Phillips was a workaholic who could stay up half the night and expected others to do the same. At 3 A.M. he would take long solitary drives to the quarry (a swimming hole) at St. Marys. He wasn't content to delegate responsibility, but he did assemble a tremendously energetic and talented group of people around him. He inspired – and demanded – absolute loyalty. "Robin is a genius" became the opening remark of Festival people to visitors from the outside world, and this became a standing joke among sceptical non-members of the faith. Under the spell of fiery sermons from the young theatrical prodigy who had once planned to be a clergyman, Stratford became a hotbed of born-again believers. Having been an actor, he understood intuitively the psychological needs of actors. Like a lover skilful at wooing, he conquered the company totally.

After his year of observing, travelling, politicking, scouting, and fence mending, it was time, in the spring of 1975, for Robin Phillips to start delivering. His first season of productions was startlingly bold. Phillips himself directed five of the eleven shows: including a sharp and nervy *Measure for Measure* on the main stage at the Festival Theatre; paired versions of *The Comedy of Errors* and *The Two Gentlemen of Verona* (which toured the country before opening in Stratford) at the Avon; an eccentric version of Bertolt Brecht's *Trumpets and Drums* which was staged at both the Festival Theatre and the Avon Theatre; and *The Importance of Being Earnest,* an

31

end-of-season romp with William Hutt in drag as Lady Bracknell.

Surprisingly, Phillips chose to open the first year of his tenure as artistic director of the Stratford Festival with William Hutt's production of *Saint Joan* – which turned out to be a perfect illustration of the things that needed changing at Stratford. Stratford had never before opened its season with a non-Shakespeare play, and taking on a big Shaw project that had been conspicuously avoided by the GBS-enshriners at the Shaw Festival down the road at Niagara-on-the-Lake was a way of emphasizing the Festival's boldness. Conveniently, the play matched the occasion. Opening night at Stratford has always been a stuffy event. The lords and ladies of Upper Canada arrive in their chauffeured limousines, and, as the trumpets blare, make their way across the lawns and through the theatre lobby in dinner jackets and long dresses. The evening represents an uneasy get-together of culture and big business. For many people in this audience, the theatre still represents what the Marx Brothers were demolishing in *A Night at the Opera* – a gala, dress-up, formal occasion; and the style of the play should ideally be in keeping with this tone of decorum. There must be a certain amount of pageantry and spectacle, and the actors are expected to march about in puffily elegant costumes, looking like stuffed vegetables and reciting the kind of elevating speeches – fragments of rhetoric about the meaning of life – that people might remember memorizing for the final exam in high school.

Shaw meant *Saint Joan* to be eclectic and provocative, offering several conflicting interpretations of the same character: a simple peasant girl, a romantic heroine, a dangerous heretic, a saint, or an ironic pawn of shifting historical forces. But in a later era the true subject of *Saint Joan* is not really the clash among these points of view but the dated theatrical contrivance itself, which sees history as material for a debating club. Shaw used ideas like pieces of heavy furniture, and the play now seems to be less about the events of fifteenth-century France, and more about the educated Edwardian mentality that Shaw represented. The dubious achievement of William Hutt's production was to reflect almost perfectly that segment of the Canadian cultural gentry whose thinking hadn't budged beyond the Edwardian aristocratic ideal. Every point of view was soberly and deliberately articulated as impartially and boringly as in a series of CBC free-time political addresses. Since Pat

Galloway as Joan didn't give the kind of performance that makes an audience lose its head, no one could guess why the other characters in the play should lose theirs. Why didn't they just humour this poor, demented girl and send her back to the farm?

This *Saint Joan* epitomized what Stratford, at its worst, had become – a museum that turned famous plays into dinosaurs. Some people wondered whether Robin Phillips might not have chosen this as an opener to demonstrate what he wanted to get away from, and as a way of giving the die-hard veterans in the company a chance to hang themselves. But to meet Phillips himself, with his boyish, persuasively innocent gaze, was to feel ashamed of harbouring such malicious thoughts. People encountering him for the first time tended to be bowled over by his energy and enthusiasm as he talked eagerly and articulately about his hopes for the company, its problems, and his responses to the controversy over his appointment.

It was in the two productions at the Avon that Phillips' vision was most clearly and freshly evident. Phillips developed a separate and more youthful (in point of view as well as age) company for the Avon. Liberated from the heaviness of period costumes and lavish, excessively reverent staging, the company gave these two early, rather flimsy Shakespeare comedies an intoxicating exuberance. The productions, taken together, had the buoyant spirit of an ideal college revue. But the approach of the Avon company, though inexpensive and youthful, couldn't be called amateurish. And in the person of Jackie Burroughs (who was new to Stratford) and Nicholas Pennell (who was not), the Avon had one of the most enchanting young comic couples to be found on any stage anywhere. Pennell was a wonder of high-style comic bewilderment – a cartoon charmer. Burroughs' eccentric looks and flamboyant sense of comedy were more suited to classical roles than anyone had guessed. Phillips and his co-director, David Toguri, were going back to the plays of Shakespeare's own youth to find a new connection with the impulses of contemporary young performers and contemporary young audiences. Taking amusing liberties – The *Comedy of Errors* looked like a frontier spoof, and *The Two Gentlemen of Verona* like an Art Deco fantasy – these productions showed that Shakespeare didn't have to be stuffy and predictable. *The Two Gentlemen of Verona* was essentially a reprise of the production that had got Phillips into trouble at the Royal Shakespeare Company five years earlier, but in Canada it hardly raised any hackles.

The second production on the Festival stage was *Twelfth Night*, directed by David Jones of the Royal Shakespeare Company. There were many good performances – Tom Kneebone's melodious Feste, Denise Ferguson's scheming Maria, Leslie Yeo's weather-beaten Sir Toby Belch, Frank Maraden's hyped-up Sir Andrew Aguecheek, Kathleen Widdoes' beguiling Viola, and Brian Bedford's show-stopping Malvolio. But the good elements didn't quite come together, and the show failed to take off.

The season's sense of promise found full expression only in Robin Phillips' own production of *Measure for Measure* on the Festival stage. This play hasn't traditionally been an audience pleaser, but Phillips made it the most thrillingly supercharged event of the season. His staging was crisp and stark, almost suspended in time. With visual embellishment stripped away, the audience was pushed to listen to the words in a new way; for the first time in many years at this theatre, the pauses and the whispers counted for something. The production gathered force as it moved along, until finally the audience was hanging on every gesture and inflection. Martha Henry's Isabella had great resonance, William Hutt's calculating Duke was his best performance in several years, Richard Monette was an amusingly cocky Lucio, and Brian Bedford was an unforgettably creepy Angelo. Phillips made the final scene a knockout both dramatically and intellectually, saving a major revelation for a silent sequence after the last words of the play had been spoken.

Trumpets and Drums, added to the repertoire at the Festival Theatre at the end of July, was a big, extravagant production, and it was also Robin Phillips' first full-scale disaster in Canada. Brecht had taken George Farquhar's 1706 comedy *The Recruiting Officer*, changed its period to the American Revolution, and used it for a didactic commentary on the evils of war and human greed. Phillips took the Brecht version and transformed it into a musical pageant. How could this heavy circus of a show, so obscenely pleased with itself, presume to offer moral instruction? The overwhelming irony was that Brecht's exposé of imperialist arrogance had become the vehicle with which a British director was bombarding the colonies with the already outdated musketry of 1960s London stage fanfare.

At the end of his first season, Robin Phillips was poised in formation, like a Shakespearean hero who had arrived to forge new order out of chaos. It would take a little boisterous breaking away and a little sense of rebellion against the crumbling old order just to get the juices flowing again. The trick was to find room to grow and develop within the confines of being a fat cultural institution. It would be madness to ignore the enormous weight of government support, the lofty status of the Festival in the school system, and the needs of audiences with wildly varying tastes which had made the Festival the longest-running hit in Canadian cultural history.

At Greenwich, Phillips had drawn attention to his young company by bringing in stars like Joan Plowright and Mia Farrow, who were attracted to his charismatic drive. It was Phillips' notion that the company would benefit from working with stars, and from the bigger audiences the stars would generate. He was shrewd enough to see what he could offer stars: the chance to feel they were escaping from the corruptions of stardom, renewing themselves, and purifying their work. Now he was ready to try the same approach in Canada.

He had already lured Brian Bedford to Stratford for the 1975 season. Bedford wasn't exactly a star, but he was a distinguished actor of international repute. Like Phillips, Bedford was a working-class boy from England. His father had worked in the post office in Yorkshire. Bedford had left school at fifteen and landed at the Royal Academy of Dramatic Art, where he was quickly established as a young prodigy. On graduation from RADA, Bedford won two prizes – a contract for a year with the Liverpool Repertory company, and a contract with H.M. Tennent, the most important independent producer in London. At Liverpool, he played Hamlet for eight pounds a week. Then he began an association with Tennent that lasted six years. His first London show was *The Young and the Beautiful,* followed by *A View from the Bridge,* directed by Peter Brook. By Bedford's own account, he was extremely self-destructive at this point in his life. "I was a bit of a maniac," he would recall years later. "I was always late for everything, and always drunk. I got into a car crash and broke my nose when I was twenty-two." He almost managed to get fired from a production of *The Tempest* at Stratford-upon-Avon directed by Peter Brook. (Bedford was playing Ariel to John Gielgud's Prospero, and would remember his own performance as an embarrassment.)

Bedford moved to the United States in 1959 to recreate the role he had played in *Five Finger Exercise* (opposite Jessica Tandy), and from that point on he would always seem like the perfect mid-Atlantic man. Although he would return to London for several acting assignments, he took up residence in the United States and began to think of himself as American. He had had the advantage, however, of being steeped in the great tradition of British acting, not to mention his having an elegantly understated accent.

In 1974, just after accepting the job of artistic director at Stratford, Ontario, Robin Phillips went to Bedford's farmhouse in upstate New York. Their paths had never crossed before. What Bedford would remember most vividly about this visit was that Phillips arrived by train with a huge suitcase and changed his clothes three times in the course of a fifteen-hour visit. As a result of Phillips' visit, Bedford made his Stratford debut in 1975, in the exciting first year of the Phillips era, playing Malvolio in *Twelfth Night* and Angelo in *Measure for Measure*. But Bedford didn't return in 1976, the year that Maggie Smith joined the company, and the lack of a suitable leading man for her was a major problem.

Phillips hardly knew Maggie Smith in England, though they had met on at least two occasions (he had forgotten one of them, and she had forgotten the other), but in January, 1975, when a tour of Noel Coward's *Private Lives* brought her to Toronto, she got a telegram from Phillips, who had just taken over at Stratford: "If you want to escape for the weekend, I'll come and collect you." Phillips sensed that since leaving the National Theatre, Maggie Smith had become a company leading lady without a company. The daughter of a pathologist in Ilford, Essex, she had attended the Oxford Playhouse School of Drama and made her acting debut in the Oxford University Dramatic Society. After scoring a New York triumph in *New Faces of 1956*, she became a West End star in *Mary, Mary*. Her period of international glory began at the National in the late 1960s, when she played Desdemona to Laurence Olivier's Othello, the title role in *Miss Julie*, and Beatrice in *Much Ado about Nothing*. One of her most celebrated performances was in a Freudian version of *Hedda Gabler*, directed by Ingmar Bergman. It was at the National, too, that she became the world's most glittering interpreter of Restoration and eighteenth-century comedy, in *The Recruiting Officer*, *The Beaux' Stratagem*, and *The Country Wife*.

By 1971 it was time to leave the National. The politics were trying, and the competition for parts fierce. Smith was miffed because after taking over the role of Masha from Joan Plowright for the Los Angeles run of *Three Sisters* she was not chosen for the film version. In addition, after asking whether she would rather do *Twelfth Night* or *As You Like It* and being told that she wanted to play Rosalind in the latter, the National management had announced it was doing an all-male version of *As You Like It*.

Smith had always been uncomfortable in movies, even after her well-earned Academy Award for *The Prime of Miss Jean Brodie* in 1969. The corrupting effect of purely commercial entertainments on her work was apparent in her overbearingly mannered performance as Aunt Augusta in the film of Graham Greene's *Travels with My Aunt* and in her facile success in *Private Lives*, which she played for eighteen months, making a caricature out of her own style and personality. The revival of *Private Lives*, directed by John Gielgud, was commercially the biggest hit she had ever had in the theatre. In 1930 Gertrude Lawrence and Noel Coward himself had starred in this comedy of sexual confusion about a recently divorced couple who meet by accident in the south of France while each is honeymooning with a new spouse. Smith had opened in London's West End in 1972, playing Amanda Prynne while her husband and frequent leading man, Robert Stephens, played Elyot Chase, the character best remembered for his wisecrack that some women need to be struck regularly, like gongs. During the run of the show, Smith and Stephens found themselves in the same situation as Amanda and Elyot: their marriage was over. When Smith undertook an American tour, starting in Los Angeles and ending in New York, it was with a new leading man, and she gave the broadest performance of her life; she seemed to have turned into a nightclub comic's Maggie Smith impression – all tics and nervous affectations. Phillips could see that the "success" she was enjoying in *Private Lives* was something that Maggie Smith needed to be saved from.

Phillips took her to Grand Bend, where they had a weekend retreat at the country residence of Barbara and Peter Ivey. Phillips showed her around at Stratford, and she was enthusiastic about the Young Company in particular. No offers were made or accepted, but probably from that weekend on, Phillips and Smith knew that they would be working together at Stratford a year later.

Maggie Smith arrived in Stratford on March 1, 1976, after a winter in Los Angeles, where she had appeared in the film *Murder by Death* – a good example of what she needed to get away from. With her second husband, librettist Beverley Cross, and her two children (by Stephens), she settled into a rambling old house on Cambria Street and got the children registered in local schools.

Maggie Smith's arrival at this point in the development of Canadian theatre raised a crucial question: why couldn't Canada develop its own stars? There were a number of actors at Stratford, including Martha Henry, William Hutt, Douglas Rain, Pat Galloway, and Richard Monette, who were not exactly unknown, and who were capable of taking on the big roles. If they weren't stars, that was because it is just about impossible to become a star without leaving Canada. Donald Sutherland, Geneviève Bujold, Christopher Plummer, and John Colicos, on the basis of their acclaim in London, New York, and Hollywood, could come home as stars. To be a star meant to be recognized all over the world, and for that you had to be working somewhere the whole world was watching. At first what seemed astonishing was that Smith would *want* to come to Canada. She had already captured New York, London, and Los Angeles.

She made her Stratford debut in *The Way of the World.* The role of glittering Millamant was a natural for her, but she had to be talked into it. She wanted the other big female role – Lady Wishfort, who describes herself as "an old peeled wall." But Smith allowed herself to be persuaded that she could wait twenty years to play Lady Wishfort. Jessica Tandy took the role of Lady Wishfort, but finding a Mirabell wasn't so easy. Among those who turned it down was Christopher Plummer, who hadn't come home to Stratford since playing Antony to Zoe Caldwell's Cleopatra in Michael Langham's farewell production in 1967. Finding leading men for Maggie Smith wasn't the only problem. *The Way of the World* was supposed to be directed by William Gaskell, who had directed Maggie Smith and Robert Stephens in *The Beaux' Stratagem* at the Old Vic, but Gaskell's ideas for the production caused some alarm. Phillips, already overworked and without the assistance of literary manager Urjo Kareda, who was in hospital for months recovering from a car accident, took on *The Way of the World* in addition to the other six productions he was directing. (On the Festival stage he was directing *A Midsummer Night's Dream, Antony and Cleopatra,* and *Measure for Measure.* At the Avon, he was reviving *The Importance of Being Earnest* and co-directing with William Hutt two Youth Company productions which had gone on a spring tour – *Hamlet*, with Richard Monette and Nicholas Pennell alternating in the title role, and *The Tempest*.)

At rehearsals, Phillips insisted that Maggie Smith was to be treated like a member of the company, not like visiting royalty. Smith would typically be the first one in the company he'd call on to stand up and tell a little joke to the others as an acting exercise. Being almost pathologically shy, she dreaded the experience. But she bore her responsibility to the company very seriously, attending voice and movement classes so religiously that younger colleagues were startled to discover that acting technique didn't come automatically even to a star. When Zoe Dominic, the photographer, who had worked with her in England, remarked that she seemed to have found a new voice and was no longer retreating into mannerisms, Smith replied, "Well, you see, I'm not acting with Larry Olivier here, and for the first time in ten years, I'm not scared."

The Way of the World was potentially the most enjoyable event of the 1976 season, but the production went wrong in a peculiarly innocent way. Faith in the text was Phillips' credo; with play after play, he had undertaken to throw out the clutter of artificial performing style and get back to a fresh, natural reading of the lines. But that approach just doesn't work with Congreve. Congreve's tortuous plot, with its crowded stage full of fops and rogues, all preening, prattling, and scheming against each other, can't be made clear no matter how simply it's presented – and the slow, deliberate pacing of this production proved deadly. With Congreve, when the dazzling surface is lost, all is lost. Jeremy Brett was dreadfully miscast, so it was impossible to understand why all the women kept falling for Mirabell.

Yet Maggie Smith's Millamant was a delicious memorable display of high comic style. From the moment she walked on, carrying her body at angles that seemed devastatingly witty before she had uttered a line, the evening was redeemed. She rang inflections that gave innocent-seeming lines a sardonic kick. Her loathing of country walks, for instance, became hilarious. When she said, "I could laugh immoderately," it was clear that she meant to point out, in mock-polite terms, how unmirthful the moment was. Her insistence on the unfunniness of it was in itself supremely funny. When she announced that conversing with fools was good for one's health, or dismissed a cretin as "this flower of knighthood," the audience could see her lethal wit for what it was – her self-protection in a zoo of folly. The melting of her armour was one of the great pleasures of the evening, ending in the celebrated marriage-contract scene where she allows herself to "dwindle into a wife."

Marvellous as her Millamant was, Maggie Smith in *The Way of the World* was doing what the world already knew she could do. In *Antony and Cleopatra* she tried something much more daring. Her Cleopatra went against the grain, challenging preconceptions about the temptress of the Nile. She didn't overdo the comedy, which might have turned Cleopatra into a cartoon. This Cleopatra was not a *femme fatale* but a woman made helpless, despite her wealth and power, by being in love. Phillips' production stripped away the peacock feathers and *Aida* sets, and there was a clean feeling about it, but once again, he failed to give Smith an adequate leading man. John Colicos had been asked to play Antony, and backed out when he was offered about $250,000 to appear in the movie *Drum* (a sequel to *Mandingo*). Anthony Hopkins was also approached before Keith Baxter was recruited to play Antony. Baxter lacked the force of personality to make the audience understand why his destiny shook the world. Smith saved the show, using her comic techniques to go beyond comedy into something moving: a portrait of the vulnerable girl, consumed by the anxieties of love, hiding inside the queenly legend.

It was with a revival of the previous season's *Measure for Measure* that the company made its strongest claim to greatness. Taking over Brian Bedford's part, Douglas Rain was an effectively despicable Angelo. With the addition of Tony van Bridge (Escalus), Jackie Burroughs (Mariana), and William Needles (the Provost), the 1976 *Measure* was even more magnificent than the 1975 *Measure*. The throwaway jewel of the piece was Maggie Smith in the bit part of Mistress Overdone – a shrill, luridly painted Cockney bawd. The production seemed to be announcing that Stratford didn't need to use imported stars as a substitute for its own achievements. This show had the nerve to flaunt Maggie Smith in a tiny role as if to say, "Look, we can afford it." This was Maggie Smith's gesture of good faith to the Festival and to the audience – an affirmation that she meant to be, above all, a member of the company.

The major failure of the season was *The Merchant of Venice*, directed by Bill Glassco, one of the leaders of the 1974 nationalist manifesto protesting Phillips' appointment. Hume Cronyn played

Shylock, Jackie Burroughs played Portia, and the cast also included the young Italian-Canadian actor Nick Mancuso, who, like Glassco, had become one of the heroes of the Toronto alternative theatre movement of the early 1970s. On the surface, this appeared to be exactly the sort of opportunity for Canadian talent that the nationalists had attacked Stratford for failing to provide in the past. But the experience proved traumatic and disastrous for several of the principal participants. Glassco had made his reputation developing and directing new Canadian plays in a tiny converted warehouse. Now he was doing a Shakespeare production on the notoriously difficult Festival stage. And at Stratford he was on his own. There was very little contact with Phillips, who was busy with his own shows. Glassco's biggest problem was that he couldn't handle Jackie Burroughs, who made her lack of confidence in him painfully clear. The production was savaged by the critics, and Mancuso had such a negative experience that he decided to leave Canada for the United States, where he quickly launched a career in TV and movies. This was the first of a number of episodes in which Canadian directors came to Stratford and failed, giving rise among the most cynical to speculation that it was part of the *function* of guest directors to fail, and thereby make Phillips look good in comparison.

The authors of the nationalist manifesto had called for new Canadian plays at Stratford, and in 1976, Phillips gambled on *Eve*, which opened at the Avon in late August, with Jessica Tandy – one of the world's most distinguished actresses – in the title role. The play was based on a Canadian novel, *The Book of Eve*, by Constance Beresford-Howe, about a geriatric feminist rebel who after years of marriage elects to set out on her own, with no money. Under Kareda's guidance, the play was written by Larry Fineberg, a promising Toronto playwright with several modest successes in the small theatres of Toronto to his credit. The show was not created without anguish. Tandy kept demanding rewrites and Fineberg had to throw out what he regarded as his choicest bits. Dramatically, *Eve* had its limitations, but running for only about a dozen performances, it became an instant hit and roused audiences who cheered at the end. (For years there would be talk of a Broadway production – Tandy, Bette Davis, and Helen Burns were among those seriously interested – but neither the play nor a projected movie based on the novel, not on Fineberg's script, materialized.)

At the end of the 1976 season, Maggie Smith had one of the great triumphs of her entire stay at Stratford, but it was not one that Robin Phillips would necessarily remember with pleasure. John Hirsch, returning to Stratford for the first time since his stormy exit in 1969, directed an end-of-season production at the Avon of Chekhov's *Three Sisters,* and Maggie Smith played Masha, the role she had once played opposite Olivier for the National Theatre's Los Angeles run. Bringing Hirsch to Stratford was part of an all-out effort during the 1976 season to win over the nationalists of the Canadian theatre who had been behind the manifesto in the wake of Phillips' appointment two years earlier.

John Hirsch was a decided exception to the rule that guest directors were supposed to fail, but his success with *Three Sisters* marked the beginning of a feud between Phillips and Hirsch which would eventually threaten to tear Stratford apart. Hirsch's *Three Sisters* opened in September at the Avon for a run of only a few weeks. The production became an instant legend and was immediately sold out. The cast included, in addition to Maggie Smith, Martha Henry, Marti Maraden, Keith Baxter, and Pat Galloway. Towards the end of the proceedings, there was a moment when the characters locked hands in a kind of chanting embrace. For an instant it seemed as if Chekhov's comic melancholia was about to burst into song and dance. This was a daring piece of staging not only because it was bound to provoke the wrath of purists who cannot abide any invention that is not specifically called for in the text, but also because if it hadn't worked it would have seemed ludicrous. But it did work, thrillingly, and the play came to an emotional crescendo.

Normally an end-of-season production as tumultously well received as this one would be revived at the beginning of the next season. But the bitterness between Phillips and Hirsch assured that Hirsch would never again be invited to work at Stratford as long as Robin Phillips was running the place. During the rehearsal period, Hirsch let people know he was offended by the lack of any attempt by Phillips to make him welcome. And in an atmosphere where members of the company were practically falling to their knees proclaiming the greatness of Phillips and their loyalty to him, Hirsch had the nerve to suggest that as far as he could see this was just another case of the emperor's new clothes. It certainly didn't help that Hirsch had the kind of success that Phillips might well envy, or that Maggie Smith was heard to say, with reference to Hirsch, that she wondered where he had been all her life. Maggie Smith became the symbolic queen whose favour these two duelling courtiers were fighting for, and when she gave Hirsch a present on opening night, Phillips was rankled.

But the major cause of the blow-up between Phillips and Hirsch was an interview Hirsch gave to John Fraser of the *Globe and Mail* a week before *Three Sisters* opened. Hirsch was talking about the plight of the freelance director in Canada, and how impossible it was to make a living. Fraser noted in his article that Phillips was directing a fearsome number of plays each season and suggested that his motivation might be the extra fee that he would get for each production. In fact, Phillips was not being paid extra for directing shows, and he flew into a rage when he saw Fraser's article. At seven o'clock on the Saturday morning the article appeared, Fraser received a call from a livid Phillips, demanding to know where he had picked up this treacherously untrue tidbit. "Where do you think?" Fraser replied, indirectly confirming what Phillips already suspected.

Fraser would say later that he should have checked his facts but he thought John Hirsch would know. According to Fraser, Hirsch asked him, "Why do you think he [Phillips] is directing so many shows?"

When Phillips called Hirsch about it, Hirsch denied that he had said any such thing to Fraser. According to Hirsch, Fraser had got it wrong, or misunderstood Hirsch. It was Fraser, according to Hirsch, who raised the question of the artistic director's fees, and it was only in reply to Fraser's question that Hirsch had recalled that when he worked at Stratford in the 1960s, artistic directors did get paid extra for each show they directed. Phillips didn't believe Hirsch's denial. A year later, before Fraser left for China to become the *Globe*'s Peking correspondent, he went to Stratford to have dinner with Phillips. "I just want you to know," Fraser said, "you guessed right about what person gave me that unfortunate piece of misinformation. And I've paid a price for letting you know that: John Hirsch and I didn't speak for months afterward."

It would be four years before John Hirsch would get another offer from Stratford. By that time, Robin Phillips would be gone.

CHAPTER FOUR

Trouble in Paradise

Robin Phillips was riding high at the end of his first two full seasons. With Maggie Smith as a drawing card, the box office had soared past half a million for the first time in Stratford history. During Jean Gascon's seven-year reign, annual ticket sales had ranged from a low of about 350,000 to a high of just over 400,000. Under Phillips, that escalated to 437,302 in 1975 and a spectacular 518,421 in 1976. There may have been a few people with doubts about Phillips' way of running the Festival, but opposition crumbled in the face of his astounding success at the box office. The Board was so ecstatic that after he had completed two years of his three-year contract, Phillips had his old contract replaced by a new one for five years. The length of the term was unprecedented, but the argument was that Phillips needed a long-term commitment in order to accomplish what he wanted to do, and that the Board was lucky to be able to hang onto this prodigy.

Having already taken control of the company, Phillips now made his rule absolute by gaining control of the Festival's administrative machinery as well. Even his most loyal supporters would admit that administrative skills were not among his great strengths, and Phillips would at times complain about his taxing workload and say that he needed help; but it was hard to imagine a strong administrator with whom Phillips could easily share power.

Only a few people had any misgivings about the dangers inherent in allowing the Festival to turn into a one-man show. William Wylie had been an administrative strong man who might have been an equal match for Phillips. After Wylie's death, Bruce Swerdfager, who had worked under Wylie and held the title of comptroller, was moved up and given Wylie's old title of general manager. Swerdfager had been with the Festival from the beginning, as a member of the acting company for the first eight seasons and then as part of the administrative staff. When Phillips arrived in 1975, Swerdfager had been in the top administrative job for three years. He found working with Phillips very different from working with Gascon, who had been content to delegate most of the details involved in mounting a season. Phillips demanded an almost unbelievable degree of control. Samples of every fabric used for costumes had to be personally approved by Phillips. He even insisted on seeing the designs and paper samples for the promotional hasti-notes sold in the theatre lobby.

There had been discussions with the Board about how authority would be divided between Phillips and Swerdfager; what became clear was that they *couldn't* share authority. It soon followed that Phillips was going to be the one in control. By the end of the 1976 season, Swerdfager felt worn down. He felt the Festival had turned into a dictatorship. The new five-year contract Phillips had won was to Swerdfager a sign of what was wrong. The new contract allowed Phillips to get out of his commitment on three months' notice, which to Swerdfager meant that the Board was putting itself in a position to be blackmailed. Was Swerdfager pushed or did he quit? Certainly he got the idea that Phillips didn't have any overwhelming confidence in him. Swerdfager decided to go into a Stratford graphics business. Before leaving, he warned the Board that the Festival could face administrative and fiscal disaster within three years. (Three years later, in 1979, the Festival did have a big deficit.)

After Swerdfager's departure, some of his duties were taken over by Gary Thomas, a Stratford chartered accountant who had moved into Swerdfager's old job of comptroller after Wylie died. During Phillips' reign, Thomas was never given the title of general manager, and he didn't have the power to challenge Phillips' authority. At the insistence of Phillips, the artistic director was the only member of the Festival staff who was allowed to report directly to the Board. This meant that when Phillips was feuding with the Board, the sole channel of communication was closed.

* * *

One of the big problems about Maggie Smith's first season in Stratford had been the lack of suitable leading men. This was solved when Phillips lured Brian Bedford back to team up with Smith for the 1977 season, the first of three seasons they would do together. Bedford and Smith had first crossed paths in England in 1958 when Smith was playing a supporting role in a West End play, *The Stepmother*, which starred Kate Reid. (When Maggie Smith's presence at Stratford was being questioned, it became a standing joke that no one in England had complained about that foreign star, Kate Reid, when Maggie Smith was playing second fiddle to her in London.) In those days, Bedford was very much the actor as angry young man. He met Maggie Smith at a *Stepmother* company party and irritated Kate Reid by pointedly telling people how much he loathed the play. Bedford and Smith had a very long talk at this party, sitting on a wooden floor and chatting about acting, sex, and other cosmic issues.

Bedford's partnership with Maggie Smith got off to a rocky start at the beginning of 1977. Robin Phillips directed them in *The Guardsman*, a Molnar comedy that Alfred Lunt and Lynne Fontanne had played both on the stage and the screen; it opened in Los Angeles during the winter before going to Stratford the next summer. They were playing a huge theatre – the Ahmanson at the L.A. Music Center – and neither Smith nor Bedford felt secure with the delicate tone of Phillips' direction. *The Guardsman* marked Maggie Smith's fifth appearance on the Ahmanson stage in seven years. Her triumphant appearance there with the National Theatre of Great Britain had helped her win an Oscar for *Jean Brodie* at a time when she was not well known to American movie audiences.

When Phillips left L.A. after the opening, Bedford and Smith quickly discarded his ideas and began acting in the style of a Neil Simon Broadway comedy. Later Bedford would recall the disagreement with jocular glee, "When we opened, there wasn't time to do what Robin wanted, and people were just sitting out there numbed by the tedium of it all. Maggie and I thought we would give the audience a show and get some laughs, and so we did this very gross thing." *The Guardsman*, written in 1910, is about a man (an actor) who decides to test his wife (an actress). While pretending to be on the road playing Hamlet, he disguises himself as a guardsman and woos his wife, hoping she'll resist. During the L.A. run, Maggie Smith signalled the audience when she wanted a laugh and then waited for the audience to respond on cue. She delivered lines with a nasal inflection to give them comic punch, and when she walked across the stage she was such a collection of tics and jerks people might have thought they were watching a farce about spastics. Her fluttery performance, unfortunately, was a regression to the self-parody into which she had slipped before being revitalized at Stratford.

A week or two after the opening, Phillips came back unannounced to check the show and was so angry that while making an explosive exit at the theatre, he slammed a door against a wall, causing about a thousand dollars' worth of damage to the wall. As Bedford tells the story, "Maggie and I were so appalled by Robin's carrying-on that we said, 'Well, fuck him, we're not *going* to Stratford next summer.' But somehow it all got sorted out. Robin had a very specific vision of *The Guardsman,* and we managed to get it right in Stratford."

Indeed, the production at the Avon Theatre a few months later was one of the high points of Stratford's rich twenty-fifth season. It was hard to believe that two stars playing the same roles under the same director could be so radically transformed. Maggie Smith, no longer burlesquing her own mannerisms and nudging the audience for laughs, gave a delicately understated performance – moving, beautiful, and funny all at once. Bedford was the perfect sparring partner for her: agile and witty. Together they reached a level of perfection that makes an audience high, holding its collective breath for fear of breaking the spell.

The Guardsman is the story of brilliant theatre people who get into trouble by misusing their acting talent but eventually arrive at an ending not merely happy but positively euphoric. That was the story of this production, too. Robin Phillips had pulled a lot of rabbits out of his hat, but this born-again *Guardsman* was one of his greatest accomplishments. The redemption of a show that courted damnation was a true miracle – a feat worthy of the heroine of *All's Well That Ends Well* (also produced at Stratford in 1977), and a demonstration of how Shakespeare's benevolent thesis about second chances applies to the stage itself.

The heroine of *All's Well* is a wilful creature who sets her heart on impossible goals and gets her way by performing acts of magic. That was a specialty of Robin Phillips, too; and Martha Henry's pushy miracle worker represented, in a way, the spirit behind the whole Festival. David Jones' production on the Festival stage did not go in for startling new interpretations, but it had the satisfying grace of a fine traditional approach, with a strong cast including William Hutt (the King), Nicholas Pennell (Bertram), and the amazing Margaret Tyzack (the Countess).

Phillips opened the season with his majestic production of *A Midsummer Night's Dream*. The show lumbered along for the first hour with ample evidence of intelligence and competence, but without the stroke of alchemy that translates bright ideas into theatrical excitement. Maggie Smith as Hippolyta wore a black-and-gold costume, her hair in crimson ringlets, and this allusion to Elizabeth I was timely as well as striking, since Stratford's anniversary celebration coincided with the Queen's Jubilee. Yet Phillips' Gloriana interpretation was somehow beside the point. There had been casting improvements since an earlier try in 1976, but this *Dream* still moved too slowly and felt curiously earth-bound.

Then suddenly, just before the intermission, the show took off. Maggie Smith, playing Titania as well as Hippolyta, did something daring in the scene where this woman under the influence wakes in a forest and falls in love with Bottom wearing the head of an ass. Instead of pushing the lines for laughs, she played the scene as pure romance. Not that the comic dimension was missing – Alan Scarfe's Bottom practically roared with robust humour – but Smith's Titania had something beyond low humour: radiance and eroticism. The scene had the charge of surprise; it brought the production to life, mysteriously imbuing the second half of the play with the electricity missing from the first half. This transformation was the first miracle of an altogether miraculous season.

Playing the title role in *Richard III*, Brian Bedford resisted the temptation to give a campy account of Richard's evil. This Richard wasn't charming, but stunningly nervy and charged with negative energy. Phillips' production, brazenly flamboyant and decorated with brilliant theatrical flourishes, was the spectacle of the season, and the critics went wild. Besides trotting out all the stars of the other productions, it showed off the muscle of the company. *Richard III* is not generally considered a play for actresses, but the women's parts have rarely been as well played as they were here by Margaret Tyzack (Queen Margaret, coming in on a billow of smoke to deliver her curse), Martha Henry (Lady Anne), Mary Savidge (the Duchess of York), and Maggie Smith (Queen Elizabeth). Several tableaux stood out: Richard manipulating a crowd by turning down the crown; a gathering of cursing women, with overlapping dialogue;

and a positively electric scene between Bedford and Smith, in which Richard, having just murdered everyone else in Elizabeth's family, asks to marry her daughter. The show belonged to Bedford's regal foul toad; as Northrop Frye observed, Bedford was exactly the Richard that Shakespeare must have wanted.

*　*　*

The absence of certain major Canadian actors was becoming an issue at Stratford, and it was an embarrassment for Phillips that Kate Reid, a Stratford regular in the early Sixties, had scored a huge success at Niagara-on-the-Lake in 1976, playing the title role in *Mrs. Warren's Profession* at the Shaw Festival. Phillips was determined to bring Reid back to Stratford for the twenty-fifth anniversary season in 1977, and once she agreed, he built the season around her. But when it came time to sign contracts, Reid had second thoughts about tying herself up for such a long season. She backed out, throwing the Festival into a panic. To replace her, Phillips went to England and recruited Margaret Tyzack. Canadian Actors' Equity threatened to block Tyzack's Canadian work permit, but Phillips pointed out that he was forced to bring in a foreigner because a Canadian had left him in the lurch. The grumblers said that importing an international star was one thing, but importing an unknown foreigner was another. "Margaret who?" became a familiar question, though not one that had to be asked again after her spectacular showing at Stratford. She played three parts – the Countess in *All's Well*, old Queen Margaret in *Richard III*, and Mrs. Alving in *Ghosts*. She was magnificent in all of them, but it was for her Mrs. Alving that she was to be remembered.

Ghosts, however, had as rocky a preparation as *The Guardsman*. The director was Arif Hasnain, who was at that time artistic director of the Manitoba Theatre Centre. Like Tyzack, Hasnain was a last-minute replacement: John Wood bowed out of directing *Ghosts* because of problems at his own Neptune Theatre in Halifax. Rehearsals began at the end of March, 1977, for an early June opening, and it would be an understatement to say that Tyzack and Hasnain did not see eye to eye. According to Hasnain, Tyzack demanded a specific concept from the director, and he held out for making the actors "discover" the right approach. Tyzack, simultaneously rehearsing *All's Well* and *Richard III*, knew that Mrs. Alving in *Ghosts* was the role that could make or break her reputation. In a state of frenzy she began telling her problems to Robin Phillips and other company members. Just before the season's openings, Tyzack did something even more extraordinary: she made it clear in interviews with certain drama critics that if *Ghosts* failed it would be Hasnain's fault, and if it succeeded it would be in spite of him. Perhaps that was why when the show opened, some reviewers seemed to feel it was, at one and the same time, brilliantly performed and badly directed.

Hasnain felt like an alien invader at Stratford. The actors had developed a certain language of work with Phillips, and he came along with a different language. Tyzack, however, felt that nothing was happening, and until the first preview, she thought the production was going to be a total disaster.

When Ibsen published *Ghosts* in 1881, it was considered so shocking that bookstores returned their copies as unsuitable for sale, and the major theatres of Scandinavia refused to perform the play (it had its world premiere in Chicago, of all places). What shocked people was the subject of syphilis, which, as an editorial in Norway put it, "has no place on the Christmas table of any Christian home." Ironically, Ibsen, who could be insufferably moralistic, resorted to the redeeming-social-value defence: "Zola," he remarked, "descends into the sewer to bathe in it; I, to cleanse it."

In the latter part of the twentieth century, the danger is not that audiences will be shocked, but that it could seem as absurdly overwrought as a meant-to-be-shocking trash movie like *Imitation of Life*.

Ibsen latches onto great clanging symbols, none more lurid than Osvald Alving's syphilis. But this production made the audience believe in it on a naturalistic level. Tyzack and Pennell were marvellous at suggesting how people dance evasively around a subject they are afraid to confront. The final scene, in which this wilful woman is forced to acknowledge precisely what she is determined not to acknowledge, was a knock-out. Hasnain, naturally, felt vindicated by Tyzack's triumph in the role. The only problem was that she went back to England remembered as the actress who gave a great performance as Mrs. Alving, and he went back to Winnipeg remembered as the director who didn't exactly direct *Ghosts*.

Hasnain wasn't the only guest director who had trouble in the 1977 season. The two unmitigated failures (both at the Avon) were *Romeo and Juliet*, staged by the English director David William (whose Stratford *Othello* Phillips had seen and disliked while he was negotiating his contract in 1973); and *Miss Julie,* staged by the respected young Toronto director Eric Steiner.

At the end of the season, Phillips directed Maggie Smith in Noel Coward's jokey romp *Hay Fever,* about an eccentric family driving their weekend guests bonkers. Smith had been in the cast when the play was done to great acclaim by the National Theatre at the Old Vic in 1964. Now she graduated to the role that had been played at the Old Vic by Edith Evans. As Judith Bliss, Smith was playing an actress for the second time that summer, and it was appallingly clear that she didn't need an excuse for acting actressy. Audiences were beside themselves with pleasure, and the show was a hit, but the comedy was forced, and heavily dependent on running gags. It was all too apparent that Stratford had hired two Maggie Smiths – the great one, and the one who overdid being Maggie Smith – and that both drew full houses and standing ovations.

* * *

The 1978 season was planned as the biggest, most extensive extravaganza in Stratford history, with eighteen productions (not counting a special one-night-only "gala Shakespeare revel" which was really a high-toned variety show) on three stages. For the first time in three years, the Third Stage was being reopened to the public. The Third Stage was a small, modestly equipped theatre, used since 1971 for low-budget and experimental presentations – new Canadian plays, contemporary European plays, chamber opera, concerts. There had been several productions there in 1975, Phillips' first year, but in 1976 it was used for workshops and closed to the public. Now it was being reopened, with a new stage design by Daphne Dare, as a theatre where young directors could work with young writers, whose scripts were being developed by Urjo Kareda. There were four productions in 1978: *Ned and Jack,* a new play by Sheldon Rosen about John Barrymore and his friend the playwright Edward Sherrin, which had already been produced in Vancouver and would get a full production in 1979 at the Avon Theatre; a new version of *Medea,* written by Larry Fineberg and directed by John Palmer, both part of the Toronto fringe theatre; a program of four short Samuel Beckett plays; and *Stargazing,* by the Vancouver playwright Tom Cone, directed by Pamela Hawthorn of Vancouver's New Play Centre.

Phillips' best production of the season was *The Winter's Tale* on the Festival stage. In the final scene of the play, there's a moment of pure wonder unsurpassed by anything in all of Shakespeare. The repentant King Leontes, who has already had restored to him the daughter he banished at birth, presides at the unveiling of a statue of his queen, Hermione, who is supposed to have died sixteen years earlier as a consequence of Leontes' jealous, unfounded rage. As we watch with Leontes and the members of his court, the statue's arm moves – and then she breathes, she speaks. It is Hermione, mysteriously recalled to life now that the wrong against her honour has been set right. Brian Bedford played Leontes, the jealous tyrant who undergoes a kind of therapy and after being cured gets back most of what he has destroyed. The play, a masterly late romance, crystallizing Shakespeare's intimations of cosmic reconciliation and forgiveness, has been maligned for centuries, and it has never been especially popular with audiences. But Phillips' rich and glittering production perfectly captured the fable's mellow beauty. Dramatically, the show stoppers were the moments when Bedford as Leontes and Martha Henry as Paulina, his miracle-working conscience, clashed head on. He was a walking cartoon of petulance made grave by the power of a king; she was an explosion of outraged virtue. One of the few problems with *The Winter's Tale* was that while Bedford and Henry were off-stage, during the long pastoral interlude in the middle of the play, they were really missed. But Graeme Campbell, singing and dancing as Autolycus, helped carry the middle section over the weak spots; Margot Dionne was fine in her first major role as Hermione; and the reliable William Needles was outstanding as Camillo.

Brian Bedford and Martha Henry emerged as a thrilling team again in *Uncle Vanya,* staged at the Avon and co-directed by Phillips and Kareda from a new translation by Calgary playwright John Murrell. At first the pacing seemed too deliberate but the production built to an exciting third act and a moving fourth act. William Hutt, Marti Maraden and Max Helpmann were all effective, but the show belonged to Bedford as Dr. Astrov and Henry as Elena.

Maggie Smith played Rosalind again in Phillips' version of *As You Like It* on the Festival stage, a revival of the production, mostly successful, that had opened in mid-season in 1977. Once the tedious exposition of the first half was out of the way, the show took off.

The Forest of Arden set, one great felled tree, was a splendid image. In the small role of Jaques, Brian Bedford delivered the Seven Ages of Man speech and stopped the show. In court gowns Maggie Smith looked a bit ripe for Rosalind, especially given an Orlando as callow as Jack Wetherall's, but once ensconced in the forest in her boyish disguise (green waistcoat and off-white straw hat) she looked good and gave an enchantingly funny account of befuddled love.

One of the real disasters of Phillips' career was his *Macbeth*, which was co-directed by Eric Steiner. Douglas Rain in the title role seemed caught in the grip of terrible depression rather than vaulting ambition. However, this may be exactly what Phillips wanted; Rain's performance was in keeping with the whole tone of the production – gloomy and flat, damp and cold. Maggie Smith managed to break through with a brave performance as Lady Macbeth, but it couldn't save the show.

At the Avon, Lotfi Mansouri of the Canadian Opera Company directed an overblown but amiable production of *Candide*, the Broadway musical version of Voltaire's satire. Most of the performers were not members of the Stratford company but outsiders brought in by Mansouri and his choreographer, Brian Macdonald. The young lovers were more insipid than absolutely necessary, but Michael Fletcher was entertaining in the double role of Voltaire and Pangloss; and Andrea Martin of SCTV had a wonderfully funny few minutes as an old lady with one buttock.

The most daring event of the season was *Judgement*, in which Richard Monette held the stage alone for an hour and forty-five minutes, without intermission. The text, by the British journalist Barry Collins, was taken from an episode recorded in George Steiner's *The Death of Tragedy*. A group of Russian officers, captured by Nazis and taken to a monastery in southern Poland, were locked in a cellar and abandoned when the Germans left. Two of the officers managed to stay alive by eating the flesh of their colleagues. The crazed survivors were found by the advancing Red Army and shot. The monologue – an account a survivor gives when he's discovered by the Red Army – is based on the assumption that one of the two officers was sane. Phillips' production was bold. The set was a chrome platform with a table on it, on which loomed a gigantic human thigh bone. Monette was dressed in off-white institutional pyjamas, nervous fingers clutching his own flesh. But it was impossible to believe this man had been locked in a cellar for eight weeks: he not only looked well fed but had a stylish haircut; he was not only lucid but downright eloquent, talking quickly and in well-formed sentences. It was hard to believe anyone could think out loud this way, let alone a man who had been locked in a cellar eating his fellows. Not so much as a participle was allowed to dangle.

During the first few weeks of the 1978 season, with the box office booming, Stratford seemed to be enjoying its golden age. The sheer volume of productions was staggering. On the Festival stage the list included The Merry Wives of Windsor, directed by Peter Moss, and two Roman plays – Brian Bedford's surprisingly lively production of Titus Andronicus and John Wood's production of Julius Caesar. Included in the repertory at the Avon were The Devils, starring Martha Henry, directed by Phillips; and Abelard and Heloise, directed by Keith Batten. Then the roof fell in. Overworked and exhausted, Robin Phillips became seriously ill. He was in the middle of rehearsing Private Lives, starring Brian Bedford and Maggie Smith, due to open at the Avon on July 9. The week before the show opened, he was haemorrhaging and going to rehearsals with his flesh held together by bandages. A few days before the opening, he left abruptly and flew to England, where his doctor told him he needed a serious operation. Phillips thought he had cancer. From England, he sent in his resignation. Stratford went into shock. The Festival was booming but it was more than ever before in its history a one-man show, and now that one man was suddenly gone.

Private Lives opened without him, but two other shows which were to have been directed by Phillips later in the season – Larry Fineberg's new play Devotion, starring Martha Henry, and Haworth, a Portrait of the Brontës, starring Maggie Smith and written by her husband, Beverley Cross – were cancelled. Eventually the cancer scare would pass and Phillips would be talked into taking a sabbatical and then returning to Stratford. But this was the beginning of the end.

At the end of 1978, the Stratford Board chose its new president. Robert V. Hicks, a Toronto corporation lawyer, had earned a reputation on the Board as a crack fund raiser. He succeeded John Heney, a Stratford man in the furniture business who had stepped in after the death of Russell Payton, who had been expected to follow John Killer as president. Hicks was the first non-resident of Stratford in five years to become Board president. The son of a United Church minister who had moved from charge to charge, Hicks grew up in southwestern Ontario, and while attending the University of Western Ontario in London, he met several people who would be his colleagues on the Stratford Board thirty years later. Hicks was Conservative with a capital C, and he had made his reputation as a corporate lawyer. He was one of the first people in Canada to move into the field of labour relations, and his specialty became advising large companies on how to deal with employees and their unions. He acted frequently for companies in collective bargaining and became an expert on the legal fine points of collective agreements – such as arbitration, safety rules, injunctions, firings, and human rights grievances.

But Hicks had social and artistic interests beyond the practice of law. He rather prided himself on his family's cultural accomplishments: his grandmother had been an artist, his mother was extremely well read, his sister was a painter, and Hicks himself listed music as his hobby. He had already been on the Toronto Symphony Board, and his administrative experience included having been chairman of the Toronto Board of Trade. But when Hicks was asked in 1974 to be on the Stratford Board, he couldn't have realized what he was getting into.

Hicks was a brilliant fundraiser, and his intimate acquaintance with the Tory coffers of Upper Canada helped keep the Festival so solvent that by the time he became president there was serious talk about breaking free of government subsidies. There had always been a tacit distinction between Stratford Board members and Toronto members, but under Hicks the two groups became polarized. When Hicks became president, one of the more active Board members, Carol Dilks (a Stratford resident), was asked to go to the Senate to make room for the new Toronto people that Hicks wanted around him. (The Senate was an advisory group of former Board members, and "going to the Senate" became a euphemism for being eased off the Board.) The bigger and more complex the Festival became, the more the Stratford people felt they were losing control; the most conservative of the Stratford Board members wanted to turn the clock back to the days of the purely local eight-week summer Festival. Hicks envisioned the company blazing a path toward international greatness, and Robin Phillips was central to that dream.

The Board was under the spell of Robin Phillips, and the biggest challenge for Hicks was to keep Phillips at Stratford. After Phillips' illness and sudden withdrawal in the summer of 1978, the Board coaxed him back, but only in a limited way. Phillips was persuaded to withdraw his resignation, on condition that he be given a complete sabbatical in 1979. Phillips was not totally absent in 1979 – he stayed away about six weeks, then came back and directed three shows – but even his partial absence was severely felt. The season was less ambitious, there were no big-name imports until Peter Ustinov's late-season *King Lear,* and box-office receipts dropped alarmingly. (The gas crisis across the continent that summer didn't help.) By the end of the season, the Festival had run up a deficit of $647,000. Even with a surplus of $400,000 from the year before, the Festival was still about a quarter of a million dollars in the red. This was taken as a warning of what lay ahead if Phillips left Stratford.

Early in 1979, Phillips wrote a letter to Hicks, explaining that his time off hadn't changed his mind about needing to leave. Phillips agreed to do the three productions he had taken on for 1979, and then come back for a full year in 1980. But that was to be the end of the line. (This meant Phillips was serving notice that he intended to quit a year before his contract was up. At the end of the 1976 season, Phillips had been given an unprecedented five-year contract, running through the end of the 1981 season, but had the contractual right to withdraw on three months' notice.) Six months after writing the letter to Hicks, Phillips was astonished to find that some members of the Board didn't seem to know about it. Phillips had given as his deadline the end of the 1980 season, but it wasn't until the fall of 1979 that there was any serious attempt to find a successor. Hicks was thrilled by the glory that Phillips had brought to Stratford, and perhaps, thinking back to the other times Phillips had threatened to go, he thought this was one more time when he would be able to talk Phillips into staying.

CHAPTER FIVE

The Searchers

When Robert Hicks became president in 1978, one of the biggest problems he faced was the distance (150 kilometres) between his office in downtown Toronto and the Festival Theatre in Stratford. He began to understand why presidents in the past had come from either Stratford or London. He asked Barbara Ivey, who was his first vice-president and projected successor, "Do you think I should spend a day a week in Stratford?"

"Yes," she replied, "even if it isn't a full day. You can diffuse a lot of problems by being around to talk them out before they get out of hand."

But a couple of months later, in February, 1979, Ivey drove to Stratford and was surprised to discover that Hicks hadn't been around. Eventually she discovered he had gone to his condominium in Florida.

Ivey realized early on that it wasn't possible for Hicks to deal with everything he had to oversee, and at first she tried to help him out. "For God's sakes," she would say to him, "let me take care of this." But Hicks didn't like to delegate. Ivey could see the things that weren't getting done – such as reporting back to people after meetings when a follow-up was expected, or keeping the Canada Council informed of what the Festival was doing. "Bob," she would nag, "we simply must pick up the phone and call Mavor Moore and tell him where we're going. That's just basic courtesy."

Increasingly Hicks found himself caught between people with conflicting demands. He found himself in a bind; this wasn't the kind of arbitration he was used to. When he learned that Phillips wanted out at the end of the 1980 season, he began a series of discussions with Phillips. They often met late at night, after Phillips had finished rehearsals. Sometimes the meeting took place at The Church, a spectacularly fine restaurant that Phillips' friend Joe Mandel had opened in what had once been a Baptist church. The restaurant instantly became the most notable gathering spot in town. Hick knews that Phillips wanted time away from Stratford, but he hoped something could be worked out that would keep him involved as a central figure. More than once he advised Phillips to cut back on his workload, do fewer productions, bring in other directors, delegate some responsibilities.

Phillips seemed to like the idea of turning Stratford over to a group rather than a single artistic director. He felt that if any prospective artistic director asked him whether it was possible for one person to do the job without killing himself, the truthful answer would have to be no. But as discussions dragged on over a period of months, Phillips shifted ground as to what his own involvement might be. Sometimes he would say, "Assume I won't be here." Other times he spoke as if he would be there. At one point, he told Hicks, "I beg you not to keep asking me to stay because I don't *want* to leave, and it's hard for me to break away from this place. It would be easy for you to persuade me to stay, but I would let you down. You must believe me. I have made my decision, you have it in writing. The decision is not that I want to go, the decision is that I have to go – for your good. You must understand that this is a decision I am giving you because I know what the consequences will be. You are putting me in a position where I will fail you."

Hicks' problems escalated when it came to shopping for the chairman of a group directorate. His style as a labour negotiator was to break up group meetings and have tête-à-têtes with each of the important people involved. He followed this procedure at Stratford, and it got him into trouble. Hicks was talking to everybody, but no one else on the search committee – which included Bryden, John Lawson, and Ivey – could be sure what was happening. Hicks' trips from Toronto to Stratford became more and more frequent; eventually he was spending more than half his time on Stratford business – for which he was not being paid.

When James Sharkey, Phillips' agent, came over from London before the opening of the 1980 season, he felt that Hicks was unprepared to believe him when he said this was the end – Phillips did not want to stay on. Hicks told Sharkey that if there was any way he could retain Phillips' services, he wanted to know about it.

Sharkey said he was sure it was not a matter of money. "The simplest solution," Sharkey told Hicks, "would be for you to accept this and find a new artistic director."

Officially the Phillips position was that his resignation, effective at the end of the 1980 season, was on record. But there was a strong feeling on the part of several people that if they could only find the right way to phrase the question, Phillips would say yes to staying on. Hicks was also discovering that a lot of the people he spoke to were interested in being part of a group directorate only if Phillips remained. Not much energy was put into finding a single artistic director. Michael Langham had a series of phone calls and in the end said he wasn't interested in coming back to his old job. Hume Cronyn and Robert Whitehead indicated they weren't interested in the job, either. John Hirsch wasn't asked.

The idea of setting up a group to run Stratford (in place of the traditional single artistic director) had been in the air since the summer of 1978. Brian Bedford phoned Phillips in England, just after his sudden departure had left Stratford in a state of shock, and suggested getting a group of people to pitch in and give Phillips some help. In the fall of 1979, Ronald Bryden – who had returned to Canada in 1976, been elected to the Stratford Board in 1978, and was now a member of the search committee – had a discussion with Phillips about using as a model the group directorate set up at the Royal Shakespeare Company when Peter Hall gave up the job of managing director in 1968. Hall wanted to go on directing plays but was unwilling to run the RSC. The solution was a two-tier structure. The company was to be run by the best of the younger directors while Peggy Ashcroft, Peter Brook, and Peter Hall served on a senior level, saying in effect: "We vouch for these young people, and if you're not satisfied, we'll come and bail them out." However, Trevor Nunn eventually emerged as Peter Hall's successor.

Certain members of the Board undoubtedly thought Stratford had to find "the next Robin Phillips." But there was a strong argument for the RSC solution, which went like this: we can't find another Robin – there isn't one around. Anyway the Festival has grown so much in four years it can't be run by one person. We want to start a school, produce our own films, have a winter season in Toronto. We need someone in Stratford to hold things together, someone else in Toronto, and a heavyweight business manager. Hicks had his heart set on finding a structure that would keep

Phillips associated with Stratford. Phillips said he would be delighted to continue directing plays, but emphasized that he needed to spend a lot of time away from Stratford, and wouldn't be able to run the place. By the end of the 1979 season, the RSC solution seemed viable, and the issue became: who will be the wizard who stays in Stratford through the winter and makes it all work? The search for an artistic director had turned into a search for a chairman, who had to be a big name to satisfy certain members of the Board. Robin Phillips was adamant: it wasn't going to be him.

In February, 1980, Hume Cronyn made an ill-fated attempt to help secure the Festival's future. Cronyn was the only person in Stratford history to be simultaneously a member of the acting company and a member of the Board of Governors, and he felt a special kinship with the place. He had grown up thirty-five miles down the road in a well-established London, Ontario, family. One great-grandfather was John Kinder Labatt, who founded the beer empire, and another was an Anglican priest from Ireland who arrived by oxcart to settle in London when it was still known as The Forks. Cronyn's father was a Victorian patriarch – a president of the Huron and Erie Mortgage Corporation, Canada Trust, and Mutual Life, and a member of Parliament. It had been almost fifty years since Cronyn had gone to New York to become an actor, but he still had ties in London, and his family connections were just the sort of thing to make the Stratford Board feel he was one of them. The offer of a spot on the Board came at the end of the 1976 season, the first season he and Jessica Tandy, his wife, were full members of the acting company.

Cronyn's connection with the Festival went right back to the beginning. In 1952, Tom Patterson received $125 from the city of Stratford to explore his idea of starting a Shakespeare Festival. He went to New York to see Cronyn and Tandy, who were then starring in *The Fourposter*. Patterson was eager to arrange a meeting with Laurence Olivier, and Cronyn put them in touch with each other (though Patterson never did get together with Olivier). Cronyn also gave Patterson a donation, for more money than he had received from any other source. Patterson wanted Cronyn and Tandy to bring *The Fourposter* to Stratford in its first year of operation, but they were committed to an American tour. Cronyn did, however, come up for the ground breaking, and he and Tandy were in the audience for the historic first performance of *Richard III* in

1953. They told Tyrone Guthrie that if he ever did anything like this again, he should keep them in mind. (Jessica Tandy had worked with Guthrie years before in England at the Old Vic.) In 1962, when Guthrie started the Guthrie Theater in Minneapolis, he wrote to them. They acted there for a couple of seasons, and Cronyn served on the Minneapolis board for six years.

There was a long period when Cronyn felt slighted and over-looked by Stratford, but in 1976, Cronyn and Tandy were finally welcomed into the fold. (Cronyn had appeared in 1969 at Stratford in a production of *Hadrian the Seventh,* which toured North America, but he was not considered a member of the regular company.) They appeared together in Robin Phillips' first version of *A Midsummer Night's Dream* in 1976, with Cronyn as Bottom and Tandy as Titania; that same year he played Shylock in *The Merchant of Venice,* and she took the title role in *Eve.* When asked to join the Board, Cronyn accepted on the understanding that he couldn't act as a liaison between the company and the Board – because he wasn't going to be with the company on a continuing basis – and that his attendance at meetings would be very limited. Actually, he was pretty good about attending; sometimes he flew in from California or Florida at his own expense.

Cronyn felt that with the matter of Phillips' successor up in the air, it would help to attract a guest director with a big international reputation who might have some long-term association with the Festival. John Dexter's name first came up one night in January when Cronyn and Tandy were having dinner with Laurence Olivier and Joan Plowright at the Wyndham Hotel in New York, where they lived. Cronyn and Tandy had recently returned from England and Russia, where they had been doing *The Gin Game;* the Oliviers were passing through town. The discussion turned to Stratford, and everyone thought it would be a smashing idea to get Dexter involved. Plowright and Dexter had been friends for twenty years, ever since sharing their first great triumph together, with *Roots.* Peter Stevens' name came to Cronyn because of the Pickering Report, a management study commissioned by the Board to recommend the most efficient structure. The number one recommendation was that Stratford find someone to take over the executive managerial function as opposed to the artistic job. Cronyn felt Stevens would be ideal. For five years he had been the general administrator of the National Theatre in London; he had also produced for the Shubert theatre chain the London version of *The Gin Game*, starring Cronyn and Tandy, and Cronyn was impressed. Stevens had then moved to New York to work for the Shuberts.

Cronyn told Hicks, "Bob, I know these two people, Stevens and Dexter. Nobody else on the Board does. I suggest I just sound them out, on an entirely unofficial basis." Hicks thought it was a good idea. Cronyn talked to other members of the Board, who were also encouraging, and he thought he even had the blessing of Robin Phillips. When Cronyn approached Dexter and Stevens in February, 1980, he thought he was taking a long shot, but to his surprise, they both expressed great interest. Dexter, then with the Metropolitan Opera, said he had a commitment to the National Theatre in the summer of 1980, but was open after that. Cronyn reported this to Hicks and Phillips, then waited for the Board to follow up. Contact was made with both Dexter and Stevens, but then they were left hanging.

The search committee at this point was looking for the chairman of a group rather than a sole artistic director, and in any case there was a strong feeling on the Board that the Festival could not recruit another non-Canadian. Yet somehow Dexter got the idea that he was being sounded out about much more than being a guest director; he thought he was being approached about being Phillips' successor. He began turning his mind toward putting together a whole 1981 season, and word went out to his network of friends, including the Oliviers, that the top job at Stratford was in the pipeline but rather hush-hush. Arrangements were made for Dexter to fly to Toronto early in March and spend six days in Stratford looking the place over and having discussions about his involvement there.

The first Phillips heard of this was during a meeting, shortly before Dexter's projected visit, at Hicks' Toronto law office. Brian Bedford was in town doing some advance work for his production of *Titus Andronicus*, and Phillips wanted to introduce him to the search committee as a candidate for the prospective group directorate. Ronald Bryden and Barbara Ivey joined Phillips and Bedford at the meeting in a plush, richly panelled suite in one of the towers of the Toronto-Dominion Centre. Afterwards, Hicks, who was vacationing at his condominium apartment in Florida, talked to the group on a conference telephone call. Bedford had just told Phillips the hot rumour he had heard from Desmond Heeley, the designer, that Dexter has been asked to take over at Stratford. Phillips was surprised. Almost two months had gone by since Cronyn had asked him about Dexter, and he had heard nothing in the meantime. Now Bedford put the question directly to Hicks, "What's this we hear about John Dexter?"

Hicks replied, "We thought it would be a good idea for Dexter to direct a production or two."

Bedford: "Yes, but he has told people in New York that he has been offered the artistic directorship."

Hicks said he knew nothing about that; if Hume Cronyn had offered Dexter that, Hicks said, Cronyn had been out of line. During the conversation it came out that Hicks was planning to pick Dexter up at the Toronto airport and drive him to Stratford. Phillips was suspicious: if Dexter was to be only a guest director, why was he being met by the president and spending almost a week in Stratford? After the discussion about the group directorate, Hicks, who was embarrassed, asked, "Well, what shall I do about Dexter?" He knew it wasn't really the Board's function to plan productions and directors for a season; that was the artistic director's job. But it was getting late, and there was no artistic director in place for the 1981 season.

The day he was to come, Dexter called and said it was impossible. He had shingles. Hicks phoned Dexter and followed up with a letter on March 3, marked *private and confidential:* "It was delightful to talk to you recently, and I hope you are well on the road to recovery. As requested I am pleased to enclose some brochures and other material pertinent to the Festival's operation. You intimated you will be providing alternate dates when we will have the opportunity of entertaining you in Stratford. I have talked privately with two members of the executive committee, and we are most thrilled with the prospect of your being with us in '81."

Dexter's visit was rescheduled for early April. This time Bryden was to meet him at the airport and drive him to Stratford, where he would be welcomed by Phillips. The morning he was supposed to arrive, Dexter phoned Bryden and said he had had another shingles attack, and he wouldn't be able to come at all. Perhaps someone could fly to New York to see him instead. No one did. Both Dexter and Stevens felt they had been left hanging, and Cronyn started getting calls in California, where he was working on the movie *Honky Tonk Freeway:* "Hume, what's going on? I haven't heard anything."

Cronyn was in an embarrassing position. He had made it clear that he wasn't authorized to offer anything; he had simply told Dexter it was obvious Phillips would be doing far less in 1981, and there would be a need for directors of substance, with the future uncertain. Certainly Dexter qualified. He was flamboyant and controversial, and theatre people liked to argue about him; some considered him abrasive and impossibly difficult, but others re-garded him as a genius, and were so fiercely loyal they would gladly cross two continents for a chance to work with him. After his early success at the Royal Court he had become an associate director of the National Theatre during the Olivier era and had directed some of its most celebrated productions, including *The Royal Hunt of the Sun* and *Equus.* As director of productions with the Metropolitan Opera, he had brought off some of its most spectacularly theatrical productions. Dexter is a robust, witty man – also demanding, irascible, and impatient. Now he was calling Cronyn to complain that Phillips wasn't returning his calls. Cronyn tried to reach Phillips but couldn't get him (Phillips was rehearsing several shows). Finally Cronyn reached Urjo Kareda and said, "Urjo, please tell Robin to answer Dexter's calls. For God's sake, get in touch with him, even if it's only to say no. Say anything – but don't let it hang in space."

Cronyn also spoke to Hicks, and Hicks asked Phillips to call Dexter and make arrangements for Dexter to direct a production or two at the 1981 Festival. Phillips told Hicks he was reluctant to do so: "I can't approach him to come as a guest director in a season for which I am not going to be responsible." The argument went back and forth, and finally Phillips was persuaded to call Dexter and at least set things in motion. Dexter and Phillips had a couple of phone conversations, in which they agreed on a production of *Coriolanus.* Dexter was thinking of having either Christopher Plummer or Christopher Walken in the title role. But Dexter also told Phillips: "I don't want to just come and do an audition piece." He asked what was going to happen in 1981. Phillips told him he didn't know, that it was really up to the Board. Dexter started to sense that Phillips might be thinking of staying on, and he didn't want to be in the position of appearing to push him out. He told Phillips he didn't want any misunderstanding between the two of them. Phillips finally went to Hicks and said, "Bob, you have got to deal with Dexter yourself. The man thinks he is coming here to do something more than guest productions, and I am obviously not the person to be talking to him."

Meanwhile Peter Stevens had been brought to Toronto for a meeting with the Stratford Board. The meeting seemed to go well, but then Stevens went back to New York and heard nothing. He had told the Board that his wife – a literary agent – wouldn't be able to work in Stratford, so he in effect would need a double salary. Perhaps the Board felt Stratford couldn't afford him; in any case, Stevens was kept on hold. Cronyn began getting calls from Stevens, and finally called Hicks. Hicks said, "Yes, we like him, but the Board isn't unanimous as to whether he's the right man."

Dexter and Stevens weren't the only people left hanging. Throughout the search, there was only one person who was communicating with all sides, and that was Hicks. Among the people Hicks approached about being part of a group were Bedford, William Hutt, Douglas Rain and Martha Henry, Peter Moss, Peter Roberts, and Urjo Kareda – many of whom were confused about their interviews. Douglas Rain, a veteran member of the company, left a meeting with Hicks thinking he had said he didn't feel he could be artistic director on his own but he would be very interested in being part of a group; Hicks told people Rain had said no. (Phillips had put Rain's name on the directorate list because he thought he had done an excellent job at the National Theatre School.) Martha Henry's name was on the list because Phillips said it must be. "Martha is absolutely first class," he would say. "She's the one person in Stratford that everyone reveres." Weeks were spent on such delicate problems as, "Well, if we have Brian, then we have to have so-and-so."

In May, 1980, Hicks chaired a meeting at Stratford's Victorian Inn at which control of the Festival was more or less offered to a trio – Urjo Kareda, Peter Moss, and Peter Roberts. Moss was the only director who had been developed by Phillips; Roberts had been the Festival's production manager for eight years; and Kareda had been the Festival's literary manager since 1975, when Phillips had wooed him away from his job as drama critic of the *Toronto Star*. Kareda, an extremely private person by nature, wasn't in the public eye; he wasn't a director of plays (except in collaboration with Phillips or Moss) but Phillips had come to rely on his shrewd instincts and judgements, and his prodigious knowledge of the acting, writing, and directing talent across the country.

Phillips had hinted earlier in press interviews that he saw Kareda as a possible successor, but by 1979 Kareda was no longer being spoken of as the heir apparent. Some people wondered whether Phillips' attitude to Kareda had changed. Kareda told Hicks in May that the proposal involving Moss, Roberts, and Kareda seemed to be contingent on some involvement by Robin Phillips which hadn't been spelled out. Hicks said the committee would get back to them; they didn't hear anything more for two months. It was becoming clear to Hicks that a group directorate wasn't going to work without Phillips, who was still advising Hicks to do what he thought best for the Festival, and not to count on his availability.

Recruiting members willing to lend their names and their part-time talents to a group directorship was no problem, but finding a chairman was a very considerable one. This elusive figure had evolved into the Godot that all of Stratford was waiting for. It had to be someone who would live in Stratford and work full time for the Festival, so that Phillips could be released from his cage. It had to be, to satisfy the businessmen on the Board, somebody with a glittering name and star presence. To avoid further controversy, it had to be someone who was already a member of the company or else a landed immigrant, if not a Canadian citizen. Brian Bedford was one possibility, but he didn't want to be tied down. He wanted to go on working at Stratford but also to go on being free to accept such lucrative offers as the national tour of *Deathtrap* and the national tour *Whose Life Is It Anyway?* – activities that earned him more than ten times his Stratford salary.

Then along came John Neville – who seemed like the perfect solution. Neville was an actor-manager in the old English tradition. He had been in Canada since 1972, he was known throughout the international theatre world, and he had made all the short lists of possible successors to Phillips. He claimed to be reluctant to leave the Neptune Theatre in Halifax, where he had gone in 1978, but no one was sure how serious an obstacle this was. Neville was a showman in the flamboyant nineteenth-century tradition; an air of mystery was part of his stock in trade. He came and went with the dramatic flourish and suddenness of biblical revelations.

One enduring mystery was what made him leave the empire he

had built and ruled for five years at Edmonton's Citadel in favour of the relatively small-time Neptune. In both Edmonton and Halifax, Neville's relationship with the community was talked about in almost mystical terms. He didn't just mount plays and occasionally act in them; he nurtured and infiltrated, even drank with, the people of his constituency. He had grown up working class in London before working class became fashionable in the theatre, and in 1963, when he created the title role in the original production of *Alfie*, he had the right Cockney accent. He had earned his reputation as a Shakespearean at Nottingham and the Old Vic, but *Alfie* was his big break, and he was disappointed when the movie role went to a young unknown named Michael Caine.

In March, 1980, the same month Dexter had been invited to visit Stratford, Ronald Bryden went to Halifax and saw Neville in Ibsen's *The Master Builder* and took part in a panel discussion on the play. Neville and Bryden had crossed paths years before in London. While they were chatting in Halifax, Neville asked what was happening in Stratford. Bryden said there was going to be a group directorate, and it would be lovely if Neville could be a part of it. He invited Neville to come to Stratford to talk about the possibility.

Neville arrived by plane from Halifax in May. Bryden picked him up at the airport and drove him to a meeting at Hicks' Toronto office. Hicks was enthusiastic about putting the Festival in Neville's hands, but when Hicks told Neville he was the only person to whom the job was being offered, Neville was sceptical. Bryden drove him to Stratford, where he had a meeting with a group of Board members, and spent part of the evening at the home of Robin Phillips. Everybody was in a buoyant mood. Phillips and Neville, who had worked together in England at Chichester (with Neville playing Macheath in Phillips' production of *The Beggar's Opera*), were very effusive with each other. They talked about how gorgeous it would be if they could work together at Stratford.

But Neville was full of misgivings that he didn't talk about that night. He had always thought that Stratford was overrated as compared to other theatres around the country, and he felt the place had grown to an unwieldy size. His instinct for self-preservation told him Stratford could kill him. It was not clear to Neville what his working relationship with Phillips would be like. Neville gathered that he was being invited to become the head of a group that might or might not include Robin Phillips, and that Phillips, if he stayed, would be responsible to Neville. But Neville couldn't tell whether Phillips was planning to stay. It was very late to be organizing a 1981 season, Neville knew. Phillips assured him the season was partly planned – John Dexter was going to do a production of *Coriolanus* – and Neville would inherit the plans. The Board people who'd met Neville seemed to regard the Neville-Phillips combination as a panacea, and Neville didn't say anything to disabuse them of the notion.

A few days later, though, Neville sent a note saying, basically, "No thanks." Hicks and Bryden were stunned. Bryden sent a letter to Neville asking him to explain what had gone wrong; Neville never answered the letter.

Perhaps Neville sensed the acute psychic tension imposed by this place. It wasn't easy to live in Stratford, especially for artists who needed a cosmopolitan environment. Stratford was peaceful, and the parkland greenery along its riverside drive gave it a certain beauty not shared by some Ontario towns where railway tracks had been allowed to spoil the waterfront. But apart from the Festival, Stratford was culturally and intellectually starved. The deprivation was hardest on those who had to stay all winter, when the snow made it seem even more isolated and even trips to nearby London or Kitchener seemed perilous. In this atmosphere, the arrival of a half-decent new movie for a day or two at the one movie house in town became a monumental event to be anticipated for weeks. Actors coming to work here sometimes felt as if they were entering a monastery; they had to cling to their colleagues and to the work itself for survival. That's what drove John Hirsch and others away. That's why Phillips and some of his actors dreamed of developing an annual Toronto season. And that's why Phillips felt a strong need to get out.

CHAPTER SIX

The Summer of Our Discontent

At the end of May, when John Dexter left for England to do a production of *Galileo* for the National Theatre, he took an enforced rest by sailing on the Queen Elizabeth 2. Dexter was in a fury because no one from Stratford had come to see him in New York. He had agreed to direct a production of *Coriolanus* in 1981, but had his heart set on the top job, and he was expecting someone to get back to him with an answer. Dexter was holding off on other projects – including a chance to direct Elizabeth Taylor in *The Little Foxes* – and he became so agitated about being kept waiting that he told Zoe Dominic, who was on her way to Stratford, "You can tell that fucking Board from me they can just piss off."

When Phillips called Dexter in London to settle the question of a designer for *Coriolanus*, it was obvious something had gone awry. (Phillips thought Dexter would want Tanya Moiseiwitsch, who often worked with Dexter at the Met, and who would have to be booked early.) "I do not want to come to Stratford to do an audition piece," Dexter said. "I will talk only when I know what my on-going commitment is going to be." He hung up. After that, Phillips couldn't get through to Dexter, who had started rehearsals for *Galileo* and wasn't taking calls.

Stratford's 1980 season opened officially on Monday, June 9, with two productions directed by Robin Phillips. At the Avon Theatre in the afternoon, there was a bizarre, chaotic production of *The Beggar's Opera,* featuring the new Stratford Youth Choir. This choir had been an obsession with Phillips ever since the Ontario Youth Choir serenaded him at Stratford's opening-night gala in 1978. Phillips seemed bent on recapturing that magical moment, and phenomenal efforts were put into raising the money for this new toy. When it was finally shown off to the public, Phillips seemed oblivious to the fact that the choir, with its fresh-scrubbed faces and best behaviour, was exactly wrong for *The Beggar's Opera*, which needs a tacky, tawdry ambience – a touch of the disreputable.

For the big first night at the Festival Theatre, Phillips had chosen a new production of *Twelfth Night*, which had been staged in this same theatre in his first season. It was a fine summer evening, and, as usual, the gentry of Upper Canada came from Toronto and London in tuxedos and evening gowns, stopping to feed the white swans that had been released from their winter cages to glide along the Avon River. The production was impressive, but curiously subdued, with a cast including Brian Bedford (as Malvolio), Patricia Conolly, Pat Galloway, William Hutt, and Kate Reid.

It was on the second night, at the Avon Theatre, that Phillips scored one of the great triumphs of his career. The play was *Virginia*, starring Maggie Smith as Virginia Woolf, and compiled out of Woolf's own works by the Irish writer Edna O'Brien. The play came to Maggie Smith through her London hairdresser, who also happened to be Edna O'Brien's hairdresser. It came to Robin Phillips from Smith, and Stratford quickly reached an agreement with Arthur Cantor, the producer who had commissioned the play.

If anyone was born to play Virginia Woolf, it was Maggie Smith. Yet some people may have felt that Woolf had earned the right to be judged on her work alone – that she should be spared the questionable honour of being turned into a character. Luckily, the fears were groundless. What's most important about *Virginia* is what is left out. The audience does not see Woolf going mad or drowning. O'Brien refrains from dragging in roomfuls of performers doing cameo turns as Bloomsbury celebrities. There are only three people on the stage – Nicholas Pennell, who plays Virginia's father and then her husband, Leonard Woolf; Patricia Conolly as her friend and lover, Vita Sackville-West; and Maggie Smith in the title role. Fragments of Virginia Woolf's life run together as they would in memory, without punctuation and scene changes to indicate the time gaps. It's the theatrical equivalent of a stream-of-conscious prose style.

The look Smith achieved in the role was stunning, her gauntness accentuated by a plain, elongated dress with a sweater over it, the hair pulled back severely in side rolls. There were unsettling moments when the audience laughed at a remark that wasn't funny, as if cued by a Maggie Smith nasal trick too often used to italicize wisecracks. But early on it became excitingly clear that this wasn't just another crack Maggie Smith performance. In *Virginia* she was testing herself, taking risks. The star was recognizable, but it was clear, too, that she had been taken over – and was giving herself up to the role. In *Much Ado about Nothing,* which opened the same week, it was sublime fun to see Maggie Smith trading witty put-downs with Brian Bedford, but her *Virginia* was on a different, and higher, level.

In other productions there had been signs that Robin Phillips' clean, crisp style could be a limitation as well as a virtue; at times, when rhetoric was used to fill the vacuum where the recognizable human emotion should go, it was wearying to hear all his well-exercised actors speak so beautifully. Sometimes his productions seemed *too* clean and *too* cool. But in *Virginia,* the crispness and the sharp, elliptical staging worked brilliantly, and the audience was caught in a kind of spell. There's a glimpse of Virginia with "a new book pumping in my brain, my mind agape and red-hot with it." The last words of the text are "something tremendous about to happen..." and the audience leaves intoxicated, aware that something tremendous has already happened. A literary heroine has been reincarnated through a theatrical heroine, and great words have been unforgettably well spoken. Robin Phillips, Edna O'Brien, and Maggie Smith did something unexpectedly wonderful by refusing to use Virginia Woolf's madness and suicide for cheap effects. By celebrating the miracle of Woolf's words, they earned the right to call her back from the grave and demonstrated their own sanity by showing the side of her that was gloriously, brilliantly sane.

Virginia was the crowning touch in a season that seemed to have been planned in the spirit of "Shoot the works; there's no tomorrow." There had been visiting stars before, but never so many in a single season. Not only did Phillips have Maggie Smith back, and her ideal leading man, Brian Bedford. He also had Cronyn and Tandy, and Kate Reid coming home triumphantly with her great performance in John Guare's *Bosoms and Neglect,* and Peter Ustinov repeating his nervily comic King Lear from the 1979 season. There were fifteen productions scheduled in all, including eight the first week. For insiders there was the added excitement of speculating what the future might hold for Stratford and Robin Phillips. On paper, the 1980 season was so dazzling that one or two people wondered whether Phillips' secret fantasy was to mount a season so brilliant that the Board would have to beg him to stay forever, and name his own terms.

Robin Phillips was, among other things, a skilful strategist, but he had a fatal tendency to overreach himself and get caught in his own manoeuvres. One of his most ingenious schemes was to get a group of the leading London drama critics brought to Stratford each year during opening week. Even the most prestigious British newspapers are notoriously penny-pinching when it comes to paying the expenses of their cultural commentators on foreign missions, but they have no qualms about allowing their writers to travel if the tabs are picked up by the host country. The critics of the *Guardian,* the *Observer,* the *Telegraph,* and the *Financial Times* came regularly to Stratford with a substantial portion of their expenses covered by the Ontario government's department of tourism.

The benefits for Stratford and for Robin Phillips were considerable. The critics were impressed. They said Stratford was a world-class company, compared it with the Royal Shakespeare Company and the National Theatre, and proclaimed Phillips one of the reigning geniuses of the English-speaking world. But in June, 1980, one of the British visitors picked up the rumour that John Dexter might be the next artistic director at Stratford, and by reporting it in England provoked an incident.

In July, Hume Cronyn received a letter from Michael Anderson, John Dexter's agent at International Creative Management in London, enclosing a letter he had written to Phillips on Dexter's behalf. "Dear Robin," it began, "I understand Michael Billington has suggested in the *Guardian* that John Dexter will be taking over from you at Stratford. Presumably he heard this story at Stratford. As there were never any further discussions between John and yourself, he has because of other pressures moved forward with other plans. The rumour is therefore something of an embarrassment, and he would be grateful if his name were not mentioned publicly in this manner."

On August 6, Cronyn replied to Anderson, "My thanks to you and John Dexter for your courtesy in sending me a copy of your letter to Robin Phillips. Please tell John there's no need to write. I understand now regrettably, and wish that I'd stifled my ambassadorial impulse. I think I shall not remain long on the Board here. I cannot for the life of me unravel what goes on in camera."

Cronyn was depressed and angry. He had been encouraged to make contact with Dexter, and then nothing had happened. It wouldn't have been so bad if a decision had been made not to proceed with Dexter or, for that matter, with Stevens. But all this business of hanging fire was getting to Cronyn.

Cronyn had another reason for being disenchanted. He had done some work for the Board on film and cable-TV rights, and he wasn't pleased with the response to that, either. Cronyn is a shrewd entrepreneur and producer. He had just made a deal with RKO for a cable-TV version of *The Gin Game*, starring Cronyn and Tandy. He knew something about the economics of the business and felt there was enormous potential not only in cable TV but also in discs and casettes. Cronyn's idea was that any losses the Festival incurred through operating the theatre could be balanced by revenues from selling, in advance, options on the rights to cable-TV versions of Stratford productions. Not only could this provide a long-term answer to the Festival's financial problems, it linked up with Robin Phillips' vision of adding a film empire to the theatre empire. On behalf of the Board, Cronyn had gone to see the heads of movie studios in California. Cronyn then showered the Board with brochures and reports, but nothing was done about it.

Meanwhile the Board was in trouble over the collapse of plans to film the 1979 production of *The Importance of Being Earnest*. Stratford had brought in Harvey Chusid to work on the administrative side of the production and had signed a contract with Norfolk, a Toronto film company which had (in co-operation with the CBC) produced *Connections*, the sensational TV documentary about the Mafia. The choice of *Earnest* was questionable from the beginning. A quite marvellous British movie, with Dame Edith Evans heading an all-star cast, was readily available to the public. The Stratford production featured William Hutt playing Lady Bracknell in drag, and though he got away with this on the stage, it was doubtful he could get away with it on the screen. Had Stratford waited too long to get into film? With the BBC going right through the Shakespeare canon in full view of the English-speaking world, this was hardly the moment to start producing Shakespeare films.

Stage One, with its schemes to construct a film production centre behind the Avon Theatre, was one of Phillips' pet projects, and the plans had been announced with great fanfare. But Hicks felt Phillips had overextended himself. Stratford also had a commitment to a season at the Haymarket in London in the fall of 1980, and this compounded the pressures that doomed the film version of *Earnest*; maybe it just wasn't possible to do everything that Phillips wanted to do.

The dispute about the *Earnest* film became terribly complicated and acrimonious, with Norfolk threatening to sue. Cronyn was shocked because it seemed to him that the Board had made a commitment it wasn't possible to honour. Looked at closely, this might have sounded an alarm. Was the Board defaulting on a commitment because something better had come along?

As the 1981 season loomed closer and closer, with no sign of a decision about who was going to be in charge, panic mounted. The only hope was a group directorate including some or all of the people that Hicks and the search committee had been talking to, though many of these had said they would be interested only if Phillips would stay on. Early in July, Len Cariou, while visiting Stratford, joined Phillips, Hicks, Brian Bedford, and Martha Henry at The Church restaurant. They sat for three and a half hours at a quiet table, kicking ideas around. Phillips stressed that if he were going to be involved in 1981, others would have to take charge for the early part of the season, so he could have some time away.

A few days later, Phillips and some of the key people around him had a meeting on the balcony terrace of the Festival Theatre. The point of the meeting was: the Board hasn't found anyone, this place is in trouble, what are we going to do about it? The group put together a very specific proposal which was submitted, after a series of meetings, to the Board for approval. Part of the proposal was the Toronto season that Phillips had always wanted. The group attempted to explain the structure of the proposed directorate so carefully that the Board would not be able to get it wrong.

The group had arrived at its eleventh hour many times before its final proposal was hammered out. There had been concessions all around. Once Hutt was included, there had to be a place for Douglas Rain. Phillips seemed to be in control but refused to be called anything like artistic director. People were being asked to acknowledge publicly that Phillips wasn't in control, while privately they clung to their assumption that he was. Phillips blew his stack once because Brian Bedford didn't seem willing to carry his share of responsibilities. Bedford, on the other hand, was upset that Phillips didn't want to be called artistic director.

After all the months of searching, the initiative was being taken not by the Board or its search committee but by the artistic group. Hicks was ill, and Ivey was in the chair on July 24 when the Board met at the Stelco office in Toronto to consider the group's proposal. Ivey kept having the secretary read the proposal to be sure that her colleagues knew precisely what they were voting on. Her friend William Turner needled her, "Oh, for God's sake, Barb, we've heard that a million times. Just call the question." The Board voted to approve and implement the proposal from the group, but attached certain conditions. "Lines of responsibility in the method of the operation of the directorate" were to be clarified and recorded. The expansion into film, TV, touring, and a Toronto season was accepted "providing they are economically feasible." The executive committee was urged to clarify the administrative structure within the group, and was authorized to approve a press release on the whole scheme.

The Board was being offered a way out of its dilemma, but only on condition that it accept certain developments Phillips had wanted for years. It was hard to attract and hold talented people, he felt, because Stratford was so isolated. The expansion would give Festival actors contact with the rest of the world. But many Board members would accept a Toronto season only if there was a guarantee that it wasn't going to place the Festival in financial jeopardy.

It was John Heney, vice-president of a Stratford furniture company and past president of the Board, who called Phillips to say that the Board had unanimously accepted the group's proposal. Everyone was terribly excited. Phillips felt relieved and pleased that he was going to get time away, that there would be a Toronto season, that the future of his staff people was secure. After two or three days, he started to press for acceptance from the Board in writing. It was then he noticed that the Board seemed to be responding to him as if the proposal had been his, rather than to a group of which he happened to be part. He told Hicks and Heney, "You must forget about one person running this place. This proposal is from a group of people. You have to understand it isn't any good to come back to me as if I were the head of it."

On July 29, the day Kenneth Tynan died, Urjo Kareda began keeping a diary entitled How It Works. His first entry was, "This is not a good day for literary managers."

The Board sent Phillips a copy of a proposed press release announcing the group directorate. Phillips thought it was dreadful. He told Kareda, "We'll have to write our own press release, explaining what our proposal was and stating that it was accepted by the Board."

They did just that, but Hicks kept rewriting the release, taking out offensive words like "collective" and putting in what the group considered mysterious lawyerese. "Doesn't he realize," Barbara Ivey asked in exasperation, "that by making *any* changes he raises suspicions?" Phillips went over Hicks' version with Kareda, making comments like, "Look, they've changed that word, that was a key word, and if they change it, the implication is…. That's why we must get their acceptance of *our* proposal in writing."

Agreement was finally reached on the fourth draft press release. But a few days later, when Hicks submitted a fifth press release, Kareda noted in his diary that Phillips had decided, "There is nothing to discuss." (This was a pet phrase of Maggie Smith, whenever angry.) In Phillips' view, there had been too much wavering by the Board, too much fiddling, too much release diddling in lieu of contracts. Phillips professed to feel helpless and made it clear that he no longer felt he could trust Hicks. He felt that Hicks had equivocated on Stage One and the Toronto season, and now was equivocating on the group. The Toronto season was the key to Phillips' continued involvement with the Festival because he kept wondering whether he was going to be stuck in a small town the rest of his life.

On August 5, Phillips sent an abandon-ship memo to other members of the group: "Since reading you a copy of the fourth press release and one that has been acccepted by the Board of Governors, a fifth version has now been submitted to our group by the Board. (They had given no warning that they were going to submit another version, only full approval of the fourth.) The subtle rewording of this – 'projected Toronto season' instead of Toronto season, etc. – it fills me with dread. I am not prepared to continue discussions with the Board. Please feel free to present any proposal of your own. You know how much I admire all of you and I hope we will all be together at some point in the future."

The argument was symbolic of the whole deteriorating relationship between Hicks and Phillips. Hicks seemed to be trying to control Phillips, and the things he said sometimes sent Phillips into rages. Pam Brighton called Barbara Ivey to say she felt the situation was getting out of control, and a meeting was hastily put together. It seemed clear to everyone that Phillips was going to pull out. Then Robin bounded into the room and began talking about plans for the 1981 season, which sounded exciting enough to top the 1980 season. Several days later, Hicks, seeming very distressed, called Brighton in and told her he thought Phillips was going to leave. Hicks went on about how he loved him like a son, how he couldn't imagine anyone else running Stratford. "What kind of pressure," he asked Brighton, "do you think would work on Robin?"

By August 12, the impasse appeared to have been resolved. Another press release was prepared. Photographs were assembled, including Len Cariou's high-school graduation picture. A meeting of the company was scheduled for 5 P.M. At 4:45 P.M., Hicks, still working on a press release, phoned Kareda to ask what Broadway shows Cariou had been in. Standing in the rehearsal hall waiting for the meeting to begin, Barbara Ivey read the announcement aloud to herself and remarked, "Any theatre should be so lucky." But Peter Moss was calling this latest configuration "the emperor's new clothes." And Pam Brighton was muttering about "the short and dark duration of this association."

The press release was headlined "Major Artistic Restructuring Announced by Stratford Festival." It continued:

On behalf of the Board of Governors of the Stratford Festival, R.V. Hicks, Q.C., President, today announced that with the co-operation of the Festival's company, the restructuring of its artistic administration has been completed. In order to consolidate and extend the ongoing vitality and growth of the Stratford Festival, the organization will be administered by a two-tiered committee working collectively.

The first tier, artistic directors, will consist of Brian Bedford, Len Cariou and Martha Henry.

The second tier, resident directors, will consist of Pam Brighton, William Hutt, Urjo Kareda, Peter Moss and Peter Roberts. Douglas Rain will serve as liaison chairman within the organization.

Both groups will be under the guidance of Robin Phillips, who as Festival director will be a member of each group.

The two-tiered committee will be responsible for the ongoing artistic policy of the Festival and for planning and executing each year's program in Stratford and a winter program in Toronto at a location yet to be determined. The group will also integrate the development of Stratford's connections in New York, in London, and in films and television.

It is anticipated that the contracting of the directors involved will soon be completed.

By being able to draw on the exceptional range of skills and experience represented by the members of the joint committees, The Board of Governors feels that the artistic values for which the Stratford Festival has become famous will be secure. These will also be brought into play in shaping the future directions of the Stratford Festival.

*   *   *

On August 13, the day of the announcement to the press, the group (except Cariou) met in the VIP room. Phillips was unnerved by the emphasis placed on his staying on but found it hard to talk about his misgivings with Hicks in the room. There had still been no acceptance in writing of the group's proposal. It was always coming, coming, coming. At one point, when Phillips confronted Hicks about this, Hicks asked, "Oh hasn't Fran [Tompkins, the Board secretary] typed it up yet?" In front of Hicks and the group, Phillips said only, "I have to remind all of you we are about to issue a press release when we have not had our proposal accepted in writing, and none of us have contracts. Therefore we are announcing publicly something that is entirely on trust."

At the end of the meeting, the press release went out.

Within a couple of days of the announcement, trouble began. Cariou was upset because the announcement was made without his being told. Phillips was furious because he had learned from Bedford that Cariou would not be available before June, 1981. Bedford had already made it known he wouldn't be available for the beginning of the season. Maggie Smith was anxious over press speculation about her plans. Phillips was beginning to see clearly that he was going to be left holding the baby after all. "I have this recurring nightmare," he told Pam Brighton. "It's the middle of the winter and there's no one else here except you and me – and we find we have to slam through the whole season by ourselves."

Meanwhile the Board had decided to hire Peter Stevens (at a salary of $75,000), the logic being that in the absence of the magic artistic chairman, Stratford must have a strong man on the administrative side. Stevens was to arrive on October 1.

The two-tier group lasted precisely two weeks, perishing on August 27 with the sudden and mysterious defection of Robin Phillips. All along, Phillips had experienced a deep ambivalence, though one thing probably contributed most to his decision to leave. Phillips was furious when he learned that Bedford and Cariou had had their contracts negotiated with Hicks; the money had been settled, but no requirement had been spelled out as to their responsibilities and time at Stratford. Phillips' five-year contract as artistic director still had a year to run, but he felt he had served notice more than a year earlier that his term was over at the end of the 1980 season. He had told Hicks several times he needed a new contract to define his quite different responsibilities under the new arrangement.

When one didn't materialize, Phillips began doubting everything that Hicks said.

"Bob and I discussed the new contract several times," he told Barbara Ivey. "I know," Ivey told him, "but no matter what he said, I know he means to hold you to your old contract."

Phillips' worst fear was confirmed: the new structure was just so much window dressing; he would be expected to go on bearing all the responsibility himself. "He can just stuff it," he told his friend Joe Mandel.

Hicks was very distressed when he got the news from Barbara Ivey on Wednesday, August 27. Ivey had received a message from Mandel: Phillips was withdrawing from the group directorate but did not wish the word "resign" to be used. How was it possible, Hicks wondered, for something that had taken so long to arrange and been worked on by so many people to collapse so suddenly and completely? Ivey felt Phillips, while exhausted and overwrought, could see clearly that he must, for his own good, leave. This time she wasn't going to be the one to talk him out of it.

Ivey said, "He means it. I know he means it. Don't even try to discuss it with him. Just accept it."

Hicks said there was a problem of timing. Should the Phillips withdrawal be announced immediately, or should it be delayed a few days?

"Don't delay," Ivey said emphatically. "He just isn't strong enough to go through any more of this. He still has *Lear* and *Long Day's*

Journey to direct. The quicker we relieve his mind by accepting his resignation, the better he'll be able to finish them."

Hicks phoned Phillips from The Church and said, "I've got some time, can we chat?"

Phillips: "I've got some company right now."

Hicks: "I just want to say how disappointed I am, but I think I understand your position."

Phillips: "Thank you."

Hicks: "I just want to talk to you about the timing of the press announcement."

Phillips: "Well, I think the sooner the better."

Festival publicist Leonard McHardy was instructed to write a press release. A few days later Hicks and McHardy took it around to Phillips' house. It was a hot day but Hicks wanted to wait in his car while McHardy went in. Hicks said he would come in if there were any trouble.

Phillips became enraged when he came to the word "resign." It was impossible for him to resign, he said, because there wasn't anything for him to resign from. He had resigned more than a year ago from his old position and the new one hadn't been contractually defined yet.

"This is rubbish," Phillips told McHardy. "This statement doesn't explain why I'm not going to be here any more. Quite honestly, they haven't given me a contract. The whole point of the new arrangement was to relieve me of my old responsibilities, and they've offered contracts to Cariou and Bedford, yet they expect me to go on with my old contract."

Hicks appeared at the door, wondering why McHardy hadn't come back out yet. Phillips said sharply: "Bob, you're going to have to come clean. You know this press release doesn't give the true explanation. You know very well you haven't tried to make any arrangement for a new contract. That is the whole point."

Hicks and Phillips began arguing about just what had happened. Phillips claimed he had been lied to, because there was no new contract.

Hicks continued, "I believe we tried on two occasions to call your agent, Mr. Sharkey, in London, but we couldn't get him. The office said he was away on holiday."

Phillips retorted, "I have just spoken to him. He is in his office *right now*."

Outside, still shaken, Hicks said to McHardy, "I guess that gives you some idea of what we've had to deal with. He's not well."

The intricate fencing match Phillips and Hicks had been conducting all summer had come to a violent end. Later, Hicks would tell colleagues that he was trying to protect Phillips, because he feared that if the Board were given the task of working out a new contract for Phillips, the hardliners would want to cut his $75,000 salary on the grounds that he no longer assumed nearly as much responsibility. When told this theory long afterwards, Phillips would say, "The silly fool, why didn't he just tell me that?" He would even write a note to Hicks months later, wondering whether he had misconstrued Hicks' motives, and whether it had all been a misunderstanding.

The next few weeks were charged with bitter emotions and confused attempts to salvage something from the wreckage. On Friday, August 29, Hicks held an emergency meeting in the rehearsal hall of the Festival Theatre with the remaining members of the two-tier group and his colleagues on the executive committee. Hicks broke the news – which was already a hot rumour – that Phillips had pulled out. According to Hicks, Phillips' resignation had been "accepted with thanks." Hicks knew it was too late to begin a search for a new artistic director for the 1981 season, so he suggested retaining the structure of the two-tier group, with everyone minus Robin "carrying on as described."

Brian Bedford announced that he was withdrawing at once. As far as he was concerned, the only point of having a group was to keep Robin Phillips on board. Bedford had had a sleepless night coming to his decision, but without Phillips as an anchor for the group, he wasn't willing to take the risk. He didn't want to be trapped into responsibilities for which he might be ill suited. Martha Henry left during the meeting to go to a rehearsal of King Lear. Long regarded as the company's leading lady, she had accepted only one role this year – as Goneril, one of Lear's two nasty daughters. In a break from their usual practice, Henry and her husband, Douglas Rain, agreed to appear in the same production; he was playing Gloucester. Rain followed her out of the meeting, asking before he left whether the Board had approached anyone about replacing Robin Phillips. Bedford suggested that Kareda was the only possible chairman of the group. Kareda indicated his reluctance. Peter Roberts speculated that the Board might be forced to choose between the 1981 season and the London run of *King Lear*.

The Festival's contract with the Theatre Royal in the Haymarket, London, was creating a fiasco almost as spectacular as the mess over the 1981 season. And these two catastrophes were fatally interconnected. Now with no future at Stratford to contemplate, and in a state of exhaustion, Phillips didn't have the reserves to get *Lear* to London. Phillips had resigned or threatened to resign many times in the past five years and had always been talked out of it. Why had this resignation been "received with thanks"? Perhaps Phillips didn't realize that Hicks had gone as far out on a limb as he could go, and that he was already being heavily criticized by colleagues on the Board who felt Hicks ought to have accepted Phillips' resignation months earlier. The future of the Stratford Festival had turned into a private struggle between these two men, each trying to budge the other. Now it was suddenly over, and neither of them could quite comprehend it. Phillips had reason to expect he would once more be begged to stay. Why should it have occurred to him that a point would come when people would say, "Right, goodbye, we'll try to get along without you"?

CHAPTER SEVEN

The Serpent's Tooth

Less than two weeks before the opening of *King Lear,* Robin Phillips went to see Peter Ustinov to advise him to withdraw. Ustinov had come to Stratford at Phillips' invitation to star in *Lear* late in the 1979 season. The limited run had been sold out months ahead of time, and the production had been a triumph. Ustinov had been lured back to do a repeat run in 1980 on the understanding that the production would then go to London. Ustinov had Phillips' personal word that he need not appear at Stratford unless there was a London run as well. On several occasions earlier in the year, Phillips had tried to cancel the *Lear* revival because he feared he might not be able to honour his promise to Ustinov. Now the London run seemed impossible again, and Phillips was counselling Ustinov to withdraw.

The consequences, they both knew, would be staggering. The tickets had already been sold. The Festival had invested about $460,000 in the production which could not be recovered. The public would be disappointed. There would be a terrible uproar.

Phillips offered to take responsibility and face the public. But instead of being grateful that Phillips was willing to put himself on the line to make good on his promise, Ustinov was baffled and angry. He was already in the middle of rehearsals; it was too late to make alternative plans. The 1979 production had been exciting for Ustinov, but this year Robin Phillips seemed like a different person. Ustinov found rehearsals strained and perfunctory. Phillips was locked into battle with the Board, and Ustinov felt like an intruder in a troubled family.

"I have absolutely no reason not to open," Ustinov told Phillips rather curtly. "I'm not going to be the one to break the contract. Go ahead and do it, and we'll all have to face the consequences. It's too late to call it off; I am already deeply engaged."

To play Lear had been a lifelong dream for Ustinov. Before he came to Stratford, he had been negotiating with Alexander H. Cohen, the American producer, for a Broadway production and had even started to work out an interpretation with Frank Dunlop, who was to direct it. But the project had been stalled. Robin Phillips heard about it from Maggie Smith, who had just finished the movie *Death on the Nile* with Ustinov. On the basis of Smith's high praise for Phillips, Ustinov sent word that he would be willing to do a production at Stratford. Phillips flew to New York on American Thanksgiving in November, 1978. He and Ustinov met at the Algonquin Hotel and struck up an instant rapport. A deal was made: Ustinov would star in a Stratford production of *Lear*, which would be "presented in association with Alexander Cohen." Cohen would have the option of taking the production to Broadway.

Ustinov's arrival in Stratford in mid-August, 1979, was awaited with more than eagerness. There was a kind of desperation about it, because the Festival needed Ustinov to bring back the ingredient that had been missing all season: star power. It had been the season of Phillips' "partial sabbatical"; Maggie Smith and Brian Bedford were also taking a year away from Stratford. The season was heavy on history plays – both parts of *Henry IV* on the Festival stage, a *Richard II* with three different Richards at the Avon – and these English chronicles had never been popular in Canada; the box office was in trouble.

Like Charles Laughton and Orson Welles, Ustinov is a large man who took decades to grow into his own body, which he now occupies with a kind of magisterial authority. Also like Welles and Laughton, he is a multi-talented person who keeps several careers going simultaneously. He is the author of twenty plays, including such hits as *The Love of Four Colonels, Romanoff and Juliet,* and *The Unknown Soldier and His Wife;* eight movie scripts, including the one for *Hot Millions* in which he starred with Maggie Smith; several novels; and the delightful autobiography *Dear Me.* He has directed seven movies, including a fine adaptation of Melville's *Billy Budd* with Robert Ryan, Terence Stamp, and himself.

Ustinov had wanted to play Lear since he was fifteen; at fifty-eight he was the perfect age. Phillips asked Ustinov at their first meeting what he thought the play was about. Ustinov said it was a military play, all about station and degree. They decided to do it in the period of 1820 to 1850, without crowns. Rehearsals were so intense that Ustinov's unending supply of entertaining anecdotes was welcomed as comic relief. Rehearsals were open to all members of the Stratford company, and they came to be dazzled and charmed by Ustinov.

Ustinov played Lear as a geriatric bungler, and he brought out the comic possibilities. It was a risky, unorthodox performance, and it worked. The 1979 production was uneven, with a few feeble supporting performances, but it had an electricity, and moments of greatness; William Hutt's Fool was especially memorable.

Duncan Weldon and Louis Michaels, operators of Triumph Productions and owners of the Theatre Royal in the Haymarket, London, had come to Stratford in 1978 to talk to Maggie Smith about doing something for them. They met Robin Phillips, and they had a conversation with him about the possibility of bringing the Stratford company to London. In August, Weldon wrote to Ustinov:

I have been asked by the William Morris office in London to write to you direct, although I know you will have already heard from them regarding the contents of this letter.

I think your appearance in *King Lear* is extremely exciting, as I am sure you must regard it. We are, as you are probably aware, the owners of the Theatre Royal in the Haymarket, and we should love, if it be your wish, to present you in *King Lear* some time next year at our theatre. We have often spoken to Robin Phillips about the possibility of such a project. We would be more than happy to bring the production as a whole for a London season to the theatre, or if you and Robin wished, to re-stage it just using you two with an English cast.

However, such details are a bit premature at the moment. All we wanted to do is let you know of our interest now so that you have plenty of time to turn it over in your mind.

Obviously I shall look forward to coming to Stratford to see the production and I take this opportunity of wishing you an enjoyable period of rehearsal and a huge success in a role you seem ideally suited for.

Weldon and Michaels arrived in Stratford on the last weekend of the 1979 season to begin serious discussions. They had dinner at The Church on Saturday, November 3, with Robin Phillips, Peter Ustinov, and Ustinov's wife. On Sunday they saw the closing performance of *King Lear*. Everyone was enthusiastic about taking Stratford's *Lear* to the Haymarket. Nothing specific was nailed down, but there was much talk to and fro about bringing other productions along with *Lear*. It was at this time that Phillips promised Ustinov he wouldn't be held to a return engagement in Stratford unless the London run became firm.

On January 31, 1980, Ustinov's agent cabled Thomas Hooker, Stratford's company manager, who dealt with contracts, questioning the number of performances that had been scheduled for Stratford and pointing out that Ustinov's Stratford appearance was "contingent on the production moving directly to London."

On February 12, Weldon wrote to Robin Phillips announcing that he and his partner would arrive later that month along with James Sharkey (Phillips' agent and a friend of Weldon) for a weekend meeting. Ustinov, who had a concert appearance in Hamilton, would join them. "Let us hope," Weldon's letter concluded, "our weekend meeting will be the beginning of an exciting future together."

Everything seemed to go smoothly at that meeting. Weldon and Michaels met Robert Hicks and Gary Thomas, who seemed to be learning for the first time that Ustinov wasn't committed to coming back unless the Stratford run were a prelude to the Haymarket engagement. The Festival was most eager to have Ustinov's name in the brochure for the 1980 season. In London *Lear* was to be part of a package, suggesting the range of the company. The other plays weren't set yet, but strong possibilities were *Virginia* and two of Phillips' most acclaimed productions from previous seasons, *Measure for Measure* and *Richard III*. Details couldn't be finalized at that point, but there was a firm understanding that a deal would be made.

Something else was percolating between Triumph and Phillips. Michaels and Weldon wanted to form a repertory company to produce about four plays a year at the Haymarket; they asked Robin Phillips to be the artistic director. The Birmingham Playhouse would also be part of the deal. Before going to the Haymarket, each production would have a pre-London warm-up in Birmingham, where it would be part of the subscription series. Phillips couldn't fail to find the offer titillating, and his agent was promoting it. Under Sharkey's advice, he had rejected several other job offers in North America and had just turned down the top job at the Chichester Festival – the one he had been so disappointed to miss out on immediately before he came to Canada. Phillips realized there weren't many moves he could make from Stratford that would count as a career advance. In England there were really only two jobs he could aspire to – at the Royal Shakespeare Company and the National Theatre – and neither showed any prospect of becoming open. According to Weldon, the Haymarket deal might make him the world's highest-paid stage director; Phillips would get a share of the profits if the shows were hits. Phillips indicated he was especially interested if Maggie Smith could be persuaded to become a member of the Haymarket company.

After the visit of the Triumph management, the signals were positive for a Stratford engagement at the Haymarket. On April 29, Louis Michaels wrote to Gary Thomas:

Thanks very much for sending the contract, which has just arrived. I have an appointment with our solicitor to put it into more concise terms as I do not think that some of the items are clearly defined. I hope to be able to send you a draft of this by the end of the week.

Trusting that all is well.

Warmest regards.

But all was not well. Stratford's Board had discovered that the cost of sending four productions to London was prohibitive, and there didn't seem to be any subsidy available to help defray it. The Haymarket season was cut down to *Lear* and *Virginia*. (This led to bitter jokes, inside the company and out, about Canada's national theatre going to England to show the British those two well-known Canadian actors, Peter Ustinov and Maggie Smith.) Even at that the Board was going to have to raise at least $200,000 to finance the venture. When the contract came back from the Haymarket, with expenses itemized, the projected cost began to escalate. A central issue became the question of who was going to pay for the rental of lighting and sound equipment – Triumph or Stratford.

Early in June, Gary Thomas sent a cable to Weldon and Michaels: "Costs for proposed tour will have to be borne as set out in our contract draft of April 1, 1980. Please confirm your acceptance by 4 p.m. EDT."

Louis Michaels replied by return wire: "Cable received, cannot accept ultimatum. Accepted practice in England and Canada that visiting management bears total responsibility for sound and lighting. Sincerely hope this is end of argument. Kindest regards, Louis."

On June 11, Stratford cabled Triumph: "Further to your cable of June 10, mutual settlement appears impossible. Therefore obliged to withdraw our proposed formal agreement sent to you under letter dated April 18, 1980. Further discussions are not warranted."

Mindful of his promise to Ustinov, Robin Phillips now tried to cancel *Lear*. He would try to do so again, but *Lear* kept being resurrected despite his anxieties. Phillips called Ustinov in California, where he was making a movie, to tell him about the contract problems. He warned Ustinov he didn't feel sure Stratford could go through with the Haymarket project. Ustinov said, "Well let me know quickly because I've got another offer here." (The other offer was a film that would have paid $500,000.) Phillips called back and told Ustinov not to worry; he said he personally would make sure the Haymarket run did go ahead.

The cables continued. On June 14, Michaels took a conciliatory tone:

While I have been dismayed by recent tone of negotiations from Stratford, which would suggest that you have either changed your mind about coming to London or have other difficulties of which we are unaware, nonetheless I want tour to go forward. I am resolved with your co-operation to find solutions to our present problems. While I continue to maintain the outstanding matters of lighting, sound equipment and insurance are Stratford's responsibilities, I would like to suspend further unproductive argument and simply seek a solution. William Morris Agency as agents of Ustinov have offered assistance in seeking third party additional finance and between us seems reasonable optimism to acquire this quickly. We must agree on amount necessary to be found. Please be kind enough to show this cable to Robin Phillips. Would be most grateful if you would call me on receipt of this cable.

The next cable was from Phillips' agent, who was to be the British agent for the Stratford company on tour. Sharkey also put his mind to seeking a solution. "Sure differences can be resolved unless there's something we don't know here," he cabled Stratford. "Imperative we talk. Please call."

But the Festival wasn't in a mood to compromise. Its next cable to Triumph insisted: "Our position unchanged. Disappointed tone of negotiation has deteriorated and terms proposed by you have changed considerably since agreement at our February meeting."

To which Louis Michaels retorted with more than a hint of pique: "Totally confused by your return cable. Our terms have never been altered since our February meeting. Please will you answer clearly the contents of our cable of June 14. Do you wish to come or not?"

All this led to several phone calls, and in the last week of June, Weldon and Michaels, accompanied by Sharkey, again made the trip to Stratford. They eventually agreed that Triumph would provide, free of charge, the sound and lighting equipment already in the Haymarket theatre, and that if additional equipment was required, the cost would be shared. Louis Michaels lost his temper once, but the tone of the negotiations was generally amicable.

On August 6, Gary Thomas sent off a signed copy of the contract, along with a covering letter:

> The signed contract arrived in Stratford in today's mail. Many thanks for returning it so promptly. I am enclosing a signed copy for your records.... As you can understand, we are all anxious to know whether or not *Virginia* will be presented as well. I know that Robin will be closely involved with those dicussions but if you have any information I would be pleased to hear from you. I hope the next time we meet will be in London. I am looking forward to that day.

Six days later a letter was mailed to Thomas from Gilbert Harrison in the Triumph office: "Duncan and Louis are away for two weeks holiday as from today but I will bring the matter to their attention on their return. As far as I am aware all is progressing well as far as *Virginia* is concerned.

* * *

On September 4, the day after advising Ustinov to call off the opening of *King Lear,* and just a week after his withdrawal from the group directorate, Robin Phillips learned that his father had died. He made plans immediately to attend the funeral and spend a few days with his family.

Flying to England to bury his father, Robin Phillips felt as if his world were collapsing on all fronts. His parents were working-class people, country people. They thought of themselves as simple and uneducated. The world of theatre was alien to them, but they had completely supported Robin and his aspirations. He, in turn, felt his parents had made it all possible for him. Now with his father dead, he felt he had no reason to go on. His father had died of cancer, and he had gone through his own cancer scare just around the time his father's cancer had been discovered. Now Phillips was feeling ill again, and wondering whether cancer was going to kill him, too.

As the plane streaked through the long darkness of the Atlantic, he remembered the letter Hicks had written two years earlier to his parents, when both he and his father were seriously ill. It had been an enchanting letter full of fatherly concern and fatherly pride. Here was Bob Hicks trying to find words to tell Phillips' parents what a marvellous person their son was, and how proud Hicks was of him, and how pleased they should be of all his spectacular accomplishments. Thinking back on that wonderful letter from a man toward whom he now felt an almost uncontrollable rage, Robin Phillips felt more alone than he had at any time in his life.

While Phillips was away for his father's funeral, the Haymarket crisis reached hysterical levels. Gary Thomas cabled Triumph that the Haymarket engagement was "becoming impossible." On September 5, Louis Michaels cabled back in a tone of panic:

Am amazed and confused by your ambiguous cable. Every sympathy with Robin Phillips' personal bereavement but must inform you Triumph has relied on and acted on and now holds Stratford bound by contract dated July 24th. Triumph are preparing without prejudice to consider some minor cast replacements but Triumph cannot accept cancellation Haymarket engagement. Please send scenic designs as early next week as possible and confirm by return Stratford will fulfil contract.

Going to London as president of the Board represented a personal milestone to Robert Hicks; he had even rescheduled the Festival's annual meeting (from the last Saturday of November to the first Saturday of December) so that he would still be in office on December 1, the day *Lear* was to open at the Haymarket. But there were more practical reasons for pushing ahead with the project: the Festival, having signed the contract with Triumph, could be liable for devastating sums in damage suits if the production failed to open. Several times Phillips had tried to cancel *Lear*, and several times Hicks had resurrected it. Now the London run of *Lear* became the final symbolic battleground for the showdown between the two.

During the first week of September, Ronald Bryden made the first of several attempts by the Board to save the Haymarket run.

He thought that Phillips was under too much pressure, and that if some of the pressure were removed, Phillips might be able to sort out the Haymarket mess. His idea was that someone else take over as director of Long Day's Journey into Night, which was the last production of the season and had been scheduled to open at the Avon during the first week of October. Jessica Tandy was heading the cast, and Bryden's notion was that Hume Cronyn – not only the star's husband but also a member of the Board and, on occasion, a director – could take over from Phillips. When he called Cronyn's Stratford house, Tandy answered the phone.

"Oh, Ron," she said, "Hume had a few days between performances of Foxfire, and he's gone to New York to get some business taken care of."

"Well, Jessie," said Bryden, "this concerns you, so perhaps I should tell you what it's about and ask you what you think of the idea."

Tandy had no hesitation in replying that she was absolutely opposed to having Phillips replaced. No matter what was going on, she told Bryden, Phillips was in great form at rehearsals.

The big problem with Lear and the Haymarket was the casting. Except for Ustinov, the actors hadn't been contracted while the issues between the Festival and Triumph were being sorted out, and many had got tired of waiting and made other plans. The British press had built the public up for a London visit by the Stratford company, and Phillips knew that the productions would have to be absolutely top drawer. He made it clear he could not handle extensive recasting of Lear. While all this wavering was going on, Peter Ustinov was getting increasingly irritated. He felt that his Lear was being used by Phillips as a battering ram to get back into the Festival. In Ustinov's view, Phillips was behaving like a child in a supermarket who makes a scene so that everyone will look at the mother accusingly, as if to say, "What did you do to that child?" Ustinov saw Hicks as the unfortunate mother getting hostile looks from the other shoppers.

Hicks and Gary Thomas went to Ustinov to acknowledge there was trouble.

"Why doesn't Robin want to go to London?" Ustinov asked Hicks.

"Your guess is as good as mine," Hicks replied.

"Well, I'll tell you what I believe," Ustinov said. "I think he's afraid the production will fail and the critics won't like it. It's his first production back in London since he left for Canada. If it's successful, I guess he's concerned I'm going to get the credit. So he doesn't win either way." Then Ustinov chuckled and shrugged.

A couple of days after Phillips returned from his father's funeral, he called a meeting of the *Lear* cast for some notes and last-minute rehearsing. Everyone assembled at the Avon Theatre, but Phillips didn't show up. After waiting an hour, Ustinov, furious, drove to the Festival Theatre, where he stormed into the office of Thomas Hooker, who was dealing with the *Lear* contracts.

"What the hell is going on?" Ustinov demanded.

"I haven't the vaguest idea," Hooker replied.

Under pressure from the Triumph people in London, Ustinov had been trying to get the rest of the cast signed up for the Haymarket. Phillips had instructed Hooker to clear all cast changes with Ustinov. Hooker had checked with Ustinov about several changes, and Ustinov, dubious about some of them, had made alternative suggestions. It was Ustinov's understanding that contracts were being prepared and were going to be offered to the actors as soon as Phillips had returned from England.

Now Ustinov asked Hooker, "Have the contracts been presented to the actors as they were supposed to be?"

Hooker: "No, I've been told not to give them to the actors."

Ustinov: "By whom?"

Hooker: "Need you ask?"

Ustinov: "Then would you do me the courtesy of finding out whether the rehearsal is on or off?"

At that moment the phone rang. Ustinov told Hooker, "I think it would be better if I wait outside. I can imagine who that is."

A few minutes later Hooker came out and said, "It was Robin. The rehearsal is off."

Ustinov: "But I'd have had no way of knowing that unless I had come to see you."

Hooker: "He doesn't feel terribly well. I told him you were furious the contracts had not been offered to the actors. He said, 'In that case, offer them.'"

Ustinov began to feel he was walking on quicksand. The situation reminded him of a union using a go-slow strategy. If you screamed, things got done; but if you didn't nothing got done.

On Friday, September 12, Hooker quit. He told Ustinov life had become infernal. Gary Thomas had been telling him they had to find a way to make the Haymarket engagement work. The Board was determined to go, but also not to spend any more money than originally planned, and the numbers kept coming up wrong.

Duncan Weldon and Louis Michaels arrived from England the same day, making a last attempt to save the Haymarket run. After a breakfast meeting with Phillips on Saturday, they told Ustinov they were very depressed. They were appalled to discover how few of the cast had actually been confirmed. And Phillips had told them that, given the number of changes required, he just couldn't do it; he wasn't physically strong enough at this point to get the show ready for London. Ustinov, feeling stubborn and angry, was adamant: the cast problems could be solved.

On Saturday afternoon a summit meeting took place in the VIP lounge of the Festival Theatre. Robin Phillips bounded in full of optimism. "I think it still *can* be done," he said. Weldon and Michaels looked amazed. Ustinov tried to make encouraging noises while privately he wondered what had precipitated this sudden change of heart. Was it the the threat of lawsuits? (Ustinov himself had earlier told Hooker he intended to sue if the project fell through.) Or was it the realization that if *Lear* failed to open in London, the offer to lead the Haymarket repertory company would go down the drain? Whatever the reason, Phillips was now playing to the hilt the role of the miracle worker who comes in to save everyone from disaster at the eleventh hour, and laying out the details of his rescue plan: "I'm going to try to get some of these people late in the day who just may be available.... We could do this.... There's a point here on which we can be astute...."

On Sunday evening, September 14, *King Lear* opened at the Avon. The 1980 production had stronger performances in the supporting roles, but some of the excitement had been drained out; perhaps too much energy had gone into the off-stage skirmishes. However, once again Ustinov gave a daring, eccentric performance.

Backstage afterwards, Phillips was running around trying to sign up cast members for the Haymarket. He was especially irritated about the reluctance of Douglas Rain and Martha Henry to go. Rain's explanation was that his elderly mother had been moved to Stratford so Rain could look after her, and he couldn't leave her. Henry, of course, had heavy responsibilities in Stratford as part of the directorate which was trying to put together a 1981 season.

Finally, under heavy pressure, she agreed to go.

Ustinov, meanwhile, had several visits from Barbara Ivey, who suggested that Pam Brighton could take over from Phillips for the London run. Ivey asked Ustinov whether he thought Brighton could do it, and Ustinov said that with his help she could. But Ustinov and Ivey both knew it was Phillips whose name would be in the program and that Phillips would have to take the blame for any problems caused by a replacement director and a replacement cast. The situation was impossible; five days after the Stratford opening, the Haymarket run of *King Lear* was called off.

Robin Phillips wrote to Ustinov: "Dear Peter, I'm angry, shocked and, for you, deeply upset. I hope one day you'll understand how hard I've worked to see that you are in the right company. Until then, I love you and love your Lear. I'm sorry. Love, Robin."

Ustinov was enraged by the letter, which seemed to him like a final stab in the back. He mentally drafted replies to Phillips, "But you *can't* be surprised by what's happened. You made it happen." During the rest of his stay in Stratford, Ustinov didn't talk to Phillips. Phillips seemed to be giving some sort of theatrical performance which Ustinov no longer even wanted to try to understand. In Ustinov's view Phillips was like the master at a strict academy, demanding absolute loyalty and obedience from his followers. Those who had given it were hardest hit when the whole place caved in. A couple of cast members spoke to Ustinov about taking a delegation to Phillips, asking him to reconsider, but Ustinov wanted no part of it. "There's no question of appealing," he said. "I'll finish my contract, and after that I don't want to hear about it."

The whole fiasco landed on the front pages of the newspapers when Ustinov announced that he was suing the Festival. A few weeks later, he told the press that the most extraordinary thing was that he had heard not a word from the Board since the collapse of the Haymarket plans.

Late in the seven-week run, Robert Hicks and John Heney went to call on Ustinov. "You don't know what we've been through," Hicks said, blaming Phillips for the whole mess. "If you knew what we'd done to protect him." Ustinov had to admit he would hate to be in the Board's position, having to deal with Phillips. But he blamed the Board for failing to control him, which had become even more difficult once it was settled that Phillips was leaving.

"Would a public apology suit you?" Hicks asked.

"I can't talk about that now," Ustinov said. "So much harm has been done. It has taken so long for this offer of an apology to come that I can't take it with any grace."

Heney said, "I can certainly understand your attitude."

(Eventually Ustinov would settle his claim against the Festival for $45,000. Counting legal fees and payments to Triumph for expenses, especially trips to Stratford, the total cost to the Festival would be $152,000. It might have been much higher if Sharkey hadn't arranged for *Virginia,* again starring Maggie Smith and directed by Robin Phillips, to fill the slot in the Haymarket schedule that *Lear* was to have occupied.)

Ustinov was still licking his wounds when there was another unpleasant incident. The CBC had planned to shoot a TV version of Stratford's *Lear,* but the Association of Canadian Television and Radio Artists refused to approve the appearance of Patricia Conolly, an Australian. ACTRA was willing to accept Ustinov, an international star, but there were to be no other non-Canadians in the cast. Stratford refused to go ahead without Conolly, and the project was called off.

A few months later, Ustinov was dining in a London restaurant when he ran into a prominent English actress who had worked with Robin Phillips at Chichester. She told Ustinov she'd heard about his trouble in Canada, and then she began railing against Phillips.

Much to his astonishment, Ustinov found himself leaping to Phillips' defence, insisting that no matter how irritating his behaviour was at times, Phillips was an exciting, absolutely first-class director. When he was at his best, Ustinov insisted, there wasn't a director in the world who could touch Robin Phillips.

CHAPTER EIGHT

The Gang of Four in Office

At the end of a Board meeting in Toronto on September 5, Robert Hicks took Hume Cronyn aside and asked him to take over as artistic director for the 1981 season. It was the third time he'd been offered the position. Years earlier, when Michael Langham was leaving Stratford, Cronyn had been approached about the job. Though he might have been surprised and flattered, Cronyn wasn't tempted. Then in 1976, while he was appearing in *A Midsummer Night's Dream*, Cronyn had been at the home of John Killer, president of the Board at the time, in the presence of Hicks and Heney. They were looking for a successor to Phillips even then and made Cronyn a specific offer. He had also been offered the equivalent job at the Guthrie Theater in Minneapolis and at the American Shakespeare Festival in Stratford, Connecticut.

Each time, it became easier to say no. Cronyn would say that he and Jessie had their life in New York, and that anyway it should be someone younger and better steeped in the classics. The truth was he just didn't want the job on any terms. At times he had pondered over what he would do if he actually took the job. In his first season, he decided, he would not direct a single play; instead, he would concentrate on bringing in the best people he could find – administrative people as well as creative people – and not worry about giving them too much power. But he knew that no matter how much help he enlisted, he would have no private life. As an independent operator, Cronyn could be a gadfly, mixing acting with producing, writing, and directing. But if he became the head of a huge institution, he knew he could never have a holiday when he didn't have to fret about the casting of a play or interference from the Board. At all hours of the day and night, no matter how far away he fled, he would be beset by nagging problems: fund-raising worries, where to dig up a director for this or that play, how to administer an operation with hundreds of employees. He had been given a close-up view of several of these monster cultural institutions, and he knew in his heart that running one of them wasn't for him.

Now, less than a year away from his seventieth birthday, here he was again, being backed into a corner by Bob Hicks and earnestly entreated, "Have you reconsidered, Hume? Have you changed your mind?"

Cronyn stared at Hicks and shook his head, speaking very deliberately. "I'm sorry, Bob," he said, "I *haven't* changed my mind. It's just not a job I want."

* * *

Meanwhile, the two-tier directorate was turning into a game of ten little Indians. Two of the Indians – Robin Phillips and Brian Bedford – had already disappeared. A third, Len Cariou, was in New York, and unavailable until June, 1981. The remaining seven gathered to assess their position on September 7. Douglas Rain felt strongly that the group shouldn't meet again without a written agenda and a written proposal from Hicks on how the Festival could be run by the group. The very next day there was a typed proposal from the Board, and the group had a meeting with Hicks and three other Board members – Heney, Oliver Gaffney, and John Lawson – to go through the draft contract. To most queries, Hicks replied, "We'll have to get back to you." It was a psychological blow to some people in the group that the Board was making a big distinction between full-time members of the group and part-time members (Moss and Brighton). The members of the group wanted a commitment in writing that would put them at least on equal footing with Peter Stevens. Board members, however, kept talking about team-work and trust. The matter of whether there would be a chairman was also becoming a sticky point. Some members of the group felt a publicly named chairman would be too clear a target for Stevens and the press (Stevens was to arrive in a few weeks and no one knew exactly what his role would be), but the group agreed to have an internally perceived chairman. It quickly became apparent that Kareda would assume this role.

The next day, Kareda wrote in his diary: "Another gloomy meet-

97

ing. We all seem very depressed and defeated, and the paranoia level is high. The favourite guess is that they're after someone who can't come until '82, and we are being set up. Douglas feels they are not acting with good intent. Meet with Hume tomorrow for blunt questions. Hume says Board wants a chairman."

On September 11, two more Indians dropped out – Peter Roberts, the Festival's production manager, and William Hutt, who said there was simply not enough time to do a 1981 season.

The remaining five Indians – Urjo Kareda, Martha Henry, Douglas Rain, Pam Brighton, and Peter Moss – met yet again on the rainy morning of September 13. Henry and Rain were upset to discover that Thomas Hooker had quit and Barry MacGregor had offered his resignation as company manager. Then everyone went to a bizarre meeting with Hicks and other Board officers. Hicks had called the meeting, but after everyone was seated he turned to Martha Henry and said, "Yes, Martha?" as if she had called the meeting. Hicks then spoke of resignations from Peter Roberts and Douglas Rain, but Rain was in the room and obviously hadn't resigned. (Hicks must have meant Hutt. Members of the directorate were unnerved by the inability of some Board members to tell one member of the directorate from another. One Board member, for example, often called Pam Brighton "Martha.")

Cronyn promised the five that they would get word by the end of the day, and in writing, of the Board's decision to proceed with them. And they did. Late that day there was a letter of intent from the Board – the closest thing to a signed contract that the new directorate would ever see.

The next day, Rain had a private chat with John Lawson, a Stratford businessman who was second vice-president of the Board, and then told the others he had decided to drop out. Henry said she would have to reassess her position. Was she willing to remain in a group from which her husband had just withdrawn?

That night, Henry and Rain were among the actors on stage at the Avon for the opening of *King Lear*. Backstage after the show, Robin Phillips kissed Urjo Kareda's hand – an odd gesture punctuating their disintegrating relationship. Phillips had told Martha Henry, "Urjo won't speak to me any more." Kareda, who had been waiting for weeks to hear from Phillips about a proposed get-together, thought it was Phillips who had stopped communicating with him. For reasons that weren't entirely clear perhaps to either of them, Robin Phillips' relationship with the man who had been one of his most trusted and valuable advisers for five years had lapsed into an uncomfortable silence.

The next day, September 15, Peter Moss wrote an extraordinary letter to Hicks:

The succession of artistic leadership at Stratford has become for many reasons an extremely public affair. From a relatively simple contractual agreement between the Board of Governors and an individual or group charged with ensuring artistic quality of the Festival, negotiations have become a public and political arena for acrimony, charges, regrets, and countercharges. From a unified group of nine, comprising two tiers with a Festival director, we have moved to a directorate of five, and now four.

While appreciating the support the Board has now publicly displayed to the remaining committee, I cannot help being aware of the circumstances involving personal sacrifices, strained friendships and loyalties, and undue public attention. I feel that by accepting this offer now, and by committing myself to working on the 1981 season at Stratford, I have taken a larger professional and personal risk than I otherwise would have taken.

Accordingly, although I am accepting this offer, I wish to make it clear that after this announcement is released, if any circumstance arises that makes the Board change its mind, or withdraw its confidence and support, unless directly due to the work of the committee, I shall feel entitled to take the matter to law for damages.

On that same September Monday, another extraordinary document was drafted. Hume Cronyn sat down and worked through four pages of recommendations on how the directorate ought to proceed. Cronyn had won a Tony for playing Polonius to Richard Burton's Hamlet, and now he was playing Polonius in real life.

"Dear directorate," he wrote in a covering letter, "this is only an attempt to be helpful – encouraged by Urjo. Perhaps it will provide useful discussion. Much of it you will have already considered. Forgive what's simplistic. If I can be of further use, call me – but as there is little likelihood of my being readily available in 1981, there is not a great deal I can offer after October 15. Good luck."

At the top of his first page of recommendations, he wrote, "No preamble. Plunge in. Perhaps that constitutes my first recommendation."

There were sixteen suggestions on the organization of the artistic directorate:

1. That the directorate have its own confidential secretary/co-ordinator whose exclusive duties are to the directorate alone.

2. That from the point where the directorate has absolute authority in regard to artistic policy (I assume it is immediate but have not read the Board's authorization) that the directorate refuse to entertain any change in its mandate regardless of new developments, possible reversals, etc.

3. That the directorate refuse to accept individual resignations from its membership during the first twelve months of its existence regardless of cause, difference, etc.; that *in extremis,* and only then, a dissenting member of the directorate file a brief with the Board *but* the first year's commitment be absolute (this, obviously, for the protection of the whole).

4. That the directorate attempt to maintain the existing Festival staff and that possible changes of *key* personnel, regardless of desirability, *not* be considered in the immediate future. (No, I am not hinting at desirable changes.)

5. That the directorate establish a rigid policy of scheduled meetings and adhere to it and to *attendance* through thick and thin.

6. That the directorate establish a firm majority rule as to its policy decisions, i.e. whether it is to be a simple majority...or unanimity, or whatever.

7. That the directorate be prepared to delegate authority in any specific area of its operations, so as not to be overwhelmed by a mass of minutiae.

8. That in all such matters of delegations and indeed, in all matters dependent on execution outside of the directorate itself, instructions be confirmed in writing and initialed by at least two members of the directorate. (Get a large supply of appropriate and distinctive forms quickly.)

9. That the directorate establish a policy of regular, formal – as opposed to men's room, or on-the-stairs informal – consultation with key Festival personnel at least once a month, so as to be kept constantly aware of departmental problems.

10. That the directorate petition the Board for representation thereon – and that in the instance of anything other than a routine

report of its activities, particularly in the instance of a critical or controversial problem before the directorate, it ask for attendance by a second member of the directorate.

11. That the directorate attempt to confine its work to decisions affecting artistic policy alone: choice and number of productions, choice of directors, casting, stage management, scheduling, etc. Areas of overlap will of course be inevitable but in doubt, *delegate*.

12. Co-opt into the directorate, but without fee or vote, any individual who may be given overall responsibility for managing the Festival's business affairs. If you want his/her vote you can always ask for it but if you are not already aware of business/ management reservations or objections, you're not only poorly informed but in big trouble.

13. The directorate should reserve to itself – and so inform the Board – the right to add *one* other individual to the directorate as he/she may emerge as a vital force within the Festival's total operation. This does not exclude a member of the Board of Directors any more than it does a member of the maintenance staff. I am tempted to enlarge on this but resist it.

14. That the directorate's designated chairman approach each meeting of the directorate with a manageable agenda and that every attempt be made to stick to it and to have the secretary record its decisions.

15. That the directorate adopt some stern policy with regard to the media, interviews, etc. Otherwise, you will be driven crazy. Perhaps Urjo, as an ex-journalist, can suggest specifics here.

16. That the directorate seek help – the Board's help if necessary – in establishing its authority during the transition from the existing regime to its own new one. Perhaps a Festival-wide directive is required.

On the policy of the artistic directorate, Cronyn had eleven recommendations:

1. That the directorate organize its own procedures – ignoring or considering the above suggestions – as a first order of business.

2. That the directorate approach Robin Phillips and ask for his participation in the 1981 season as the *first* of a number of guest directors who may be invited to participate.

3. That the directorate call as immediate a company meeting as

possible to announce – in general outline and without reference to any specific except for the one immediately preceding – its intention for next season.

4. That the directorate establish its priorities with regard to its commitments for the 1981 season – whether to directors, actors, designers, etc. – and proceed accordingly but that in every instance and without exception, it place a deadline on the acceptance of the individuals so approached.

5. That the directorate give careful consideration to the number of productions to which it can do justice in its first year of operation – without inhibiting reference to the pattern of former seasons.

6. That the directorate try to define for itself and for its tenure alone – however long that may be – the nature of the Festival; whether it is to be international in scope and recruitments or purely Canadian; whether weighted in one direction or another; that a guiding principle once established not have to be continually debated.

7. That the directorate give consideration to a program so balanced in its first season that it risk popularity even at the expense of purity. (If that is to be construed as a cowardly suggestion, so be it.)

8. That the directorate try to avoid the necessity of double casting directors.

9. That the directorate not hesitate to engage immediately those actors it feels are of indisputable value to the Festival company, even though the roster of productions and directors may be incomplete. (A problem here is, of course, whether actors will accept a contract under such conditions.)

10. That the directorate give due recognition to the fact that it is the director and role, not the company, or the facility, or money that is the strongest magnet for the experienced actor; that it do all in its power to encourage Canadian directors but beware of substituting chauvinism for excellence. (Forgive this bit of pedantry.) A list of a dozen directors other than those who are members of the Stratford directorate follows: There is bound to be wild disagreement on certain names – and certain of them have had unhappy experiences or histories at the Festival. Nevertheless, in the writer's opinion, they are all talented and all approachable: John Dexter, John Schlesinger, John Hirsch, Mar-

shal Mason, Ronald Eyre, John Neville, Vivian Matalon, Gordon Davidson, Ellis Rabb, Arthur Penn, Brian Bedford, Len Cariou.

11. That the directorate establish a proceeding for welcoming guest directors that provides tea and sympathy as well as whisky and Aspirin; that they be introduced to key personnel and generally be made to feel that they are indeed welcome.

Two days later, Urjo Kareda wrote to Cronyn, thanking him for his proposals, which Kareda considered "shrewd" and "useful." The letter ended with an expression of personal gratitude for Cronyn's generosity, and was signed, "Love Urjo."

The same day that Cronyn wrote his manifesto, he and three other Board members (John Lawson, Oliver Gaffney, and John Heney – the three Stratford businessmen in charge of negotiating a contract with the directorate) met with Kareda, Henry, Moss, and Brighton. The meeting was so positive that afterwards Kareda wrote in his diary: "It seemed possible at this meeting to believe in the Board's good intentions." The four did not want to be an interim measure and had decided to reject a one-year commitment. The Board members assured them that the Board was committed to a three-year term. They also let the group know that the Board had felt left out by Robin Phillips and needed more communication from the new directorate.

Martha Henry, who had been wavering, was so encouraged by this meeting that she agreed to stay on. She had had a long-distance phone conversation with Len Cariou, and they had agreed that since he wasn't going to be available until June, there would be no point in including him in the group charged with responsibility for the 1981 season. There were now only four Indians left. Moss and Brighton, who had come from Toronto for the meeting, stayed the night at Kareda's house, and the partying went on until five in the morning.

* * *

These four survivors of the ill-fated two-tier group became known almost immediately as the Gang of Four, though only Kareda and Henry were full-time Stratford employees. Pam Brighton – always an outsider in this group – had been recruited for the earlier directorate by Robin Phillips partly because she was a director in vogue in Toronto, and Phillips wanted Stratford to develop a winter home there. Originally from Yorkshire, Brighton got involved with the

English theatre in the late 1960s, having dropped out of the London School of Economics. In the 1970s, she became both professionally and personally involved with Guy Sprung, a young Canadian who was running the Half Moon, an exciting fringe theatre in London. Brighton took over the Half Moon when Sprung decided to return to Canada. In 1977, she followed him to Canada, and when their marriage broke up, she settled in Toronto. Brighton's productions of *The Club* (at Toronto Workshop Productions), *Ashes* (at the Phoenix), and *Dusa, Stas, Fish and Vi* (for Theatre Plus) soon gave her a cult following, and she even became the darling of the Toronto critics for a season or two.

In 1978, Robin Phillips asked to meet her, and they got on well from the start. Though they were both from England, their experiences in English theatre were very different. Perhaps because her projects were so experimental, there was no question of competing with Phillips. He invited her to do a production of *Yerma* by the Spanish playwright García Lorca. After reading the translation of it, she called back to say she didn't like it, although she would be prepared to do a production of improvisations inspired by *Yerma;* to her surprise, Phillips said yes.

In the summer of 1979, while she was in Stratford preparing the show, she spent a lot of time with Phillips, having supper with him a couple of times a week at The Church. Brighton was aware that Phillips had an appalling record with guest directors, and she felt lucky to be an exception. Once they became friends, Phillips told Brighton he had been frightened of her at first, that she seemed very aggressive, and that he had been relieved to discover she wasn't a monster after all. Brighton was given a plum for the 1980 season – a marathon production of Shakespeare's rarely produced *Henry VI*, telescoping parts one, two, and three into one play. It was one of the largest, most ambitious productions ever attempted at the Third Stage, and toward the end of the summer Brighton was made a member of the two-tier directorate.

Peter Moss, the other part-time member of the Gang of Four, had the distinction of being the only Canadian director developed by the Festival during the Phillips era. He grew up in Montreal's Jewish community, then got his theatre training in England, where he was associate director of the Crewe and Phoenix theatres. At Stratford he directed or co-directed *Henry IV, Parts One and Two,*

Henry V, The Merry Wives of Windsor, Ned and Jack, The Woman, and *The Servant of Two Masters.* He had just taken on a full-time job as artistic director of the Young People's Theatre in Toronto when he was recruited for the Stratford directorate.

Urjo Kareda and Martha Henry, the two full-time members of the directorate, are both by temperament withdrawn. Kareda, whose first language was Estonian, grew up in Toronto and then went to King's College, Cambridge, on a scholarship for graduate studies in modern drama. Returning to Toronto in 1970, he held down two full-time jobs, as a movie critic for the *Toronto Star* and an English teacher at the University of Toronto's Erindale College. When the legendary Nathan Cohen died suddenly in February, 1971, Kareda (at twenty-seven) stepped into his job as *Star* drama critic and played an important role in the explosion of the small theatres and the development of Canadian plays in the early 1970s. This was the dream that Cohen had nurtured for nearly twenty-five years, though he got to see the Promised Land only from a distant mountain top. People who knew both Cohen and Kareda were astonished by the physical similarities between them. Both were large men whose weight seemed to lend authority to their critical pronouncements; both gave the impression of being older than they were.

Phillips shrewdly recognized Kareda's talent and lured him away from the *Star* in 1975. A few months after moving to Stratford as the Festival's literary manager, Kareda was almost killed in a car crash and spent most of the 1976 season in hospital.

Martha Henry is so unassuming that it seems ridiculous to call her a star, though after playing major roles with shining distinction for sixteen seasons she has earned the right to be considered the company's leading lady. She grew up in Detroit, studied theatre at the Carnegie Institute of Technology in Pittsburgh, and came to Toronto in 1959 to work at the Crest theatre. It was there that she met Powys Thomas, the actor, who persuaded her to attend the National Theatre School in Montreal, which was just being established. While at school, she landed a part at the Manitoba Theatre Centre, beginning a long association with John Hirsch and the city of Winnipeg. (One of the legendary characters in her life is Ann Henry, the Winnipeg playwright, columnist, and mother of her first husband, actor Donnelly Rhodes, who dropped his family name, though Martha kept it, even after the marriage was over. Her second husband, Douglas Rain, whom she married in 1968, is also from Winnipeg.)

Henry made her debut at Stratford as Miranda in *The Tempest* in 1962, and even a partial list of her Stratford credits is staggering: Cressida in *Troilus and Cressida* (1963), Cordelia in the 1964 *King Lear*, Dorimene in *Le Bourgeois Gentilhomme* (1964) and Elmire in *Tartuffe* (1968), Viola in *Twelfth Night* (1966), Desdemona in *Othello* (1973).

At the end of the 1968 season, Henry went with Douglas Rain to England, where he played the title role in *Hadrian the Seventh* in the West End, and she, after a lot of trouble finding work, landed a part in a bad but commercially successful West End thriller, and played the leading role in a six-part BBC television series based on *Daniel Deronda*. Before returning to Canada, she spent six months in New York, appearing in three plays at Lincoln Center, where Hirsch was a regular director. Back in Stratford, she and Rain settled into a domestic routine. They had a child and bought a house. When her daughter was old enough to start school Martha Henry went back to working at full throttle, moving into the richest phase of her career as she approached forty. Stratford regulars by this time had come to regard her as the epitome of grace, nobility, and quiet intelligence.

* * *

When Martha Henry agreed to stay on in the group directorate, one of her conditions was that the Board would have an open meeting and answer all questions from the company. That meeting began in the rehearsal hall of the Festival Theatre at 11 A.M. on September 18. Sitting on the stage along with the Gang of Four were several members of the Board, including Robert Hicks, John Lawson, and Hume Cronyn. The room was filled with about seventy members of the company—Jessica Tandy and Brian Bedford in the front row, and Maggie Smith very noticeable in dark glasses.

Hume Cronyn gave a pep talk, urging his fellow members of the company to throw their complete support behind the new group. These four people could do the job, he said; they were intelligent, dedicated, and familiar with Stratford. "There may have been a great many mistakes made," he said, "but these four people deserve your support."

During the question period, Richard Monette asked about contracts for the four. Hicks replied, "We're looking at a three-year term." Brian Bedford was openly sceptical. He asked whether government by four would not inevitably lead to chaos. "Where does the buck stop? Who's in charge?" Bedford's pessimism hung like a cloud over the assembly.

At the end of the meeting, a press release was distributed:

The Board of Governors today confirmed that Robin Phillips will relinquish the position of Artistic Director of the Stratford Festival at the end of the present season. Mr. Phillips confirmed his resignation to the Board in writing in January, 1979, to become effective in November, 1980, and the Board respects his decision.

"Robin Phillips has built the Stratford Festival into one of the most significant theatrical organizations in the world," said R.V. Hicks, president, announcing the resignation. "His dedication, talent, energy and sheer brilliance have been an inspiration to everyone connected with the Festival Board, staff and audiences alike."

The Board has now authorized an Artistic Directorate to succeed Mr. Phillips. The new Artistic Directorate, chosen from the present artistic community of the Festival, comprises: Urjo Kareda, Pam Brighton, Martha Henry, and Peter Moss. They will immediately begin to plan and execute the 1981 season.

"We are totally committed to this cohesive new group," said Mr. Hicks, "and it is a matter of pride that they have been chosen, and have accepted their role, from within the present Festival ranks."

Mr. Phillips said, "I am extremely grateful for all the opportunities that the Board of Governors have given me during my time with the Stratford Festival, and for the wonderful support of the staff and company. I shall miss the Festival enormously. All best wishes to the new team and I know they will call on me for advice and support if they need it."

Hicks' words—"totally committed to this cohesive new group"— would come back to haunt him. The Board should have realized that the Gang of Four were being placed in a position that was not merely difficult but almost impossible. They were following a superstar, Robin Phillips, and they weren't inheriting an artistic or administrative structure that had been planned to survive his departure. It was alarmingly late to be starting to put together a season for 1981, and, contrary to what some Board members may have thought, there was no part of the 1981 season already in place. Even the most seasoned artistic director, even Robin Phillips, would have had trouble getting a season together as fast as the Gang of Four would now be required to do. And Phillips, with his emphasis on stars, had established expectations which would be very hard to meet. The stars were a drug without which the box office might drift into a coma.

The Board must have known that for all their talent, intelligence, and dedication, the four people now stepping into the breach were not experienced *as artistic directors* of a huge theatre. Given two or three years, they might turn out to be highly successful, but they would need more than talent, intelligence, and dedication to put together the 1981 season starting at this late date – they would need luck and a great deal of support, especially from the Board. Surely any Board that truly understood the situation would have confronted the risks and come to terms with them at this crucial moment. If these people were to accept this terrifying appointment and carry this heavy burden, the Board must for its part be prepared to accept the consequences and stand behind them, at the very least through the end of the 1981 season. It seemed implicit in Hicks' remarks that the Board understood all this, but later it would become apparent that the Board had not understood at all.

* * *

The next day, the same day the Haymarket run of *Lear* was cancelled, with both Phillips and the Board claiming to be blameless, Martha Henry went to talk to Kate Reid about the 1981 season. She had already spoken to Daphne Dare, the head of design, who had told Henry that out of loyalty to Phillips, she couldn't remain at Stratford. Urjo Kareda went to see Beverley Cross, Maggie Smith's husband, about Smith's plans for 1981. Kareda wrote in his diary: "Contracts to be signed next week."

On September 22, Urjo Kareda flew to New York. The morning of his departure, the *Globe and Mail* had a front-page headline about Ustinov's lawsuit. In New York, Kareda had lunch with Lynne Meadow of the Manhattan Theater Club, who was interested in hiring him as literary manager. He told her that tempting as the offer was, he was committed to Stratford. After lunch he had a long-distance phone conversation with Martha Henry, who said she was getting more worried about the Board's intentions. She suspected that the Board was planning to set up Peter Stevens as the Festival's *supremo*, which would make the Gang of Four's position untenable. The test, she felt, would be the budget. If it was split in favour of Stevens, she thought the Four should resign. Henry also told Kareda that she had spoken to Robin Phillips, who had agreed to become an associate artist, but not while Hicks was still president. (Among the others approached by the Gang of Four who agreed to let their names stand as associate artists were Brian Bedford, Maggie Smith, William Hutt, Kate Reid, and John Hirsch.)

That night Kareda had dinner with Michael Langham and Langham's wife, the actress Helen Burns, at their Manhattan apartment. It was a very emotional occasion. Langham, who had succeeded Guthrie as artistic director of the Festival in 1956 and stayed until 1967, had become, since Guthrie's death, the great patriarchal symbol of the Festival's history. But he hadn't done a guest production there since *School for Scandal* in 1970. After leaving the Guthrie Theater in Minneapolis, where he had once again succeeded Guthrie, Langham had settled into a teaching job with the Juilliard School in Lincoln Center. He had been approached by the Stratford search committee a year earlier about taking on his old job as artistic director, but he really wasn't interested. Now Kareda was telling him the place was in trouble and needed him to rally round. Langham said of course he would help: he would come as a guest director in 1981. Langham, Kareda, and Burns all talked about their strong feelings for Stratford, and the urgency of its survival.

The next afternoon, on September 23, Kareda went to Sardi's to have lunch with John Dexter. No one at Stratford had heard from Dexter since the curt letter from his agent asking not to have his named bandied about in connection with Stratford, adding that Dexter had gone forward with other plans. In the interim, Dexter had made a quick, unannounced visit to Stratford, flying to Toronto and driving down in a rented car to see Maggie Smith in *Virginia*, then leaving town without visiting anyone. Dexter's *Galileo* was a big success at the National Theatre in London, and now he was back in New York directing a Broadway musical, *One Night Stand*, and waiting to see whether the Metropolitan Opera was going to solve its union problems in time to save its season. Dexter, the

Met's director of production, had several of his own productions scheduled for the 1980-81 season, including *Lulu* with Teresa Stratas, and *Parade*, a triple bill of three short modern French works, on which Dexter was collaborating with the artist David Hockney.

The question in Kareda's mind was whether Dexter was still interested in coming to Stratford as a guest director, or whether he was so miffed by his dealings with Phillips, Cronyn, and Hicks that he wouldn't come near the place. Dexter is not a man to mince words, and during lunch he made it instantly clear that he was still smarting from what he regarded as insulting treatment. But Kareda couldn't be held responsible, so he was able to begin talking to Dexter with a clean slate. Dexter said there were only four or five plays that he was keen on directing, and he was prepared to go anywhere in the world to do them. He suggested doing *Henry V* and *The Shoemaker's Holiday* with the same cast, but Kareda pointed out that Stratford had done a production of *Henry V* for the 1980 season which was still running. Dexter then proposed *Othello*, which he wanted to do with Christopher Plummer in the title role, and Ibsen's *Little Eyolf*, which he wanted to do with Kate Reid and Roberta Maxwell. Dexter emphasized he would want total casting control and said he would be much more interested if he knew he could definitely have Plummer.

The meeting went well. Dexter said he would need a few weeks to think about it. He assessed Kareda as astute but a little inexperienced. Kareda left feeling optimistic about his chances of snaring Dexter. It would be a major coup: Dexter was undoubtedly one of the greatest stage directors in the English-speaking world. What Kareda couldn't have realized was that this meeting planted the seeds of destruction for the Gang of Four. Stratford had been out of Dexter's mind. Now he mused once more about its temptations.

CHAPTER NINE

Dexter in the Wings

There was some good news as work continued feverishly on putting together a 1981 season. Christopher Plummer, probably the most internationally respected classical actor ever to come out of Canada, seemed interested in coming back to Stratford. The great-grandson of a Canadian prime minister, Sir John Abbott, Plummer had grown up in the cloistered grandeur of one of Montreal's most proper anglophone families. After serving his acting apprenticeship with CBC radio drama and the Canadian Repertory Theatre in Ottawa, Plummer landed on Broadway in 1954 and came to Stratford two years later.

His mentor at Stratford was Michael Langham, who directed him in *Henry V, Hamlet, Henry IV, Part One, Much Ado about Nothing, Romeo and Juliet, Cyrano de Bergerac,* and *Antony and Cleopatra.* After leaving Stratford, he spent several years in England, appearing with the Royal Shakespeare Company and the National Theatre. He began making frequent movie appearances, specializing in arrogant aristocrats.

His movie villains – the sadistic bank robber in *The Silent Partner,* the Israeli conspirator in *Eyewitness* – tended to be deliciously decadent monsters, preening over their own stylish wickedness. In *The Royal Hunt of the Sun,* Plummer turned the Inca king into a hissing, high-camp vaudeville turn. In *Murder by Decree,* he was right at home playing Sherlock Holmes as Victorian dandy. As Rudyard Kipling in *The Man Who Would Be King,* he gave a toned-down performance, but there was still more than a trace of the bemused fop. Even in the role that, embarrassingly for him, gave him his greatest exposure, he didn't play it straight. Arching his eyebrows fiendishly as Baron von Trapp in the movie

111

of *The Sound of Music* (which he privately calls *the Sound of Mucus*), he was a touch of sourness in a morass of artificial sweetener.

It had been twenty-four years since Plummer astonished Stratford with his bold debut there in the title role of *Henry V*, and thirteen years since his last performance there as Antony to Zoe Caldwell's Cleopatra. When Martha Henry approached him, he said he was thrilled at the idea of coming back to Stratford, that it was time for him to come home. Henry agreed. While still a schoolgirl from Detroit named Martha Buhs, she had visited Stratford with her mother in 1957 and been dazzled by Plummer's Hamlet. It had seemed revolutionary to discover that Shakespeare could be spoken in a way she could understand. Five years later, in her debut season at the Festival, she played Lady Macduff to his Macduff. For her, there was a special honour in bringing Plummer back to Stratford.

Henry also went to see her old friend John Hirsch, who had been conspicuously absent from the Festival since his row with Robin Phillips in 1976. Hirsch and Henry knew each other well. One day in the late 1960s, while preparing for a play they were doing together at Lincoln Center, they went for an incredible marathon walk through Central Park, starting early in the morning and finishing late at night – and just talked. They had worked together often, in Winnipeg and Stratford as well as New York. Now she went to him and asked him to come back to Stratford to do a production for the 1981 season.

Hirsch was on Maggie Smith's very short list of acceptable directors, and Henry asked whether he could suggest a vehicle for Smith. Hirsch suggested *Madame Sans Gêne*, an obscure French play which had been a great vehicle for Sarah Bernhardt. However, when Henry mentioned the idea to Smith, the response was negative. Then two days later Smith came to Henry's office and said, "You know, the funniest thing has just happened. Beverley has been telling me for years about this wonderful play I should do, and you know it's exactly the same play John Hirsch was talking to you about. And Beverley says it would be a marvellous part for me."

Plans were quickly made. Kareda would commission Beverley Cross to write a new adaptation of the play. The play would be provisionally scheduled for the end of the 1981 season, by which time Smith might be finished with her film commitments.

Meanwhile, the departure of Robin Phillips was turning into a lingering drama. On the opening night of *King Lear,* Hicks had told a journalist who was critical of the Board's handling of Phillips, "If you knew what we'd done to protect that man!" Phillips was so upset by remarks about his mental stability that he began going to his friends and asking, "Am I crazy?" He knew he was tired, he knew he might even sometimes be described as temperamental and impossible to work with. Late summer was often the time of year he was most exhausted and short-tempered because of the strain involved in opening the season. But mentally unstable? It didn't seem possible. During a rehearsal of *Long Day's Journey* he told the cast, "It may be I'm unaware of it and I'm not functioning as well as I should. I know I'm tired and I'm not one hundred per cent, but it seems to me I'm doing okay. But please if you have any reservations, say so, and I will happily step aside." The actors tried to reassure him. Jessica Tandy said without equivocation she would like to have every single second of the rehearsals preserved on tape.

At the annual Guthrie awards ceremony on October 1, there was a wretched attempt to honour Phillips. A stage doorman presented a gift from the company. No one from the company seemed to know what the gift was, and Phillips refused to open it. Later that evening, he told Pam Brighton, "I'm going to start a company in Toronto, you know. Then we'll see who gets the best actors."

At the company farewell for him on October 7, Phillips seemed tense. The champagne was late, and everyone stood around uneasily. Rod Beattie and Nicholas Pennell made speeches – Pennell somewhat tactlessly quoting the line from *Love's Labour's Lost* about the words of Mercury being harsh after the songs of Apollo – and Phillips said his official goodbye, urging the company to support the new team. Then everyone lined up to say tearful goodbyes, as if over an open coffin.

Long Day's Journey into Night, a play whose title was all too apt for the experience many people in Stratford were having, opened on the evening of Saturday, October 4. Earlier that day, Peter Moss burst in on Kareda with a copy of Gina Mallet's long report in the *Toronto Star,* "A midsummer day's Stratford nightmare." Mallet, who had been recruited to fill Kareda's old job as drama critic at the *Star* after Kareda left for Stratford, wasn't his biggest fan, and now she was reporting that Kareda was the first to rush in to fill Phillips' shoes, and that he refused even to speak to Phillips. In an interview a few years earlier, Kareda had been quoted as saying, "I would kill for Robin." Now, Mallet joked, people were saying Kareda had removed the preposition.

Kareda more or less went into shock. Then he was handed a note: Phillips had called the theatre to let Kareda know he was free to see him that afternoon. Obviously, he too had seen the *Star*. Kareda went to Phillips' house, where they both tried to pretend that things between them were the same as always. Phillips was playing with his new Cartier watch, a gift from Maggie Smith, who called him twice to ask whether Phillips could give her the right time.

* * *

The same weekend that *Long Day's Journey* opened, Peter Stevens arrived in Stratford to assume his new job as executive director. Stevens had been shocked at the news of Phillips' departure, and the prospect of working with a group of four unknowns instead of an international superstar made him extremely nervous. But in the last week of September, he had flown up for a day, and been taken by Hume Cronyn to Kareda's house to meet the four. On the basis of that meeting he had told Cronyn, "Okay, I'll give it a try."

Stevens grew up in Cumbria, near the Lake District in the north of England, the son of a pubkeeper. As a result of a law passed in 1944, he was in the first generation of English school children who went to grammar school without paying fees – creating something of a social revolution. Stevens went to university in Nottingham and then served with the Royal Air Force in the Middle East. He was working for the British Council in Africa when John Neville arrived in February, 1963, with a touring troupe from the Nottingham Playhouse. Neville was so impressed with how efficiently the dressing facilities had been arranged at an open-air cinema in Kaduna, Nigeria, he asked who was responsible. It was Stevens, then assistant to the chief of the British Council. As it happened the Playhouse was looking for a general manager to run its new theatre, and when Neville came back from his tour he announced he had found just the right man. Stevens was flown in from Africa for an interview, and he got the job. Neville and Stevens worked together for six years; they both left when Neville had a row with the Board in 1968.

Stevens went briefly into television, as a current affairs producer for Granada in Manchester. Then he opened two new theatres in

Newcastle and Leicester before landing a job in 1973 with the National Theatre, first as personal assistant to Peter Hall and then as general administrator. His mandate in the latter post was to organize the move into the National's new home, built at vast public expense as part of the South Bank arts complex. Stevens was sometimes referred to as Peter Hall's hatchet man, but he had a reputation as being an extremely efficient, if somewhat abrasive, administrator. The nastiest part of the job involved his negotiations with unions representing workers at the National; at one point there were threats on the life of management.

The situation became unpleasant enough that Stevens was ready for a change when he got an offer in 1979 from the Shubert organization, which owned sixty per cent of the Broadway theatres as well as touring houses in Philadelphia, Boston, Los Angeles, and Chicago. The empire had passed into the hands of two men who used to be the Shuberts' lawyers – Bernard Jacobs and Gerald Schoenfeld. The Shuberts, as they became known, weren't important theatrical producers but they had a great deal of influence over producers because they owned so many important theatres.

While working for the National, Stevens had served as executive producer for several shows, including *Equus, No Man's Land,* and *Bedroom Farce,* that transferred from the National to the West End. When he took the job with the Shuberts, he was under the impression they wanted him to pick up promising London shows and bring them to New York. But things didn't work out that way. For one thing, the West End was collapsing about the time that Stevens began working for the Shuberts. For another, Jacobs and Schoenfeld enjoyed doing the wheeling and dealing for the hot shows. Why should they let Stevens handle the negotiations for, say, *Nicholas Nickleby* or *Amadeus* when they had so much fun doing it themselves? Peter Stevens uprooted himself and landed, along with his wife, in New York, where he didn't really feel comfortable, and he found himself with basically nothing to do. His contract with the Shuberts had another eighteen months to run, but he couldn't get warm to the prospect of handling the paperwork for the Shubert chain of theatres, which was really all that was left for him to do. His job so depressed him that one day he went to Charley O's bar at eleven o'clock in the morning and stayed there all day drinking Scotch until he was asked to leave at four o'clock the following morning because it was closing time.

The production of *The Gin Game* that Stevens produced for the Shuberts had closed in the West End in October, 1979, and after that Cronyn and Tandy had taken it to Russia. They had only recently returned to New York when Cronyn called Stevens in February, 1980, about Stratford. Cronyn said that since things were so quiet for Stevens in New York, perhaps he would be interested in going to Stratford. According to Cronyn, it was not certain whether or not Robin Phillips was going to stay, but either way the Festival would need a top administrator. If Phillips left, the administrator would work with a group of artistic associates. If Phillips stayed, his talent would be used where it belonged, on the stage, and not trying to run the whole place single-handed.

Stevens jumped at the idea and visited Stratford toward the end of March. He had a meeting at The Church with several Board members, including Hicks, Heney, Ivey, Lawson and Bryden; Phillips joined them for coffee during a rehearsal break.

Stevens wasn't keen on running the theatre as it was; after all, he had already spent years at similar jobs in England. What excited him was the Festival's ambition to expand – to have a Toronto winter season, to produce its own films, to do more contemporary work. It wasn't until much later that Stevens realized there was a faction on the Board opposed to this, and that those who wanted to maintain the Festival as a purely local community event also resented the idea of bringing in an outsider over the current top administrator, Gary Thomas, who was a Stratford boy. Stevens was kept on hold for months and assumed the Board was simply preoccupied with Phillips. When, in midsummer, Stevens was called back to Stratford, he met Robin Phillips on the stage of the Avon Theatre, and they talked out the details of their relationship. Phillips said he was going to be called Festival director but that he wouldn't be around a lot of the time; he would assemble a group of associates who would look to him for artistic leadership. It was on this basis that Stevens was offered, and accepted, the job of executive director.

Stevens was in England when he got an urgent call on September 9 from his wife, Rochelle, in New York: "Bryden has just phoned. Phillips has resigned for the umpteenth time, and this time it has been accepted. It has all collapsed. There used to be nine of them on the artistic end; now there are only four. You've got to get up to Canada and secure your position."

Stevens didn't try to find out exactly what had happened. He was aware of the mutual mistrust between Phillips and the Board and assumed that Phillips had finally decided to bail out after a series of spats. He knew Phillips claimed the Board was acting in bad faith by refusing to give him a new contract to reflect his new responsibilities. He also knew the Board claimed Phillips just wanted an excuse to get out, because he was upset to discover that some of his associates – especially Bedford and Cariou – had contracts that didn't spell out their responsibilities.

It must have seemed like an answer to Peter Stevens' prayers when he heard that John Dexter might be available to take on the job of artistic director at Stratford. Andy Phillips, an old friend of Stevens from England, broke the news to him over drinks at Charley O's. It seemed that on September 23, after his lunch with Kareda at Sardi's, Dexter had discussed Stratford with Andy Phillips, the lighting designer for Dexter's Broadway show, *One Night Stand*. Dexter has a reputation for being as restless and irascible as he is brilliant, and that afternoon he let his frustration show. *One Night Stand* was on the brink of disaster, and Dexter felt he was watching it crumble, million by million. His future at the National Theatre in England was in doubt despite his success with *Galileo*. He had had a *rapprochement* with Peter Hall after many rows in the past, but now Hall was facing a financial crunch; future projects on the scale Dexter wanted were in question. It didn't help the relationship that after Dexter had quarrelled with playwright Anthony Shaffer (whose play *Equus* Dexter had made into an international success) over a new play about Mozart, Hall had taken over *Amadeus* and made a big success of it.

Dexter's future with the Metropolitan Opera was also murky. He had, along with Anthony Bliss and James Levine, been one of the Met's ruling troika, but this arrangement was dissolving. Dexter had staged some of the Met's biggest successes, but he was regarded as a man of the stage rather than a musician, and there had been run-ins with singers who complained that his ideas conflicted with musical values. Bliss was ready to assume the title of general manager, and Levine, the brilliant conductor, was emerging as the artistic decision maker. What wasn't clear was Dexter's place (he later accepted the title of production adviser). Then on September 30, 1980, disaster struck: as a result of an impasse with the musicians' union, the Met's opening had to be called off, and there was a question as to whether there would be any season at all. All this rankled Dexter. He told Andy Phillips he was sick of the freelance life; he wanted a regular arrangement with one company.

"What about Stratford?" Phillips asked.

"That's last year's cold mashed potatoes," Dexter said. "They don't want me." But Dexter did admit that Stratford would be the solution *if* the Board would really make a commitment to him, and Andy Phillips passed this message to Stevens.

When Peter Stevens arrived in Stratford the first weekend in October, John Dexter was very much on his mind. Though the Board had made a commitment to the Gang of Four, it wasn't Stevens' commitment, and the need to honour it was not uppermost in Stevens' mind. Once again, Stratford was being plagued by the "them" and "us" mentality which had traditionally divided the creative people from the business people. The four had agreed to go on working without contracts rather than hold up planning of the 1981 season, but while they were negotiating with Lawson, Heney, and Gaffney, they discovered that Stevens was negotiating directly with Hicks. The implication seemed clear to them: the four wouldn't get the authority they needed, especially in matters of taste. And Stevens wasn't forging a friendly alliance with them. The problem was that Stevens had thought he was going to be working with a superstar director. Despite his promise to Cronyn that he would try to work with the Gang of Four, his heart was never really in it.

When Martha Henry said she wanted to be included in any discussions on the new company manager, Stevens told her, "This is a management decision, let me do it." Kareda wrote in his diary, "Stevens seems keen to balance his ignorance of how the Festival works with a demonstration of how powerful he personally is."

Stevens didn't have a deep understanding of Canadian culture or Canadian politics and didn't notice how people winced when he referred to Canadian drama as "your own native plays," making it very easy to portray him as a colonizer bringing the British cultural tradition to the bush. Pam Brighton saw in Stevens a hard-nosed, working-class British male she knew all too well. One day when Stevens had given her a lift in his car, he began carrying on about the evils of Canadian nationalism in the theatre, and she decided to confront him.

"You can't actually *say* things like that," she told him, speaking as one working-class Brit to another. "This is not a paper tiger you're dealing with, it's something that's absolutely real. You have to understand what people feel about it and why if you're going to be able to work in this country."

But Peter Stevens didn't want that kind of advice.

Hume Cronyn was in the Festival offices one day early in October when Stevens (who was fond of referring to his benefactor as "Gloom Cronyn") stopped him in a corridor and said, "Hey, I want to tell you something that will interest you." Stevens took Cronyn into an empty office and closed the door. John Dexter, he told Cronyn, was ready to come to Stratford as artistic director.

Stevens assumed that in Cronyn he had an ally. He knew it was Cronyn who had originally approached Dexter, and he knew about the nasty letter from Dexter's agent asking that Dexter's name never again be mentioned in connection with Stratford. Now Cronyn stared at Stevens coldly: "Peter, I don't know where you got this information, but I will tell you that if it comes up now, I'll vote against it." In Cronyn's mind, the matter was closed; the Board had made its commitment to the Gang of Four.

A day later, Cronyn saw Stevens again and said, "About that conversation we had, I really meant it. I've been very closely associated with these people. A commitment has been made, and it has to be sustained. It is not a question of who could do the job better. I could not support a change just because something better has come along."

That same weekend, Stevens spoke to Hicks about Dexter. "I think you should know," he told Hicks, "that Dexter could be available if you decide to make a change."

Hicks gasped and then replied: "I wouldn't touch that with a barge-pole." A day or two later, after conferring with one or two other Board members, Hicks called Stevens and reiterated, "It's too hot. I'm not going to do anything about it."

*   *   *

On October 8, John Dexter sent a brisk letter to Urjo Kareda on Metropolitan Opera stationery:

Thank you very much for your letter of 26th September. I very much doubt Chris [Plummer] would be attracted by a *Tempest* or *Timon* and I do not agree that the Ibsen would work better in a smaller theatre, but, to put you out of your misery or expectation as soon as possible, I said I would give the matter three weeks' thought and give you an answer. However, I do not think my state of mind is going to change during the next three weeks so can see no reason for wasting your time.

The real truth of the matter is that I am not responsive to working in committee or, for that matter, working with a permanent company unless my control of casting, designers and choice of play is absolute, and I doubt if that is something Ontario can offer now or in the future....

Stevens flew back to New York on October 8, and on October 10 he went to visit Dexter at the Nederlander Theater, where One Night Stand was scheduled to open. They sat in the empty theatre and chatted for half an hour during a rehearsal break.

"Andy says you're thinking of switching gears," Stevens said. He made it clear that he was not in a position to offer Dexter the job at the moment, but he wanted to know whether Dexter would be available if there were an offer. Dexter said it was just possible he would be available, but he was still smarting from the run-around he had from Stratford earlier. This time there had better be no messing around. "For the next few weeks," Dexter told Stevens, "all things are possible. Then I have to make a definite decision. So there must be no dithering about. You must get back to me in the next few weeks and give me an answer." Dexter also emphasized that he didn't want any misunderstanding about why he had written Kareda refusing to do productions for the Gang of Four. "I didn't say no with the idea that if I held back maybe I'd get the top job. It's not that. I just made my mind up that I'm not going to go on doing guest productions. I want my own company and my own theatre, and that's the only basis on which I would go to Stratford. If I don't go to Stratford, I'll go somewhere else. I've just reached the point in my career where I've come to the decision that this is the way I want to work."

Stevens said, "Well, there are four people there doing it. I don't know how well they're doing it, but I'll find that out when I get back. I know your interest, and if it becomes appropriate for the Board to approach you, I'll tell them it has to be in the next few weeks." The one person who might have been able to bring Stevens and the Gang of Four into a comfortable working relationship was Hume Cronyn, but Cronyn left Stratford at a crucial time. In mid-October he went to Massachusetts to work with Susan Cooper, his Foxfire collaborator, on script revisions.

Only a week after he left Stratford, Cronyn received a handwritten letter from Christopher Plummer, written from his Connecticut farm. Plummer, it seemed, had been talking to Dexter about Stratford, and Dexter had told Plummer that it was Cronyn who had originally approached him. Now Plummer in effect said to Cronyn: how brilliant of you to think of Dexter. Wouldn't it be wonderful for the Festival, and couldn't you use your influence on the Board to see that the dream comes true? Plummer did mention that he had been approached by the directorate about appearing in the 1981 season, but he felt sure Cronyn could sympathize with his notion that if you were going to go somewhere, you wanted to know who was guiding the ship. Plummer wasn't sure who these four people were or what their policies were.

Cronyn, deeply involved in his own work, didn't want to take time out to write a letter. He called Plummer and said, "Look, Chris, this is out of the question for 1981. That group has been put in. They've been given every assurance. They're planning a season. You're one of the people they want. Unless they decide to invite Dexter in, there is no way." Cronyn's stance had nothing to do with his opinion of Dexter, whom he considered a great director. It *would* be a coup to get Dexter, but the Board had made its commitment and was set on another course.

Martha Henry was the first to suspect that the ghost of John Dexter was coming back to haunt the Gang of Four. Christopher Plummer's agent had told her that Plummer was pleased by the idea of returning to Stratford, and she had agreed to call him at his Connecticut home on Saturday, October 11. She also knew that he wanted to work with Dexter – and the day before she was to call Plummer, Kareda had received Dexter's letter turning down the directorate's invitation. She called Plummer on the appointed day anyway. He didn't seem to know that Dexter had rejected the Stratford invitation.

Henry told Plummer, "I think you should know, Chris, that we've just had a letter from Dexter, and he doesn't want to come."

Plummer said, "Oh yes, but I'll talk to him." Plummer told Henry he felt he could talk Dexter into it, and said he would call her back on Monday. Plummer called at exactly the appointed time, still sounding positive about coming to Stratford.

Meanwhile, Martha Henry had spoken about Dexter to Kate Reid, who knew Dexter well, and Reid had said, "Why don't you go to New York and talk to Dexter? He really likes women who do things." Henry was prepared to go. Like Helena, the miracle worker she played in the 1977 production of *All's Well That Ends Well,* she thought she could solve the problem through an act of will. She knew Dexter was rankled, and she knew he would demand *carte blanche.* She said to herself, "Well, if he wants me to come over every morning and shine his shoes before rehearsal, I'll do that."

But by the time Martha Henry spoke again to Christopher Plummer on October 15, things had taken a turn for the worse. Plummer now said that a man of Dexter's stature couldn't possibly be expected to come to Stratford unless it was as artistic director.

"That's not possible, Chris," Henry said. "The job of artistic director isn't open."

Plummer seemed confused, and asked who the artistic director was. Henry had already explained the directorate to him, so she simply said, "It's me, Chris."

Plummer replied that Dexter had been approached by someone from the Stratford Board and had been promised an answer within two weeks. Dexter, Henry was told, was waiting to hear back.

Henry asked Plummer the name of the Board man who had approached Dexter.

"I don't think I should tell you that," Plummer said.

"Well, if I give you the right name, will you nod into the phone?"

"Yes," said Plummer, "I'll nod."

Henry knew she only had one shot. "Was it Bob Hicks?"

Plummer said no, that name didn't mean anything to him.

That very day, Martha Henry interrupted a meeting of the Board's executive committee, to submit a memo asking whether anyone on the Board had been in touch with Dexter. She said that Dexter seemed to think he was in the running for the job of artistic director, and that this was interfering with the directorate's attempt to hire him as a guest director. The next day she had a written reply from Hicks:

> In reply to your inquiry of yesterday, the executive committee knows of nobody on the Board who has talked to Dexter on any basis since last spring and, if anyone has, they have no authority to speak to him regarding any arrangements at Stratford. Knowing of Peter Stevens' prior association with Dexter, and with Peter being in New York, I called him to inquire if perchance he knew anything about it, and he advised as follows:

Dexter called him yesterday as a friend to tell him that he had written to Urjo a few days ago to the effect that he would not accept engagements anywhere where there is an artistic committee involved, such as at Stratford, and he wished Peter to understand his position – he reiterated to Peter that he would not vary his practice for us. Dexter said he had learned from Plummer of Plummer being approached by someone at Stratford so that Peter understood, while Plummer and Dexter had earlier been discussing plays involving Dexter as director and Plummer as senior principal, Dexter was not prepared to make these available to us for the reasons mentioned above.

I wish I could have reported more favourable news.

Several days later, when she raised the matter with Peter Stevens, he told her, "Don't worry, I've taken care of it."

He certainly had.

CHAPTER TEN

Hatchet Time

When Peter Stevens arrived in Canada, he knew that one person was extremely unhappy about his presence. For four years Gary Thomas had held the top administrative job at the Festival, but the title of general manager had been denied him. Because he reported to Phillips, not to the Board, Thomas had never been allowed to challenge Phillips' authority. Thomas, who had lived in Stratford all his life, was a chartered accountant who had handled the Festival account and subsequently been hired as an assistant to Bruce Swerdfager when Swerdfager took over the top job.

When Swerdfager left, the Hicks faction of the Board wanted to bring in a heavyweight theatre administrator from outside, as recommended in the Pickering Report. But the Stratford faction on the Board was reluctant to do anything that might upstage Thomas, as the only "townie" in the upper echelons of the Festival's organization. When a new top administrative position was created, Thomas had written to Hicks and said he thought he could handle it. Thomas let it be known he wasn't thrilled by the idea of bringing in an outsider. But John Heney broke the news to him one day when the appointment was getting very close: the Board had decided to hire Peter Stevens. Heney said that Thomas would find Stevens a very good person to work with. "Give it a try," Heney advised.

In order to secure work papers for Stevens, the Festival had to go through a little charade, posting a notice of the job vacancy in the Stratford Manpower office in order to demonstrate that qualified Canadians would have a chance to apply for it. People all over town were gasping at the salary listed for the job described as general manager: $75,000. Shortly before he resigned as company manager, Barry MacGregor applied for the new job, feeling he had the right combination of theatrical and administrative experience. A Board member told MacGregor to stop making trouble; later Hicks wrote him a letter saying he regretted MacGregor's application had not been received in time to be considered.

Gary Thomas, nervous about having a new man brought in over him, did something extraordinary. He called Walter Learning, the theatre officer at the Canada Council, and suggested that perhaps the Council could stop the Board from bringing a foreigner into a top Festival job. Learning was surprised, to put it mildly. "After all the times you've made it clear you don't want the Canada Council interfering with Stratford," he told Thomas, "you can't really expect me to intervene on this."

But Learning did make a call to the minister's office at Employment and Immigration Canada to inquire about what was going on. A department official told him solemnly that Stevens' work papers had been approved and added that Stratford, complying with Canadian immigration laws, had made a thorough search for a qualified Canadian and found there weren't any, before offering the job to Stevens. Learning laughed and said, "I think you've been snowed."

The conversion of Gary Thomas was a political challenge that Peter Stevens handled smoothly. Coming into a job cold, knowing virtually nothing about Stratford's operations or Canada, Stevens realized that he would need to depend on someone who did know. Gary Thomas was potentially his most useful ally. Stevens went out of his way to make it clear that Thomas should think of him not as a threat but as a benefactor. The two men got out the organizational charts and went through them together. Sorting out the administrative duties, they realized that Thomas could keep right on doing what he had been doing. Those duties, after all, involved exactly the sort of day-to-day, nuts-and-bolts affairs that Stevens had grown tired of doing elsewhere. With Thomas taking care of the minutiae, Stevens imagined that he could move onward and upward to the things he cared about – making the big deals. Stevens told Thomas that he was assuming the title of executive director and asked what title Thomas would like. Thomas replied that he'd like the title of general manager – the one that had been denied him all these years. Like a stroke of magic, it was done.

Barbara Ivey gasped when she heard about Thomas' new title at the end of an executive committee meeting on October 15. The meeting was over, but people were still sitting around. It was left to Thomas himself to break the news, and it was obviously awkward for him. He said he thought the committee members should know there was going to be a press release about his promotion the next day. Ivey couldn't believe that Hicks could be presenting this as a *fait accompli* when she, the first vice-president of the Board and the chairman of the executive committee, hadn't heard a word about it. The official explanation was that this was an administrative, not a Board decision: Stevens was merely exercising his prerogative to deal with his own staff. But according to the press release that went out, it was Hicks who was making the announcement.

Ivey was very aware that the Board had previously decided that no one would have the title of general manager until there had been a complete reassessment of the Festival's organization in light of the Pickering Report. Ivey made a formal protest to Hicks about this, but he responded with a memo which in her view dipsy-doodled around the point. He was sorry to learn of Ivey's objection, he wrote, but she must realize there were many people who thought of Gary Thomas as highly competent. Is it possible, Barbara Ivey asked herself, that Hicks really thinks the competence of Gary Thomas is the issue rather than the procedural methods of Robert Hicks?

By the third week in October, after the Gang of Four had been in office little more than a month, the 1981 season had more or less taken shape. There were to be five productions at the Festival Theatre: *Hamlet* (with Stephen Ouimette), *The Merchant of Venice* (with Jason Robards), *The Rivals* (with Douglas Campbell, Pat Galloway, and Nicholas Pennell), *The Tempest*, and *Madame Sans Gêne* (with Maggie Smith, directed by John Hirsch). At the Avon Theatre there were to be six shows: *Ring Round the Moon* (with Brent Carver), *Who's Afraid of Virginia Woolf?* (with Kate Reid and Douglas Rain), the *Wild Duck* (with R.H. Thomson, Clare Coulter, and Gary Reineke), *Colette – the Colours of Love* (with Pat Galloway), *Waiting for the Parade* (to be directed by Pam Brighton, with Kate Reid, Martha Henry, Fiona Reid, and Clare Coulter), and one other production, to be directed by John Neville, with William Hutt. (All this was still tentative.)

Within the directorate, the most controversial item on the program was Pam Brighton's *Hamlet*. Brighton was determined to do one production with her own directorial stamp; that was her justification for being involved with Stratford. She was keenly aware of being an outsider in the directorate but thought she had more varied experience than the others. Their problem, she analyzed, was that they were too firmly stuck in the mould of Robin Phillips, who in Brighton's opinion had failed to solve the central problem of how Canadians could play Shakespeare in their own style. Stratford, she had decided, was inherently full of contradictions, and Robin Phillips had tormented himself by trying to internalize these contradictions: on the one hand he was a passionate believer in the company above all; on the other hand, he had an eye on the box office and liked to attract stars. Brighton thought it was healthier to have a group directorate, so that each side of the contradictions could be represented by a different person. Kareda, for example, could take the responsibility for bringing back Maggie Smith, and Brighton could have a chance to try out her radical ideas. It was crucial, in her mind, to bring in some of the young talent from Toronto. She was absolutely convinced that Stephen Ouimette – who was not just an unknown to general audiences, but little known even among Toronto theatre insiders – was absolutely the right person for the title role in *Hamlet*, and she was prepared to go to the wall defending that choice. Her three colleagues were somewhat doubtful but they agreed that Brighton should be given some turf of her own.

One of the big disappointments the directorate received early on was that Michael Langham wouldn't be coming after all. Three weeks after Urjo Kareda's evening at Langham's apartment, Martha Henry phoned Langham to settle on a production; she was told that he couldn't be available at the beginning of the season but might be available for a mid-season opening. According to Langham, he had explained to Kareda right at the start that, because April and May were the most important times at Juilliard, he couldn't rehearse a show opening in June. Kareda's recollection was that Langham indicated he could be available for a June opening. By the time Langham spoke to Martha Henry, the Gang of Four couldn't offer him a show for a mid-season opening. The Gang of Four had made commitments to five Canadian directors in addition to Pam Brighton: John Hirsch, John Neville, Scott Swann (to stage *Colette*), William Lane (*The Wild Duck*), and Sheldon Larry (*Ring Round the Moon*). Offers had also been made to three British directors. Michael Bogdanov, a sensationally gifted National Theatre regular (whose production of *The Romans in Britain* was the scandalous success of the season in London), was being invited to direct *The Merchant of Venice*; Colin Graham (who had replaced John Dexter as director of the Metropolitan Opera's new production of *La Traviata*) had accepted an offer to direct *The Tempest*; and Peter James, who was experienced at staging classics on the Sheffield stage, modelled on Stratford's, was asked to direct *The Rivals.* James' agent, James Sharkey (who also represented Maggie Smith and Robin Phillips), wasn't sure whether the dates could be worked out. There was also a scheduling problem with Bogdanov, who would have to return to England for a National Theatre commitment before *Merchant* had started its previews, then come back to Stratford to make last-minute adjustments while the show was in previews.

Martha Henry was also running into problems getting a name American director for *Who's Afraid of Virginia Woolf?* Kate Reid's involvement was contingent on getting a director on her short list. At Reid's suggestion, Henry tried Mike Nichols, who was not only a celebrity director on Broadway but also the director of the popular movie version of the play. A secretary in Nichols' New York office told Henry that Nichols was in Washington and could be reached over the weekend at the Watergate Hotel. She sent a telegram to Nichols advising him that she would call on Sunday, and she told Peter Stevens she was doing so. She thought it was odd that Stevens, who had been closely associated with Nichols on *The Gin Game*, couldn't give her Nichols' phone number, but she got it elsewhere with no problem, and Stevens told her to give Nichols his regards. She did, and was stunned by Nichols' abrupt dismissal of her offer. It wasn't just that he said no; it was that he told her next time she should get in touch with his agent first.

Next on Henry's list was José Quintero, who had made his name directing Eugene O'Neill plays. He expressed interest but said a number of details would have to be worked out.

There was a fall-back position: if the right director couldn't be found for *Who's Afraid of Virginia Woolf?*, Kate Reid was willing to appear in a production of *The Little Foxes* instead.

The Gang of Four presented its provisional 1981 season to the planning committee of the Board on October 21. Hicks said he hoped there weren't going to be any plays with naughty language like *The Gin Game*. Afterward, Peter Stevens, who had just come back from a ten-day trip to New York, began telling members of the Board how unimpressed he was by the projected season. Actually, what should have been astonishing was how much the directorate had been able to pull together in just over a month. No Stratford season had ever been organized in so short a time.

The Gang of Four knew that to achieve a balanced budget for their 1981 season they would have to draw about eighty per cent of capacity at the Festival Theatre and seventy-five per cent at the Avon. When it came time to make a submission to the Canada Council, Stevens told Kareda, "We'll have to stick in eighty per cent on the Canada Council application. Those figures will do for now, because everyone knows they're very provisional, and the important thing is to get an application in, but there is no way we are going to do that kind of business. This season of yours is not going to do better at the box office than Robin Phillips, but that's what our budget says."

Stevens blew the whistle on the Gang of Four at an executive committee meeting on Friday, October 31. The main business on the agenda was the Canada Council submission. (Two days earlier, Kareda had discovered that the names of the artistic directors had been omitted from the report, which had been written by Kareda for Hicks.) Before the meeting, Stevens had a brief discussion with Thomas about the figures in the Canada Council submission. "Their season is not going to do this kind of business, is it?" Stevens asked.

"No, I guess not," Thomas said.

"What would you guess – ten per cent less?"

"More like fifteen," Thomas said.

They both knew that the Festival had landed in financial trouble in 1979, the year of Phillips' partial sabbatical. (Attendance at the Festival Theatre that year was only sixty-six per cent of capacity, though it was eight-two per cent at the Avon, largely because of the sold-out run of the Ustinov *Lear*.)

The executive committee meeting was held in the reception room of the Festival Theatre. Barbara Ivey chaired the meeting, and others present were Hicks, Heney, Lawson, Gaffney, and Donald MacLeod. Stevens dominated the meeting. He said he thought the 1981 season was not looking good, and he felt it was going to get a lot worse. In Stevens' view, some of what the Gang of Four planned was achievable and some was not. He had prepared a rundown of the season, dated October 30, which went through each of the eleven productions reviewing the status of the directors, designers, and principal actors mentioned by the Four. According to Stevens, for instance, Michael Bogdanov's schedule made his engagement "extremely ill-advised," and the designer's commitment was dependent on Bogdanov. Stevens also said both Maggie Smith and the new translation of *Madame Sans Gêne* were unlikely to be available until 1982.

Then he brought up the real issue – the numbers. Gary Thomas was asked to draft a budget using attendance figures that he and Stevens considered safely achievable, given the risks of the program as Stevens had outlined them. The figures were staggering. Committee members went into shock when they realized what they were discussing was a deficit of well over a million dollars. The meeting lasted three hours, and by the end several people were ashen faced. But really all they were being told was that there was more financial risk involved in a season programmed by four new people than there was in a season programmed by Robin Phillips. Was it possible this hadn't occurred to them before they made a commitment to the Gang of Four?

While executive committee members were still reeling from the numbers, Stevens introduced a ray of hope. He said he thought he would be failing in his duty to the Board if he didn't let them know they had another option. He understood that John Dexter was available and felt that if he were given an immediate go-ahead he could pull together a 1981 season. At the mention of Dexter's name, as one observer would put it later, Bob Hicks' face lit up like a dying plant given a sudden drink of water.

Ivey shared the distress of the others at that meeting, but she insisted that the Gang of Four be confronted immediately with these figures and given a chance to respond to them. Her understanding was that the same Board members who had been negotiating a contract with the Four – Lawson, Heney, and Gaffney – would get in touch with them as quickly as possible. She assumed that meant the following Monday. But if this decision was agreed upon, it did not appear in the minutes of the meeting.

Meanwhile, Stevens was asked by the committee to get in touch with Dexter and see whether he really was available, and if so arrange a meeting with him as soon as possible. That meeting took place two days later, on the afternoon of Sunday, November 2, at the Bristol Place Hotel near Toronto International Airport. Dexter flew up from New York and rented a car at the airport. When he got to the hotel, he had to register under an assumed name; the Board was taking a cloak-and-dagger approach to the matter. Dexter felt he was in the middle of either a very bad James Bond movie or a Kafka nightmare, and either way he didn't like it. Stevens was present, along with four Board members – Hicks, Heney, Lawson, and Gaffney – who, to Dexter, were indistinguishable.

Dexter told the Stratford group that he had a season in place because he had been thinking of accepting an invitation to become artistic director at Stratford, Connecticut. He said, in fact, that he had to have a commitment from Canada soon or else he might accept the offer from Connecticut. If he came, he told the Board members, he wanted to use a completely Canadian company. He said Christopher Plummer was excited at the prospect, and that he thought he could get Roberta Maxwell and Kate Reid. Dexter said he would want to stay three years, try to stabilize the operation, and then "piss off."

Dexter emphasized the importance of hanging onto Kareda, Henry, Brighton, and Moss, but when asked whether he would consider working as a member of the directorate, he said no, he didn't believe in rule by committee; the Board would have to offer him the artistic directorship or nothing. Even the Berliner Ensemble, he joked, was run by one person with an iron fist. Someone has to be in control, he said; someone has to have the final say. Yet he saw himself serving as friend, father figure, guide, and philospher-king to the Gang of Four. They were good people, lacking only experience, and they must not be sacked. "You've got to find a way to hang onto them," he said.

Dexter would say later he found the meeting most peculiar. The Board people grilled him about politics, his personal life – everything except religion. He felt as if he were being subjected to something like a police interrogation. They told him they thought there would be no problem getting him a work permit, and at the end of the meeting they shook Dexter's hand. The crucial meeting of the full Stratford Board was set for the next Wednesday afternoon, November 5, at the Hotel Toronto. On Tuesday afternoon, Hume Cronyn was at the Wyndham Hotel in New York, conferring with the producers of *Foxfire*, when Hicks called to say there was an emergency meeting of the Board the next day in Toronto. Could Cronyn be there?

Cronyn replied that he was locked into appointments. What was the nature of the emergency?

Hicks: "Well, there's been a projection drawn by Gary, and it looks as though we stand to lose $1.3 million, and that is extremely serious. We also think we could get Dexter. He's come up here to talk to us, and he could bring some big-name people, which the group has so far not managed to do."

Cronyn: "But Bob, they've only been functioning together for six weeks."

Hicks: "Well, that is what is going to be discussed tomorrow."

Cronyn: "I can't be there. I'm sorry. Have you discussed this with the directorate?"

Hicks: "No."

Cronyn: "Well, the only way I can see that you can conceivably proceed is to bring them in, make these facts known to them, show them what the problems are, discuss their program with them, and if you feel Dexter is the answer and he is indeed available, then ask them if *they* will invite Dexter."

Hicks: "Well, yes, I guess that's one thing that might be done."

Cronyn: "Bob, if it ever gets out that you're considering dismissing the directorate and engaging another artistic director right after the collapse of the two-tier structure, the shit is going to hit the fan."

Cronyn wasn't the only Board member missing from the fateful meeting on November 5. Only nineteen Board members turned up (on very short notice), barely a quorum. Ronald Bryden had a class he couldn't cancel. Barbara Ivey said she had urgent business in London on Wednesday morning but that she would do her best to get there. She had even hired a car and driver before realizing that there was no way she could get to Toronto in time for a two o'clock meeting.

On Wednesday morning, Pam Brighton, who was in Stratford for a few days, called John Lawson to ask why after weeks of pressing the matter, the Board had suddenly become silent on the subject of contracts. She was quite suspicious; as she put it, the line seemed to have gone dead.

Brighton: "What's going on? I feel insecure because of this contract delay."

Lawson tried to soothe her. He told her not to worry. She got the impression he was going to have the contract ready in a couple of days.

Brighton said, "I've got an hour this morning. Maybe we could meet and straighten it out."

Lawson said that wouldn't be necessary.

Brighton ran into Urjo Kareda just as he and Martha Henry were about to leave for Toronto to appear at the Board meeting. "I've just had a conversation with Lawson that makes me very nervous," she said.

"Now, Pam," Kareda assured her, "don't be paranoid."

At the beginning of the meeting in Toronto that afternoon, Kareda and Henry were invited to present their season to the Board. They had been given no inkling that their presentation might serve as a preamble to a motion calling for their dismissal. Indeed, only a few of the Board members present knew what was coming. But there was a tip-off: Peter Stevens changed seats rather than sit next to Martha Henry.

There were a number of questions from Board members after Kareda and Henry made their presentation. Hicks asked, "Yes, but are any of these people committed?" Kareda and Henry said emphatically yes. Then Hicks queried, "Are they contracted?" The answer to that was, of course, no. But it was embarrassing for Kareda and Henry, with Stevens sitting there, to explain why not. Didn't Hicks realize that there was one only one person empowered to do the contracting? And that that person was Peter Stevens? Indeed, the Gang of Four had been pressing Stevens to follow through by sending contracts to the people they had been lining up. They couldn't understand why he wasn't doing so.

Kareda and Henry weren't comfortable with the Board. They didn't live in the same world as these people, who were mainly rich, establishment businessmen. The discomfort was mutual. Kareda and Henry must have seemed subdued and distant. If they had made one major mistake, it was probably political rather than artistic or administrative: they had failed to establish a rapport with anyone on the Board. If the Gang of Four had managed to attain the sort of on-going representation on the Board that Hume Cronyn had suggested in his September memo to them, it wouldn't have been possible for the Board to dismiss the Four without giving them a chance to reply to the case against them. In retrospect,

Cronyn's advice on this point would seem grimly prophetic.

After Kareda and Henry left the room, Stevens delivered a lethal appraisal of their proposed season. He suggested that their plans were extremely shaky. Michael Bogdanov couldn't really be in Stratford when needed, according to Stevens, and Peter James was merely a possibility. The Canadians lined up – William Lane, Scott Swann, Sheldon Larry – he didn't regard as first-class directors. Pam Brighton herself he considered just a fringe director trying to step out of her league. Kate Reid had director approval, and if the Four couldn't land someone she accepted for *Who's Afraid of Virginia Woolf?*, she might drop out not only of that show but also *Waiting for the Parade*. Stevens didn't deny that John Hirsch was first-class, but he was very sceptical about getting *Madame Sans Gêne* for 1981. Maggie Smith's agent had told Stevens it was a 1982 project: when her husband finished doing the translation, Smith would read it. She would be ready to discuss a commitment *if* she liked it. (But as far as Martha Henry was concerned, Maggie Smith was as firm as it was possible to be.) Stevens knew that the Board, conditioned by the way Robin Phillips had operated, believed in the magic of stars and might be thrown into a panic by the suggestion that in 1981 there might not be *any* stars. Jason Robards, he implied, wasn't really serious about playing the lead in *The Merchant of Venice*; he was just trying to be polite when he said he'd try to work the dates out.

Stevens was strong and smooth. To several Board members, he seemed more confident than Henry and Kareda. He warned that the 1981 season would be far below the usual Stratford standards. His assessment of the Gang of Four was: They don't seem to be working out, their support has dropped away, they're over-extended. Some Board members realized that the directorate had had no indication from anyone that their work wasn't satisfactory. If Stevens' criticisms had any validity, shouldn't the Gang of Four have a chance to face them and answer them?

"It's no good going back to the Four," Stevens told the Board. "It's not that they're not doing their best. The problem is that they *are* doing their best." In Stevens' opinion, there was no point in cutting their budget, either. It wasn't that the shows were too extravagant, he argued. The problem was that the program didn't have the strength to draw enough revenue. If the directorate were confronted with this criticism, according to Stevens, they would be bound to say, "This *will* make money." They had to believe in what they were doing, even if no one else could, Stevens said.

Given the personality and the personal history of Peter Stevens, it wasn't entirely surprising that he took the position he did. What was surprising, though, was how readily the Board allowed itself to be led by Peter Stevens, a man they hardly knew, who hadn't spent more than a month of his life in Canada at this point. He saw himself as a major-leaguer, and he was going to share a little of his finesse with these people if they wanted to fly with him. Stevens had become the magic chairman that the Board had always wanted. He was stepping into a vacuum.

The way Stevens presented the situation, the Board had three choices: stick with the Four and take a disastrous loss; cancel the 1981 season; or bring in John Dexter and save Stratford from ruin. There could, however, have been other ways of looking at the situation. Wasn't it possible that Stevens and Thomas might be wrong about the projected deficit? Wasn't it true that Stevens had been sold on the idea of bringing in John Dexter before he ever started working with the Gang of Four? Whether or not it had been a good idea to appoint the Gang of Four in the first place, once the commitment had been made shouldn't the Board honour it? In fairness to the Gang of Four, shouldn't someone have pointed out that no wizard – not Robin Phillips, or John Hirsch, or John Dexter – could have put together a dazzling season in six weeks and have all the details nailed down? Shouldn't someone have said that the Gang of Four had stepped into a terrible mess and made an impressive recovery in a short time? An astute Board member might have said, "We knew when we appointed these four people that the first season would be rough, but maybe if we get behind them, things will be right again by the time they start their second season." Or, "Peter Stevens doesn't understand the forces at work in this country, and has no sense of the repercussions this move is going to have." Or, "We aren't going to get away with this. Given the political situation in this country at the moment, there is going to be a terrible public uproar." Or, "John Dexter is a great director, but we have no way of knowing whether he is the right man to head a company like Stratford."

One or two Board members did have misgivings, but they sensed that the pressure was on for a show of solidarity, that if the Board were split on this matter, there would be a rash of resignations and the whole place could come crashing down. During a break in the proceedings, Mona Bandeen – who had made her mark on the Montreal Symphony Board, and whose husband, the president of Canadian National Railways, had preceded her on the Stratford Board – asked Arnold Edinborough, who had seemed sceptical about the move to bring in Dexter, whether he was going to vote against it, and he said no, he didn't feel free to do so.

The motion to disband the directorate and bring in Dexter was formally proposed by H.N.R. Jackman (chairman of the board of the Empire Life Insurance Company and a key figure in several other major companies) and seconded by E.G. (Ted) Burton (then in the process of stepping down as president of Simpsons). The vote was unanimous.

The Board members who might have spoken against the removal of the Four were all absent: Hume Cronyn, Barbara Ivey, Ronald Bryden. Also absent from this crucial meeting were Hope Abelson of Chicago; George A. Allan, a Hamilton businessman; L.A.L. Garvie, president of the Stratford-based Dominion Chain; Dr. Reva Gerstein, a professor of psychology at York University; W. Darcy McKeough, president of Union Gas; Derek Mitchell, chief executive officer of BP Canada; Alfred Powis, president of Noranda Mines; and W.H. Young, president of the Hamilton Group.

Those who did attend the meeting and voted to dismiss the Four included Mrs. Bandeen; Edinborough; Hicks; Lawson; Gaffney; Heney; Jackman; Burton; Mrs. D.S. Davis of Stratford; Robert Gordon, owner of a Stratford men's clothing shop; Robert Heneault, vice-president of Stelco; Perry Hill, a Stratford lawyer; Donald G. MacLeod, president of a Cambridge, Ont., shoe company; Judge Arthur Mullen of Stratford; R. Thomas Orr, a Stratford insurance executive; David A. Rae, president of the Stratford-based Mirror Press; B.J. Sibold, owner of a Stratford car dealership; W.I.M. (Bill) Turner, Jr., chief executive officer of Consolidated-Bathurst of Montreal; and Peter Widdrington, president of John Labatt of London, Ont.

Only a handful of these people had been involved directly with the crisis as it had developed day by day throughout the year. Those who were neither on the executive nor residents of Stratford were inevitably distanced from the events, and relied on the judgement of colleagues more closely involved. Many of them functioned mainly as fundraisers.

The decision was actually made very quickly – in about half an hour. Afterward, though, the meeting continued for another two hours, with a great deal of agonizing about what would become of the Four, what strategy to use to get Dexter into the country, and how embarrassing it was going to be that only two months earlier this same Board had heavily endorsed the Gang of Four.

Why did the Board go along with Peter Stevens, a man who had always been second banana to someone who could overrule him – John Neville at Nottingham, Peter Hall at the National, the Shuberts in New York? Why did no one say, "Hang on a minute, you just got here, we don't think you're qualified to make this decision"? Was the answer partly that the Stratford Board – encapsulating Canada's long history of a colonialism so deeply ingrained that people weren't even conscious of it – was just doing what it had almost always done, bowing to the presumed higher authority of a British overlord?

CHAPTER ELEVEN

Swan Songs

When Ronald Bryden got the news from Robert Hicks of what had happened at the Board meeting, he was stunned. Knowing that the political consequences would be disastrous, he asked Hicks whether Dexter really understood the climate of opinion in Canada and suggested that Dexter be asked to join the directorate. Hicks replied that at the Bristol Place interview Dexter had made it very clear he would be either artistic director or nothing. Bryden, however, felt that Dexter's decision must have been made without knowing very much about the situation in Canada, and he told Hicks that someone should try to give Dexter some inkling of what the consequences would be. Hicks suggested that Bryden call Dexter, but by the time he phoned Dexter in New York the next day, Dexter had already left for a ten-day holiday in the Caribbean. Dexter did realize there would be an uproar, and he had promised the Board he wouldn't talk to the press. He needed a complete rest and wanted to be unreachable while sitting by the sea planning the 1981 Stratford season. Dexter stayed in St. Martin until November 17.

Having decided on a startling change of course, the Board was now faced with working out a strategy for gaining government approval and public acceptance of it. Hicks decided in consultation with his closest advisers (a category that no longer included Barbara Ivey) that the Board's decision should be kept secret until he could sound out the Department of Employment and Immigration and get assurances that Dexter would be given a work permit. Stevens and Dexter had both pressed Hicks to get things settled with Immigration before proceeding further, but Hicks was nervous about this aspect of the operation. He feared that news of the decision would leak as soon as anyone from Stratford began lobbying the Department of Employment and Immigration, and that there might be a terrible public row before the Board had a chance to make its announcement. But he reluctantly agreed that the Ottawa mission was mandatory.

When Hicks phoned Ottawa, he wasn't able to reach Lloyd Axworthy, the Minister of Employment and Immigration, so he called Bill Jarvis, member of Parliament for the Stratford area. Jarvis called back to say he couldn't get a commitment from Axworthy, but that he could arrange for Hicks and his delegation to have a meeting the next day with two senior officials of Employment and Immigration.

On Friday, November 7, Hicks flew to Ottawa with Lawson, Gaffney, and David Rae, a past president of the Board who was asked along because he was known as a strong Liberal. They spent two-and-a-half hours with two officials of Axworthy's department, Ian Hamilton and George Lambert, outlining the situation as they saw it. The officials said they couldn't give any guarantees, but the Board had their sympathy and support, and they would convey that to the minister.

Hicks said, "I would like to communicate directly with the minister, confirming what we've discussed."

"How soon can you do it?" one of the Immigration officials asked.

"I'll have a letter in the mail tomorrow," Hicks said.

What Hicks and his colleagues didn't realize at the time was that they had gone to see the wrong people. Every Cabinet minister had two kinds of staff: a personal staff who advise on policy issues and are political appointments; and departmental bureaucrats who keep the machinery running no matter what party is in power or who the minister is. Hicks should have been talking to someone in the former category – probably Joseph Stern, one of Axworthy's top advisers. Instead he was dealing with people in the latter category.

The Stratford Board members left Ottawa under the mistaken impression that they had taken care of smoothing the way for the admission of John Dexter. Because they couldn't get a flight from Ottawa to Toronto (always difficult on a Friday afternoon) they decided to rent a car and drive back. The rental car was in bad shape, and on the road, the one thing that hadn't yet gone wrong for Bob Hicks did go wrong: his back, a chronic problem, gave out. The next morning, Hicks, still suffering terrible back pains, dictated a letter several pages long to Lloyd Axworthy. After discussing it with Lawson and making a few changes, he sent it off by courier to insure it would be on Axworthy's desk on Monday morning.

The same day that the Board people were in Ottawa, Peter Stevens, for the first time, made the gesture of walking over to the office of Kareda and Henry for a chat. He knew Dexter wanted them to stay, and it would take some diplomacy to keep them once news of the Board's decision broke. Stevens tried to make small talk with them; he asked Kareda where in Stratford he got his hair cut.

There was a slight buzz around the office. Gary Thomas had told someone that Festival employees should all hold onto their hats: a big announcement was coming. When Peter Stevens got home later that night, he heard the voice of Robert Hicks on his telephone answering machine, reporting that all was going well in Ottawa.

That same evening, Hume Cronyn and Jessica Tandy kept a date they had made long before. They had dinner at The Church restaurant with Urjo Kareda and his wife, Shelagh Hewitt (who also worked for the Festival, as its education co-ordinator).

Cronyn had just returned to Stratford after three weeks in Massachusetts to see Tandy's last performance as Mary Tyrone in Long Day's Journey into Night. The two planned to spend a few days tying up loose ends, pack up and move out of the house where they had been living for the summer. They were going to drive back to New York. At the age of sixty-nine, and with only one good eye (the other lost to cancer twelve years earlier), Cronyn wasn't fond of long drives, but there seemed no other way to move all the things that had to be taken back to New York.

That morning, Cronyn had gone to the Festival Theatre to get a receipt from Gary Thomas for a contribution he had made to the Festival. Thomas asked Cronyn whether he had heard what had happened at the Board meeting, and Cronyn replied that he hadn't. When he found out that the Board had voted unanimously to dismiss the directorate and bring in Dexter, Cronyn was dismayed. It was he who had introduced the name of John Dexter to the Stratford Board nine months earlier. But in September he had thrown his complete support and loyalty to the four people who were now being dismissed. Indeed, he had become one of their closest and most trusted advisers.

As they drove to The Church, Cronyn said to Tandy, "Oh, God, I hope they don't talk about the 1981 season." But he knew they probably would. It was on everybody's mind. That evening at The Church turned out to be one of the most painful Cronyn had ever sat through.

Cronyn had first met Kareda seven years earlier, when Kareda was the drama critic at the *Toronto Star,* but it was Stratford that had cemented their friendship. Cronyn had worked closely with Kareda on *Foxfire,* and gave Kareda full credit for getting the play produced. When offered the awesome responsibility of the directorate position, Kareda had relied heavily on Cronyn's support. It was largely because of Cronyn's presence on the Board that Kareda had agreed to accept the offer at a time when there was every reason to be wary of the Board. It was Cronyn, too, who had been instrumental in bringing Peter Stevens to Stratford, and who had urged the Gang of Four to work with Stevens.

Cronyn knew that Kareda had been to New York to see Dexter, and at one point during the dinner, Kareda leaned across the table and said, "Oh, incidentally, Hume, Dexter has turned us down." Cronyn was acutely aware that Dexter had not only turned them down but was now waiting in the wings to take over. He knew Kareda did not suspect that he was about to be fired from a job to which he had been appointed less than two months earlier. Cronyn knew this was going to be a traumatic blow for Kareda and the others, and that later on Kareda would find it hard to forgive Cronyn for sitting across the table from him on this night at The Church and failing to warn him. But Cronyn had been through all this in his mind on his way to the restaurant. He felt it would be as unethical of him to tip off Kareda as it would be to let the Board know something Kareda and Henry had told him in confidence.

"By the way," Kareda said toward the end of the evening, "Martha is very anxious to talk to you. Will you call her?" The next day Cronyn tried two or three times to reach Martha Henry, but failed. That night, after the final performance of *Long Day's Journey,* he and Tandy did their final packing.

Peter Ustinov was also packing up. It was the closing day of the 1980 season, and that night *King Lear* had its final performance. Before the performance began, Ustinov received a note from Urjo Kareda that touched him deeply:

I do not know whether or not it will be possible for me to see you tonight: it will be an emotional evening at any rate, and there will be many who wish to say farewell. I do want you to know, however, how grateful I am for your commitment and loyalty to our company, and for what you have brought to all of us. I know that it has been a bewildering and painful season for you. I can only guess the extent of your pain and bewilderment by judging my own from not entirely dissimilar experiences. You have my deepest affection, admiration and support. Please know that. It would be wonderful if, some day, you felt free and confident enough about your experiences here to return to us. You must know that you will always be welcome. Even for so extensive a world-traveller as you, there may remain a small area of the heart for which Stratford means a "home": I hope to see your return to that home some day. Keep well, keep in touch, and remember your friends here. They are legion.

During the tumultuous curtain calls after that night's performance, Ustinov gave a speech. "I've been happier this year than last in some respects, and very much unhappier in others. *King Lear* shows how difficult it is when you're dealing with a divided kingdom. But at least let us give every support to the quadrumvirate. Lear has only three daughters to cope with; there are four of them now." Martha Henry, still in costume, was standing in the wings. Ustinov brought her out and handed her some flowers that had been thrown at him from the audience. "This is a new leader anyone should be happy to serve," he said. "This is the finest company in the world. The king is dead. Long live the king. All best wishes to the new artistic directorate." The audience went wild.

On Sunday morning, as Cronyn and Tandy were getting ready to leave for New York, Martha Henry called. "Would you and Jessie consider coming back to Stratford for the 1981 season?"

Again, Cronyn experienced the dilemma of dealing with a friend on less than honest terms. He knew Henry would feel humiliated when the truth became known. Very quietly, Cronyn replied: "Thanks, Martha, but it's just not possible."

After the call from Henry, Cronyn and Tandy had lunch with Cronyn's eighty-three-year-old sister, who had driven up from London to say goodbye. Then he drove to the home of John Heney, the chairman of the Board's nominating committee. Cronyn had planned to step down from the Board when his three-year term was up at the end of 1980, but Heney had persuaded him to stay on.

Cronyn, after all, was a strong supporter of the directorate, and the link between the Board and Peter Stevens. Cronyn had earlier told Heney that he would stand for another term if the Board thought his presence would help. Now he reversed that decision.

Cronyn: "I'm sorry, John, but you'll have to withdraw my name. I can't stand because I don't approve of what the Board is doing. Whether I would have had the balls to stand up against the unanimous vote of nineteen other people I don't know, but I don't approve of it. We've made certain commitments to the directorate. I understand the problems, but we said we'd do certain things, and I think we should be sticking to them. If that means missing Dexter, well, I'm sorry. And if it means taking a loss, well, then, we take a loss."

Heney: "Hume, that's unrealistic. If the directorate does not manage to come up with something more promising, then we'll be discussing their dismissal in June. And that will be infinitely more critical, and we won't have somebody else around who can do the job."

Cronyn: "Well, I feel those are the chances you have to take. But you've voted unanimously to go in another direction, and I don't want to continue. I'm out."

There had always been tension between the creative community and the business community in Stratford. Cronyn had a foot in each world. Fancying himself a bit of an elder statesman, he had tried to bring them together. Now, leaving Stratford perhaps for the last time, it was with a sense of "a plague on both your houses."

Cronyn could see now that his good intentions had contributed to a catastrophe. He had given Kareda and Henry his full support and some excellent advice, but then he had absented himself at a time when only his presence might have saved them. Unwittingly, he had introduced the Festival to the two people who brought about their downfall—Stevens and Dexter.

Cronyn was experiencing a Stratford syndrome with which many people over the years had become painfully familiar. Because this was, after all, a very small place, when things went wrong, they took on an exaggerated importance. In New York or London or Toronto, a professional setback could be balanced by the context of life going on around you, but in Stratford a professional setback was all-consuming. Everyone would know about it and talk about it. Cronyn, like other people who have felt hemmed in by Stratford, felt a need to escape from this environment, to breathe the air of the outside world, where there might be a chance to be diverted by other people with other interests.

The day before his talk with Cronyn, John Heney had had an awkward conversation with Barbara Ivey. Since communications had broken down between Hicks and Ivey, it was Heney who was regularly in touch with her. A month earlier, Heney had received a shock when he started organizing his nominating committee in preparation for elections at the annual meeting of the Festival foundation on December 6. As first vice-president, and a veteran of the Board, Ivey was a natural choice to become the Board's next president. But she had told her colleagues the previous March that her deadline for making a decision about the Stratford presidency was the end of June. On several occasions she had asked Hicks and Heney to convene the nominating commitee. Hicks said things like, "Oh, Barb, we couldn't get along without you," but nothing was done. When the nominating committee finally was convened in October, Ivey reminded Heney, "You know, John, you've lost me. I told you months ago I had a deadline. You knew that. Bob knew."

Heney urged her to reconsider. They had a guarded discussion about what her conditions would be *if* she were to reconsider.

Ivey: "Look, if I were going to reconsider, I couldn't wait until December 6, I'd have to start right now. I'm afraid Mr. Hicks would have to take his bad back down to his condominium in Florida."

Heney: "You mean you want me to ask him to resign?"

Ivey: "No, I don't want him to resign. Just ask him to go away."

For two years Hicks and Ivey had been working together as president and vice-president, trying to gloss over their conflicts. Now their mutual disenchantment was out in the open. She conceded that Hicks was a great fundraiser, and that somebody, not her, had to do it. But she had grown impatient with Hicks, and she thought the records were appalling. Hicks was the only person talking to everyone, and no one else could ever be sure what was happening. She knew she was regarded by certain colleagues on the executive as "that hysterical woman." She also knew that some people said she was too emotionally committed to Robin Phillips to be clear-headed. Sometimes she suspected that Hicks blamed her for not pulling Robin Phillips out of the hat one last time to save the day.

It was Heney who had phoned to ask her to come to the critical

Board meeting on November 5 in Toronto, and when she heard what was up, she said to him, "My God, are you crazy?" Yet two days after the meeting she had still not heard the result. On Saturday she finally called Heney and found out that the Board had voted to disband the directorate and bring in Dexter.

"Who talked to the Four?" she asked Heney. As far as she was concerned, it had been decided at the October 31 executive meeting she had chaired that Heney, Lawson, and Gaffney were to speak to the Four the following Monday (November 3), advise them of the committee's concerns, and give them a chance to respond. (This decision, however, does not appear in any official Board records.) She was outraged when Heney said that no one had spoken to the Gang of Four. She felt the whole procedure was immoral. It was standard practice in the case of budget problems to go back to the people responsible and ask for changes. "You can't dump these people without giving them a chance to discuss the problem! You just can't treat people that way."

Heney replied that the Four were going to be called in and given the news the following Monday night (November 10) at eight o'clock. There was going to be a meeting at six o'clock in Lawson's office to work out strategy, and Heney asked Ivey to attend.

"Okay," she said, "but I don't think you'll like what I have to say."

That Monday, Ivey started out in her car along the road from London to Stratford, and at ten minutes past five she lost control of the car and wound up in a ditch. When she got the car out of the ditch, she set off again in the direction of Stratford, but after a couple of minutes she was still feeling shaky. "I've got to go home," she thought. She turned the car around and drove back to London.

Ronald Bryden received a phone call on Monday from another Board member, Arnold Edinborough, asking Bryden to attend a meeting in Stratford that night. Bryden, who still had in mind the idea of making Dexter part of the group, saw this as the last chance to work out a compromise. At the meeting at Lawson's office, attended by Heney, Bryden, Edinborough, and Lawson, there was a discussion about whether the Four could be kept on and Dexter given a different title, such as Festival Director. But they couldn't agree on how this would affect Peter Stevens, and finally they decided simply to tell Kareda and Henry what the situation was, say their season simply wouldn't fly, and ask them to go back to doing their old jobs.

Heney had called Kareda that afternoon to ask whether he and Henry could meet a few members of the Board at eight o'clock in the VIP lounge of the Festival Theatre to go over plans for the 1981 program. A distant alarm rang in Kareda's head, but Henry told him not to worry. When the meeting began, Heney, reading from a prepared statement, broke the news. Kareda and Henry were offered a year's salary and asked to meet with Dexter the following week and "continue to give him your artistic input." Which prompted Henry to ask, "Whatever can you mean, John?"

Kareda and Henry asked a few pointed questions: why hadn't they been told about this major deficit until ten seconds ago? How was Dexter going to know enough about what had been done at Stratford to decide what he wanted to keep of the planned 1981 season and what he wanted to discard? Kareda warned there were problems ahead that the Board couldn't even guess about: "You've given four people two months to put something together, then pulled the rug out from under them."

Arnold Edinborough asked Kareda to call Pam Brighton and Peter Moss and give them the news. Kareda replied tersely, "I think that's your job, Arnold."

The firing was all wrapped up within twenty minutes, and the victims, all things considered, had received the news fairly quietly. The Board members hoped that after a few days of being upset, the Gang of Four would go back to doing their old jobs, thus smoothing the way for John Dexter. But before adjourning to the Victorian Inn for drinks with Kareda, Henry called her husband, Douglas Rain. He flew into a rage and was on the phone for the rest of the evening, calling, among others, the Toronto newspapers. A public uproar was imminent.

Henry and Kareda chose the Victorian Inn because they knew no one would find them there. They had three drinks each. Snow was starting to come down when they left. They were both out of work – he at the age of thirty-six, she at forty-two. By the time Kareda got home two hours later, word had spread all over the world, and the phone didn't stop ringing. Maggie Smith called from Paris, where she was filming Quartet, to commiserate. Robin Phillips called from England to say he was "stunned and amazed." Kareda and Phillips spoke for an hour. The thought ran through Kareda's mind that what he had once regarded as Phillips' paranoia about the Board was now starting to seem like reality.

146

Peter Moss got the news from John Heney at 1 A.M. Moss, who had regarded Heney as one of the friendlier Board members, replied: "You making a big mistake. You've been listening to very bad advice. This is going to haunt you for the rest of your life."

Pam Brighton had been unreachable the night of November 10, but the next morning a phone call from Heney woke her up.

Heney: "I've got some bad news for you. We've decided to disband the directorate and hire John Dexter."

Brighton: "That's shocking. I mean it is really appalling. How *can* you behave like that?...Well, do you think you can get Dexter a work permit?"

Heney: "That's all under control. It's going to be fine."

Brighton: "I suspect it is *not* going to be fine."

Brighton decided on the spot to phone John Lawson. Lawson, she recalled, was the one who had done so much chatting about good faith and everyone working together and trusting each other. On the very day the Board was voting to dismiss them, she had had the impression that something was wrong even as Lawson tried to soothe her. When she heard Lawson's voice on the line her rage exploded.

Lawson told her how famous and well-regarded Dexter was, citing the rave reviews for his production of *Galileo* at the National Theatre in London.

Brighton said, "We're never going to have a national theatre in this country if you don't stop reading notices from the English press. You're a parody of what a theatre board is supposed to be."

On Tuesday, November 11 – Remembrance Day – Martha Henry went to her office and began calling people to say she was no longer empowered to make offers to them. When she reached Len Cariou and broke the news, he burst out laughing and shrieked, "They're incredible." John Hirsch called from Seattle in a flap: "What's all this about? What about my project? Who am I supposed to talk to?" Maggie Smith sent a message saying how distressed she was. There was also a message from Peter Stevens saying that Dexter was very eager to work with the Four, but Martha Henry was in no mood to take messages from Peter Stevens seriously. Despite being a public performer, Martha Henry was a very private person. At this moment she felt more exposed than she ever had before. And she had to do something very difficult: with the headlines about the firings in the newspapers, she had to fly to Vancouver to act in a

CBC radio version of *A Month in the Country.*

Hume Cronyn arrived in New York from Stratford on the night of November 11, and the phone was ringing as he walked into his hotel suite. It was Greg Wanless, one of the actors in the Stratford company, That's how Cronyn learned the whole matter was out in the open. He paced around for a few minutes, then said to Tandy, "Well, I have to call Martha and Urjo." To Kareda, he said, "You realize that when we had dinner on Friday night, I knew about this situation."

"I realize it now. I didn't realize it before. I assumed you didn't know." He was clipped, terse, letting Cronyn know he was hurt.

Cronyn: "I don't think I have the heart to call Martha right now. I'm dog tired. I've been driving for two days. But I will call her later, and if you see her, please tell her I'll call."

Cronyn was very depressed as he put down the phone. It rang a minute later, and he heard Douglas Rain, calling to suggest that he resign from the Board. Cronyn was enraged by what he interpreted as Rain's unjustified moral superiority. He said, "Thank you, Douglas, I've already taken the steps I feel are appropriate" – meaning, he had withdrawn from the Board. Rain asked why.

Cronyn: "Because I don't want to walk down the street in Stratford and see either Urjo or Martha coming in the other direction and feel that I have to cross the street."

Rain: "You told me last week at a party at Bill Hutt's that the Board was not Machiavellian. Can you honestly say that now?"

Cronyn: "Yes, Douglas, I can honestly say the Board is not Machiavellian. The Board may be in serious error. It may have done something extremely unwise, or even unconscionable. But it is not Machiavellian."

Rain said something about "having made your confessional...."

Cronyn was livid: "I've made no confessional. I have absolutely nothing to confess. It's a bloody mess. I regret it has happened. Now I'd like to speak to Martha."

She was already on the upstairs phone. "I just want to make one thing clear," she told Cronyn. "You do realize that the conversation I had with you a couple of days ago about your coming back to Stratford has no validity."

Cronyn gulped. Martha Henry's style was kind and thoughtful, but it was obvious she was deeply wounded. "Yes, Martha," said Cronyn, "I do realize it."

John Dexter was furious when Peter Stevens called to say the Four had been sacked. Dexter had emphasized that he wanted them kept on, and he felt that if he could have talked to them they would have agreed. It never occurred to him that he had made it impossible for them to stay by insisting he couldn't work as anything less than sole artistic director.

Robert Hicks, still laid up with a bad back, was also unhappy with the results of the November 10 meeting. He couldn't help thinking that if he had run the meeting things might have turned out differently. He would have kept the meeting going as long as it took to work out an alternative.

Peter Stevens was shocked by the public reaction. He had had no idea how touchy Canadians could be about these things. He had assumed that after a day or two, the fuss would all blow over, and the Four would realize it was in their own best interests to go back to their old jobs. When he and Neville had been squeezed out at Nottingham, there had been a public row and the press had been on their side, but it hadn't done them any good. All week long Stevens kept trying to make an appointment to see the Gang of Four. Finally he sent a memo asking how they intended to deal with all the people they had approached with offers for the 1981 season and begging them at least to meet with Dexter.

On Wednesday, November 12, the dammed part of the Avon River next to the Festival Theatre was drained, and Stratford's famous white swans were gathered up and put away in their cages for the winter.

CHAPTER TWELVE

The Shit Hits the Fan

Hume Cronyn wasn't wrong when he warned Bob Hicks that the shit was going to hit the fan. The most breath-taking aspect of the Board's miscalculation was the notion that they were going to get away with it. Cronyn, Ivey, Bryden, and Edinborough had all expected there was going to be a dreadful uproar, but the Board was taking its cues from Peter Stevens, who had spent less than a month in Canada, and knew little about the Canada Council, Canadian Actors' Equity, the media, the theatre community, or the government's immigration policies. Yet the strength of the outcry came as a surprise even to those who knew a great deal about these matters. Canadian nationalists had been used to symbolic protests and futile gestures. The Stratford Board, almost unbelievably, had provided an issue around which the outrage was so clear and dramatic that the dissidents could sense that here was a battle they could win.

Dan MacDonald, an Equity past president and vociferous spokesman for the nationalist position, got the news when Pam Brighton called on Tuesday morning. She was livid: Equity had had its skirmishes before with the Stratford Festival, but this time the Board had gone too far. Brighton and MacDonald agreed that the Board's action constituted an intolerable insult to Equity members. The issue was not only the mistreatment of the Gang of Four; there was also the matter of Equity members who had been offered work for the 1981 season in shows that would not be produced. What compensation did the Board plan to offer? (None, as it turned out.)

It may have seemed ironic that Pam Brighton, herself a British director, could initiate an Equity protest against the appointment of a British director. But Equity drew a big distinction between someone like Brighton, who came to work in the Canadian theatre and became an Equity member, and the case of someone like John Dexter, who was being parachuted in not just to direct plays but to take over one of the country's most important cultural institutions. In Equity's view, there was a correct way for outsiders to behave, and Dexter wasn't observing it. If he was sincere about joining the Canadian theatre, let him spend a couple of years working here, directing plays, acquainting himself with the country, and then perhaps he would be ready to run a theatre.

John Neville had spent several years working as an actor and director in Canada and had become a landed immigrant before he presumed to become artistic director of the Citadel Theatre in Edmonton and later the Neptune Theatre in Halifax. His commitment to Canada was by then clear. Indeed, Neville showed a greater respect for the local constituency than many home-grown artistic directors. Even Robin Phillips, whose appointment was so hotly contested at the time, had spent a year in Canada as an observer, getting to know the country, meeting people, seeing shows, becoming familiar with the talent resources, before he attempted his first Stratford season.

Dexter's situation was preposterous. Without knowing the strengths and weaknesses of the Stratford company, of which he had seen so very little, how could he possibly make intelligent casting decisions? Never having had a chance to observe the actors, writers, designers, directors, and technicians working at theatres across Canada, how could he possibly make intelligent judgements about what they were capable of doing? It was all very well to speak of the theatre as international, but would anyone dream of importing a Canadian or an American who had never worked in England to become the immediate head of, say, the National Theatre of Great Britain? Yes, it had been great that Tyrone Guthrie was available when the call came from Stratford in 1952. But things had changed since then.

In 1952, Canada was a country with virtually no theatrical past, and with a very small body of people working in the theatre. Dora Mavor Moore, the pioneer of Canadian theatre and a great champion of the notion that it was always better to nurture and develop your own talent than to bring it in from somewhere else, had understood that when she put Tom Patterson in touch with Guthrie. All this had been clear to Guthrie, too. The great excitement for him had lain in the opportunity for a fresh start, without the weight of tradition. He had preached the gospel of Canada's finding its own way in the theatre, developing its own talent, running its own affairs. "We must be careful," Guthrie had remarked, "to avoid creating another Boston tea party here."

Now that latter-day Boston tea party was finally starting. Stevens expected that people might scream for a few days, but he thought if you were brash and aggressive enough, you could plug your ears and barrel right through. Hicks relied on Stevens' advice and brought the rest of the Board into line. Many of the Board members were at home in corporate boardrooms, where they were used to seeking the counsel of just the kind of high-powered expert that Stevens seemed to be. Few had any rapport with people in the cultural community, and so they weren't prepared for the reaction.

The Canadian Actors' Equity Council called an emergency meeting for Thursday afternoon, November 13, in Equity's downtown Toronto quarters, a former whorehouse. The mood of the dozen delegates was extremely militant. The "soft" position of the minority was that maybe Equity should try to work out some accommodation with Stratford. But most delegates felt things had gone too far; there had to be a showdown. Equity had played nice and backed down too many times. The argument the association heard was always the same: "Of course we understand your concerns, and next time we can assure you things will be different." There could be no more "next time." (When the meeting broke up after more than four hours, TV and radio reporters were waiting downstairs for a statement.)

The council decided to take a series of strong and immediate steps to protest the actions of the Stratford Board. It was resolved that "Canadian Actors' Equity cease to negotiate the agreement which was to be effective April 1, 1981, on the grounds that the Board of Governors of the Stratford Festival is an unfair employer...specifically that the president of the Board of Governors pledged full support to the directorate and subsequently fired the directorate without just cause. We require the Board to repudiate this action with the resignation of the members responsible and the Board's reconstitution in accordance with principles which would prevent a recurrence. Until this is done, no further negotiations will take place."

Another resolution called on the government of Ontario to inquire into the conduct of the Stratford Board and make such changes "as might be necessary to prevent the further humiliation and financial embarrassment of our members." (This resolution seemed ill-advised, since the Ontario government had no jurisdiction over the Stratford Board.)

The Equity Council instructed its president to inform the Stratford Board in writing that the Festival's agreement with Equity was due to expire in a few months, and that Equity felt it was unlikely the Festival would be able to present a credible negotiating team.

"Until such time as Equity can come to believe that the traditional trustworthiness with regard to employment of our members has been restored, the Stratford Festival is to understand that Equity regards the normal good relations between us to have been gravely prejudiced. No further contracts for the services of our members will be recognized by Equity until we are satisfied that relations with the Stratford Festival have been normalized."

The word "normalized" was defined: there must be a Canadian resident in the position of artistic director empowered to negotiate in good faith with Equity. All members of Equity were to be told not to enter into any contractual agreements with Stratford until further notice. (One of the finer points was that Canadian Actors' Equity was not a trade union and had to be careful to avoid the word "boycott." Ironically, despite the care taken to avoid this word in the formal resolutions, it was the one word used over and over in reports of the Equity stand.)

Equity also requested that Lloyd Axworthy, the Minister of Employment and Immigration, demand specific details of all interviews conducted by the Stratford Festival with Canadian nationals regarding the position of artistic director, and that he publicly pronounce himself satisfied with the exhaustiveness of this search. Finally, Equity asked the Canada Council and the Ontario Arts Council to review the Stratford situation.

It was hardly necessary to prod the arts councils. They had both swung into action as soon as word reached them of what had happened. November 11 was a government holiday, but it would be remembered as the day that all hell broke loose inside the Ontario Arts Council's walls. William Lord, the OAC's theatre officer, had had a call late the night before from a friend in the company. Within hours, the OAC's chairman, Arthur Gelber, had pulled together an emergency meeting. Ronald Bryden came in to explain the Board's position to Gelber, Lord, and Ron Evans. While the discussion was going on, the Remembrance Day guns were fired at Queen's Park, as if to symbolize the hostilities now breaking out.

The Ontario Arts Council people complained that they had had no communication from the Stratford Board. It was no secret that the Festival resented its dependence on the arts councils. Of its $8-million annual budget, all but $2-million came from box-office revenues. Just over a million dollars came from private donations, and less than a million came from government subsidy – $500,000 from the Canada Council and $310,000 from the Ontario Arts Council. There was some talk at Stratford of breaking free of the arts councils, but the Festival had never become quite wealthy enough. Indeed, early in 1980 Hicks had had to go to them on his knees. After the 1979 season there was a big deficit to clear up, and Hicks had told the Canada Council that the Festival was in a state of distress: it was up to the Canada Council to provide emergency funding, or there might not be a 1981 Stratford Festival at all. The Canada Council had resisted that pitch, pointing out the Festival had other resources to fall back on. Thanks to a phenomenally successful 1980 season, the crisis passed.

Now the Festival was in trouble again. But the Board had failed to keep the arts councils advised of what was happening, and this was taken as a severe breach of protocol. Tim Porteous, associate director of the Canada Council, told the *Toronto Star* bluntly, "What the Board has done is not right.... We can't say the information that we've received from the Stratford Board is satisfactory....When things are seriously wrong with arts organizations, and that happens often but never as badly as at Stratford, it's normally our practice to tell them in private."

Mavor Moore, the chairman of the Canada Council, was widely quoted as saying, "Every time they do this kind of thing, they endanger our principle of not interfering with the independence of our clientele." Moore wasn't just another arts council official sounding off. His mother, Dora Mavor Moore, was the legendary matriarch of Canadian theatre, and had been instrumental in bringing Guthrie to Canada. It was while visiting Toronto's Exhibition grounds with Mavor Moore that Guthrie got the idea of using a tent at Stratford. And Moore had been involved at Stratford both as an actor (under Guthrie) and then as a Board member.

The Board was looking worse every day. Jason Robards told the press that he had very much wanted to play Shylock at Stratford, and Maggie Smith's husband, Beverley Cross, had been reached in Paris by the *Globe and Mail* and said, "Maggie was more than willing to come back for the 1981 season." (Later he would explain this willingness was tentative: she wasn't sure when she would be through filming *Evil under the Sun;* she was still considering an offer to star in *Virginia* on Broadway; and she would have to read *Madame Sans Gêne* when Cross finished translating it.)

In the Ontario Legislature, Reuben Baetz, the minister of Culture and Recreation, rebuked the Board and suggested that the Ontario Arts Council might have to reconsider whether provincial taxpayers should go on funding the Festival. "Methinks there is something rotten in the state of Stratford," he told the House. Michael Cassidy, provincial leader of the New Democratic Party, asked Baetz to intervene in the Stratford crisis. According to Cassidy, more than 500 jobs and $30 million in revenue would be lost if the Festival failed to mount a 1981 season. Blaming the Board for passing over Canadian talent, he asked Baetz to advise the Stratford Board that the Festival must be in the hands of Canadians.

Of all the extraordinary developments in this week of heated reactions, few were more startling than the emergence of the drama critics of the two most important Toronto daily newspapers as participants, rather than observers, in the Stratford affair. Two days after the story broke, the *Globe and Mail* turned over the whole of its page seven, opposite the editorial page, to a manifesto by its drama critic, Ray Conlogue. Conlogue was young, but he had a manner that was half Methodist minister and half absent-minded professor. These traits were emphasized by his looks. Tall and scrawny with a red beard and rimless glasses, he suggested a young Bernard Shaw. Now he was assuming the role of spokesman for the outraged theatre community:

> Looking back over the Stratford mess this week, it's hard to understand just what the Board of Governors had in mind. They appointed a directorate two months ago to take over the season abandoned by Robin Phillips; now, just ten weeks before rehearsals are to begin for that season, they have kicked out the directorate and appointed a foreign director who knows nothing about theatre in this country.

John Dexter has an international reputation, but has never directed here. How will he know what actors to hire? Where to find designers, technicians, stage managers?...What can this Board of Governors have been thinking? The answer is just one thing: they were thinking of how famous John Dexter is....

The people on the Stratford Board are mainly businessmen. In this country, businessmen can get an MBA without reading a play; and the Stratford Board members run to form. But instead of appointing a search committee of experts, they madly insist on doing it themselves.

That ignorance accounts for the huge John Dexter miscalculation. They expect the theatregoing public to overlook the perfidy of firing the present directorate without giving it a chance; the humiliation of seeing their flagship theatre handed to a succession of foreign directors; and the damage caused by blocking our theatre community out of what is in effect our national theatre. Conlogue went on to single out two Board members for special abuse – Arnold Edinborough and Ronald Bryden – on the grounds that with their background in the arts, they should have known better. "Today my contempt for these two men knows no bounds," was the way he put it. In stating that these two had voted to dump the directorate, Conlogue made a serious error that was to set off yet another furor. Bryden hadn't been at the meeting at which the issue was raised.

Meanwhile, the *Toronto Star*'s Gina Mallet was moving in another direction. Earlier in the week she had asked, "How do you fire a board?" But by Saturday, November 15, Mallet had become a militant anti-nationalist, a Dexter advocate, waving the banner of international excellence and scoffing at the directorate as a bunch of amateurs. According to her, "the directorate behaved like a graduate seminar when it came to choosing a season....The directorate went ahead without contract, a clear indication of how unrealistic the atmosphere must have become. Any student of management tactics knows that you don't do any work until you've signed on the dotted line." Mallet said there was no excuse for keeping Dexter out of Canada, and that the Equity boycott shouldn't be taken too seriously. "Nationalists should recognize that the notion that the directorate was going to Canadianize Stratford seems delusory. Why all the foreign directors?"

The importance attached to the *Star* drama post went back to another era, when the late Nathan Cohen was drama critic and entertainment editor, and the paper published the most interesting cultural section in the country. In the early 1970s, Cohen's old spot was occupied by Urjo Kareda until Kareda left to go to Stratford. Mallet was recruited by Edwin (Ted) Bolwell, an Australian who had spent much of his career in Canada and had gone to New York to work for the New York Times and Time magazine before returning as managing editor of the Star for a brief, explosive period.

Mallet, who had grown up in England and worked several years for Time in New York, arrived in Canada at a time when the issue of foreigners was already touchy. When she took the Shaw Festival to task for its program before she had even been there, the protests began. Thirteen major figures from the Toronto small theatres banded together and called a press conference to announce that "We the undersigned members of the theatre community find the employment of Gina Mallet as working drama critic completely unacceptable." This development, of course, only steeled the Star's will to keep Mallet. When she called the Nephesh Theatre's Children of Night obscene junk, John Juliani, a principal actor and producer, sent a messenger to the Star to challenge her to a duel. (The messenger mistook an editor for Mallet, and challenged her instead.)

The day after Mallet's analysis of the Stratford crisis appeared, Urjo Kareda wrote a letter to the editor of the Star pointing out eleven factual errors. Among them: Mallet had said that earlier in the year Kareda had been considered as a possible artistic director but not offered the job; Kareda said he was offered the job, at a meeting chaired by Hicks on May 13. [On that occasion Kareda was one of a trio including Peter Moss and Peter Roberts.] Mallet had written that Kareda had taken a lofty view when Robin Phillips suggested bringing in David Soul of Starsky and Hutch for the 1981 season. Kareda replied that he had never even heard of the suggestion of David Soul at Stratford, so could hardly be lofty about it. Mallet had said Moss and Brighton had no real experience with large-scale classics. Kareda pointed out that in the past three years Moss had directed, on the Festival stage, The Merry Wives of Windsor and Henry IV, Parts One and Two – productions singled out for praise at the time by Mallet. Seven of the eleven productions in the directorate's season were to be directed by Canadians, so why was Mallet asking "Why all the foreign directors?" Could she not add? It was Kate Reid, not Martha Henry, who was to star in *Who's Afraid of Virginia Woolf?* And so on. That letter was never published.

At the urging of Arnold Edinborough, chairman of the Board's public relations committee, the Board hired a Toronto public relations firm—Tisdall and Clark—to present its case. (Leonard McHardy, who was then in charge of the Festival's press coverage, was considered too close to the discharged directorate, and he had been quoted in the paper to the effect that anyone who joined the Festival Foundation and paid twenty-five dollars would be entitled to speak and vote at the December 6 annual meeting.) Explaining the Board's case to Gina Mallet was one of Charles Tisdall's main objectives, and Ray Conlogue was inadvertently helping by occupying the territory of outraged nationalist. The other side was unoccupied ground. What more natural than for Mallet, who had been in a position not so different from Dexter's when she arrived in Canada, to become his advocate?

On Monday, November 17, the Board, at the urging of Tisdall, held an extraordinary press conference at the Hotel Toronto. The strategy was to be as open as possible about its reasons for making the change. A Board meeting was held earlier in the day to ratify the official written statement to be issued at the press conference. Among the points covered in that statement:

The Stratford Festival has always accepted as its major obligation the nurturing of Canadian talent. It provides employment each year for as many as ninety-five Canadian actors and actresses. More than ninety-eight percent of all performers and creative workers have been Canadians or those who have landed immigrant status. The Festival provides year-round employment for one hundred and twenty people which peaks to five hundred during the season. In 1980, the amount paid to actors and actresses was 1.5 million dollars. The Stratford Festival is the single most important economic entity in the city of Stratford.

Especially intriguing is the account offered in this statement of the October 31 executive committee meeting:

When the executive committee was presented with the program, it was faced with a dilemma. It could have accepted the sketched-in program, suffered the loss and then some months from now be severely criticized for bad judgement. After exploring all possible alternatives and with the future of the Festival paramount, the committee unanimously agreed to recommend to the Board that the program should not be proceeded with and the artistic directorate be disbanded. The decision was taken with much regret and soul-searching, as the executive and the Board has the highest regard for the contribution made to the Festival over the years by the group, each in their own specialty. The members were indeed asked to remain with the Festival in their previous capacities, without any reduction in their compensation which had been substantially increased in 1981 for their additional responsibility.

This interpretation would certainly come as a shock to Barbara Ivey, who chaired that meeting and left with a very different understanding of what had been decided. Everyone present was distressed by the prospect of a large deficit, and the executive committee did vote to arrange a meeting with Dexter and assess his situation. At the same time, Ivey understood the Four were to be given a chance to comment on the projected deficit and offer their suggestions on how to deal with it. As far as she was concerned, any recommendation at that point to disband the directorate or offer the job to Dexter would have been premature. It would be up to the full Board to decide what next.

Where was Ivey when the Board voted to approve the press statement on November 17? Ivey had come to the Board meeting that morning prepared to deliver a major speech, and Hicks had greeted her warmly, as if her very presence were a show of support. But she could see the situation was hopeless. The wagons were drawn in a circle. She decided to forget about her speech and left before the meeting was over to catch an early train back to London.

The Board's statement continued:

For the record, when it was recognized eighteen months ago that Robin Phillips wished to resign, a search was undertaken for a new artistic director. Every senior Canadian director was considered and four were interviewed. For a variety of reasons no one approached wished to assume the obligation. John Dexter has been the only non-Canadian contacted by the Board other than Michael Langham, a former artistic director of the Festival.

As artistic director, John Dexter has agreed to engage in an even more aggressive search for a development of Canadian artists than the rigid standards historically demanded by the Festival and its Board. It is the Board's conviction that John Dexter will make a positive contribution to Canadian theatre through his direction of the Festival....

The Board views with regret the decision taken by the executive of Actors Equity to recommend to its membership a boycott of the Stratford Festival. There is a contract currently in force with Equity. The Board has been a good employer and has enjoyed good relations with Equity. Over the years the Festival Board, despite the tensions inherent in the creative dynamic of the theatre, has managed the Festival well. The Board hopes that when Equity understand the full circumstances, they will remove the suggested boycott in the interests of Canadian theatre, Canadian performers, the Canadian theatre-going public and the citizens of Stratford.

One need only consider the financial difficulties in which many cultural institutions find themselves in Canada and then note the financial soundness of the Stratford Festival. It is the Board's responsibilty to ensure this continues.

Despite all the care that was taken in setting it up, the press conference did not go well for the Board. The waves of hostility against the Board were almost tangible. Hicks looked wilted; the strain was taking its toll. In response to a question, Hicks said the Board could hold out only a few more days against the Equity boycott before it would have to give serious consideration to cancelling the 1981 season. When Ray Conlogue asked whom the Board had consulted about Dexter's qualifications, aside from Stevens, Hicks replied that it had been a senior Canadian actor but refused to give a name. When Conlogue thundered, with the indignation of a hell-fire preacher, "What, sir, is the actor's name?" Hicks gave in and said it was Roberta Maxwell.

Maxwell's comment about Dexter had been very off-hand. It was the night *The Seagull* opened in the second week of August. Maxwell was playing Nina ("the last of my *ingénue* roles," she joked), and the cast also included Maggie Smith, Brian Bedford, and William Hutt. It was a kind of homecoming for Maxwell, who had started her career as an apprentice at Stratford in 1957 when she was a fourteen-year-old schoolgirl. She had gone on to a career of international distinction, but had acted at Stratford only once in more than a decade, and then only for a few performances. After the opening performance of *The Seagull* there was a cast party, and Hicks gave her a lift to The Church restaurant. He seemed to know of her previous association with Dexter, and he asked how she liked working with him. She said, "I loved it. He's a great director."

Gina Mallet wasn't at the Hotel Toronto press conference; she was in New York getting an exclusive interview with John Dexter, who had just returned from St. Martin. "I remember what Laurence Olivier said when he was starting the National Theatre," Dexter told Mallet. " 'We are going to be running the National Theatre,' Olivier said, 'so put on a heavy suit of totally fitting armour and then all this shit they throw at you will just roll off.' "

Dexter told Mallet that he had several productions to do in the next few months for the Metropolitan Opera, which had resolved its union difficulties and was belatedly about to open the season. He would not be able to move to Stratford until early 1981, but the Festival's production team was going to fly down to confer with him. Christopher Plummer would be playing either Macbeth or Coriolanus in 1981, and perhaps starring in Noel Coward's *Present Laughter*. Roberta Maxwell would be playing Saint Joan and Imogen in *Cymbeline*. Kate Reid and Tony van Bridge would be starring in *The Merry Wives of Windsor*. And Dexter wanted to go ahead with Pam Brighton's production of *Hamlet,* with Stephen Ouimette.

Roberta Maxwell had indeed agreed to do the season, but when she realized how acrimonious the situation was at Stratford, she changed her mind. When Dexter first called to invite her to work with him at Stratford, she was in a hotel room, and she didn't fully grasp what had happened in Canada. Later on she sent him a telegram saying she would have to withdraw until the dispute with Equity could be resolved. Kareda and Henry were her friends; she didn't think it was appropriate for her to appear at Stratford in 1981 given the way she felt about the place. This incident, she sadly realized afterward, cost her an important relationship; communication with Dexter stopped.

Feelings were running high inside the Festival Theatre. When Jane Edmonds, a member of the Festival's clerical staff, heard about the Dexter controversy, she placed a Canadian flag on the window outside her office (which was often used as a place to post photographs and clippings of interest to the staff). Peter Stevens expressed his displeasure to a senior secretary, suggesting that Edmonds might be fired unless the flag came down. "Emotions are running high," the secretary told Edmonds, "and there's been enough trouble around here. Don't you value your job?" Edmonds burst into tears. A few minutes later, the secretary came in to apologize. The flag stayed up; indeed it was still there more than a year later.

On Wednesday, November 19, Robert Hicks, John Heney, John Lawson, Gary Thomas, and Peter Stevens went to the Ontario Arts Council to try to explain their position. Ron Evans, the OAC's director of policy and planning, and William Lord, its theatre officer, had already heard a persuasive argument from Equity. Dan MacDonald had gone to lunch with them and given an electrifying pep talk. "In the historical context," said MacDonald, "we've lost so much, we just have this terrific conviction that if we don't take a stand now, we're going to lose much more. We are prepared to stop that Festival, to lose a hell of a lot of our members, to take in effect a public black eye."

Arthur Gelber, chairman of the Ontario Arts Council, had been involved for years in the formative stages of Toronto Arts Productions and the National Ballet, and he had strong views about arts boards. In his opinion, they were dominated too often by the wrong kinds of people. It was dangerous to have a board heavily weighted with businessmen who were good fundraisers but knew nothing about the arts. There had to be a balance; artists and people who knew something about the management of the arts were needed on every arts board.

Gelber was to become an important go-between in the Stratford crisis. Mavor Moore, an old friend, was talking to Gelber because the Canada Council had no direct communication with the Stratford Board. Gelber was also briefing the Ontario government – not only his minister, Reuben Baetz, but also the premier. William Davis was worried that the government was going to be blamed for the mess. And there was great pressure from the Tory business establishment of southwestern Ontario to help the Board get through the crisis and secure a 1981 season.

Even John Hirsch was calling Gelber, furious that Gina Mallet had mentioned him in a list of potential Canadian artistic directors who had been considered and rejected by the Board. "What are you going to do about this?" Hirsch demanded. Gelber and Hirsch had been friends ever since Gelber had tried to recruit Hirsch in the mid-1960s to save the Crest Theatre, and Hirsch had turned down the job. Now Gelber was barking right back into the phone, "What do you mean, what am I going to do about it? It has nothing to do with me. What are you going to do about it?"

Hirsch: "Well, what can I do?"

Gelber: "Phone her, or give a statement to the papers."

Hicks wanted Gelber to play mediator. Gelber said the OAC could facilitate a mediation but could not itself assume the role of mediator. Evans emphasized that Equity wasn't going to back down; if there was to be a solution, it would have to be agreeable to all sides. The Board people outlined the history of their problem. Gelber questioned them persistently on why no possible successor had been developed during the Phillips era. Afterward Gelber would say he felt a little sorry for Hicks. Stratford was like a distraught family in which the father had died suddenly and the mother didn't know how to carry on.

At the end of the meeting, Ron Evans took Stevens aside and asked, "Peter, what the hell happened to this Board? I mean, how do you explain how could they act this way and give that appalling press conference on Monday?"

Stevens replied, "I think Robin just emasculated them so effectively that now they're trying to demonstrate they do have balls."

CHAPTER THIRTEEN

Daggers

When Martha Henry came back from her radio-taping session in Vancouver, the Board made one last try to woo back the Gang of Four as helpmates for Dexter. The meeting took place on Sunday, November 23, in Henry's room at the Park Plaza Hotel in Toronto. She had arrived by plane from Vancouver and was spending the weekend in Toronto before returning to Stratford. Douglas Rain had come in to meet her, and on Saturday night they had had dinner at the home of Peter Moss. Urjo Kareda was also in Toronto for the weekend and also a guest at the dinner party. Kareda, Moss, and Henry speculated about what the point of the next day's meeting could possibly be. Moss didn't go to the meeting, but Pam Brighton was there with her son, who watched a football game on television while Brighton, Henry, and Kareda talked to the Board spokesmen – John Lawson, John Heney, and Oliver Gaffney, the same team that had been negotiating their contracts.

The gist of what the three men had to say was: you all made such a wonderful contribution, and we don't want to lose you. Gaffney was the spokesman, and he spoke vehemently, insisting that the Board had been right to disband the directorate. Kareda got the impression it wasn't even so much the financial loss the Board feared as artistic failure. Gaffney urged the Gang of Four to come back in their old jobs, serving under Dexter.

Kareda replied sharply, "What could I possibly do? One of the main things I did as literary manager was choose plays. I chose the plays for Robin, and I would be choosing the plays for Dexter. And our choice of plays was just what you fired us for." Afterward, Henry told Kareda that he sounded so angry his voice aroused fear even in her.

Kareda wrote in his diary, "They are like provincial buffoons in a play by Ibsen or Brecht – weak, apologetic, and powerless."

That same day Moss called Kareda with a new scheme which had come to him from Robin Phillips: Garth Drabinsky, the flamboyant Toronto show-business entrepreneur, was willing to come to Stratford as executive producer, backed by Phillips plus the Gang of Four. Drabinsky suggested making this proposal to Hicks and announcing the offer to the press. A few hours later, Phillips called Kareda to say it was urgent to respond to the Drabinsky scheme, which would, he added, include a Toronto season.

Drabinsky was bidding for control of Toronto's Winter Garden, an historic downtown theatre which had been closed since the 1920s but was going to be reopened through a deal engineered by the Ontario government. Phillips had been discussing with Drabinsky the idea of bringing to the Winter Garden productions that Phillips expected to be staging at the Haymarket with its new resident company. There was a great deal of speculation as to what Phillips' next move might be. He had just returned from Edmonton, where his presence set off rumours that he was making a deal with the Citadel Theatre.

Kareda was wary. He replied that he didn't know Drabinsky, would have to meet him, and couldn't commit himself in advance. Martha Henry also said she wanted a day to think about it. Kareda could tell that Phillips was hurt by their lack of enthusiasm. "Don't we all want it to happen?" he asked. Phillips said he would arrange a meeting with Drabinsky, but a secretary called later with a message from Phillips that the meeting was off. That was the last Kareda heard about the venture.

Pam Brighton was the only one of the Four who was tempted to have any continuing association with Stratford. After the firing, she had gone into shock and stayed in bed for several days, and then Peter Stevens had called to say, "I've just spoken to Dexter and he's very keen to keep your *Hamlet*." Brighton was torn. She felt it *would* be a pity to lose her *Hamlet*, although Stevens didn't seem to have any idea how upset she was. He kept speaking of the whole furor as a storm that could be weathered. "We'll sort this all out when Dexter gets here," he said. "It's going to be okay, Pam." Stevens was being chummy, in the manner of one British working bloke trying to cheer up another over a pint of bitters. Brighton told him he didn't understand how serious the situation was, that he had miscalculated everything. Stevens called back several times to soothe her, saying things like, "We don't need your answer yet, take your time, just so you know Dexter still wants you...." Brighton thought that if Dexter was getting his information on Canada from Stevens, then he must have no idea what he was walking into. She wondered whether she should call Dexter and warn him, but she decided not to.

John Dexter wasn't the only observer waiting anxiously in New York to see what would happen. On November 19, after learning of the Equity boycott through a report in that day's *New York Times*, Hume Cronyn dictated a letter to Timothy Bond, a member of the Equity executive and a prominent young Toronto director:

I beg the Equity executive not to take punitive action against the Festival–despite the temper of the membership–that may be self-defeating. I hope you agree that the Festival is a uniquely Canadian undertaking (by far the most important of its kind in North America) that it would be a pity to injure.

I do not happen to agree with the recent actions of the Festival's Board in its dismissal of the directorate, although ironically I was responsible for bringing both Stevens and Dexter to the Board's attention. It might have been personally satisfying (and might have salvaged a couple of valued friendships) if I had stood up and screamed on November 7 when, on my return to Stratford, I discovered what was afoot. This, however, is precisely the sort of action that I think is damaging and contributes only to further contention. In view of the Board's unanimous vote, nothing was going to reinstate the directorate; and I couldn't and wouldn't deny Dexter's unique qualifications.

What's more to the point is I believe the opportunity that now presents itself to Equity to require company representation on the Festival Board and to insist on a specific program for the training and development of Canadian directors in regard to the particular demands of the Festival's stage and operations. That is the thrust of this letter. I hope you will not consider it either meddlesome or impertinent.

Perhaps I should add that I am *not* advocating a Canadian theatre by and for Canadians only. Forty percent of the Festival's audience is from the U.S.A. Besides, a purely chauvinistic policy, if followed to its absurd but logical conclusion, would be both parochial and stultifying; Canada exposed to *only* Canadian writers, painters, designers, actors and so forth. I saw something of such policy results last year in the U.S.S.R. – hopelessly insular and old-fashioned.

Timothy Bond replied to Cronyn on December 1:

I was very pleased to receive your letter, since I had been wondering, quite frankly, where you stood in all this mess.... We are faced with a management that has cancelled a tour to England having negotiated a large number of contracts and then failed to produce the paperwork; fired the directorate having failed to produce the paperwork after negotiating three-year contracts; hired John Dexter without advertising the position and after considering, by their own admission, only six or eight candidates, after which they announced to the press that no Canadian was suitable for the job. Equity does not feel it should have a business relationship with such an untrustworthy management. In addition, we were promised when Robin was brought in that a Canadian would be trained, and Robin's successor would be a Canadian.

Why I support the boycott: Canada still runs its theatres as though it were a British colony. We continually reach to the outside for expertise, and the result is that our theatres look like poor copies of theatres elsewhere. What makes a theatre "international" is the exportability of its thought, not its willingness to import experts to direct all its operations. There may well be no Canadian as good as John Dexter, but we will never know until we look, and until some far-seeing management takes the kind of chance on someone that they took on Robin, and that many have taken on Dexter. No one argues with Dexter's abilities, or with the desirability of mixing the occasional star performer of unique ability into a Canadian company. No one would seek to prevent Dexter from directing as a guest here. But ninety percent of the artists in Canada feel that now is the time for Stratford to be run from the top by a Canadian.

By the last week of November, pressure was mounting on Lloyd Axworthy. The Stratford Board was pushing not only for a work permit but for a fast one: John Dexter was an important man, and he shouldn't be kept waiting by the likes of Axworthy. He had other offers – especially from Stratford, Connecticut – and he had to know whether or not he was going to Canada.

Interestingly, when Dexter dropped out of the running for the job of artistic director at Stratford, Connecticut, the job went to Peter Coe, who had been considered a likely successor to Michael Langham until his badly received production of *Macbeth* in the 1961 Festival. His appointment as artistic director at the Citadel Theatre in Edmonton in 1978, succeeding John Neville, set off a bitter dispute. Cultural nationalists went hysterical, Equity complained, and the Department of Employment and Immigration embarrassed the Citadel by giving Coe a one-year visa (with a one-year extension only), then rejecting his application for landed-immigrant status. That drama subsided when the cast of characters changed in Ottawa: the Liberal government which ruled against Coe was replaced with a Conservative government, and Coe was given landed-immigrant status. But in Edmonton the controversy about Peter Coe went on for years – even after Coe fought with the Citadel Board and left Edmonton in October, 1980. Beyond Edmonton, it was an issue but never became a national crisis on the scale of the dispute at Stratford. The difference was that nobody regarded the Citadel as Canada's national theatre.

At first, things in Axworthy's department seemed to be going the way the Stratford Board wanted them to go. Axworthy took the Board's claim at face value: a thorough search had been conducted, and unfortunately there just wasn't a qualified Canadian available for the job. He was relying on the information coming to him through the regular channels in his own department. The Stratford Manpower office was satisfied, and its report went through the regional headquarters in Toronto and came to Axworthy as a recommendation to let Dexter in. Manpower officials even went so far as to have a meeting with Equity representatives, trying to persuade them that it had been sufficient to post the job in the local Stratford office.

But Axworthy didn't like the pressure the Board was exerting for a quick ruling, and the longer he took to consider the evidence, the worse things began to look for the Board. Axworthy spoke to Tim Porteous and learned that the Canada Council was not at all satisfied with the way the Stratford Board had gone about making this appointment. The minister's most trusted advisers weren't satisfied either. Joseph Stern, Axworthy's executive assistant, was very aware of the rigorous procedures laid down by law: before bringing in a foreigner, an employer had to provide "reasonable opportunity" to qualified Canadians, and to conduct a thorough search.

Denise Ommanney, Axworthy's press secretary, spoke to Jamie Portman, the arts commentator for Southam News, and Portman happened to mention, almost in passing, that the Board wouldn't be having such a hard time if it had undertaken a proper search. Portman didn't think he was saying anything that wasn't already common knowledge, but Ommanney seemed surprised by his view. Axworthy was starting to perceive that many theatre people didn't trust the Stratford Board. At this point, he realized he had to make a basic decision. Was he going to be the kind of cabinet minister who lets his department run itself? Or was he going to take the initiative to make his own judgement, even if it went against the reports that were coming to him through departmental channels?

Axworthy remembered how, as a political science professor in Winnipeg, he had watched professors from Michigan bring in their American friends when teaching jobs came open, bypassing equally well-qualified Canadians. He wondered whether something similar was happening in the theatre. To find out, Axworthy ordered his department officials all the way down the line to take a closer look. Had the Stratford Board really done all the things they were required by law to do? Had they really considered all the Canadian candidates at the time when the job came open, rather than a year earlier when they started looking for a successor to Phillips?

It was going to take time for the department to complete this check, and the Board was threatening that if it couldn't get a quick decision, the 1981 season might be lost, and with it millions of dollars of tourist revenue. Axworthy was himself getting names of candidates from Equity and various private citizens who were writing and phoning him. There was an articulate letter from Skip Shand, an English professor at York University whom Axworthy had known well in Winnipeg, stating the case against the Board and urging Axworthy not to give in on Dexter. (Shand was a friend and one-time teaching colleague of Kareda.)

Axworthy knew he had to be careful not to appear to be forcing any particular candidate down the Board's throat. But his checks established that there were a number of people who might have been interviewed and weren't. As a Winnipegger who had grown up on John Hirsch's Manitoba Theatre Centre, he didn't need to be told that Hirsch's name should be on any list. The Stratford Board had said that Hirsch had been "considered," but it turned out that this meant his name had come up and he had been ruled out without being interviewed or even spoken to. If this was the way the Stratford Board went about conducting a search, then something was very wrong.

On Tuesday, November 25, Axworthy spent the day in Toronto, and after a series of meetings he arranged to have a drink with David Silcox at the Park Plaza Hotel. Silcox, an ambitious cultural bureaucrat, had worked at the Canada Council, was on the board of the Canadian Film Development Corporation, and had created a high-profile job for himself as a kind of cultural czar for Metro Toronto. Axworthy and Silcox had become friends the previous summer when they were both part of an all-male camping expedition to Algonquin Park. Axworthy wanted to get a reading from Silcox on how the Stratford situation looked to insiders in the world of arts administration. Silcox assumed that Dexter's admission was more or less a *fait accompli,* but he was very critical of the Stratford Board. He suggested a compromise solution: let Dexter in on a one-year permit only and warn the Board that this sort of thing wouldn't be tolerated again.

The next day, Axworthy huddled with Ommanney and Stern and thrashed the issue out. They were urging him not to bow to the pressure from the Stratford Board. Axworthy also conferred with Secretary of State Francis Fox, the minister responsible for most cultural affairs; Fox was willing to go along if Axworthy wanted to deny the work permit. That same day, Dan MacDonald of Equity flew to Ottawa to meet Lambert and Hamilton, the same two officials the Board delegation had seen on November 7; MacDonald was trying to stave off a decision in Dexter's favour which was rumoured to be coming by the end of the week. Robert Hicks was telling people he was very confident of the outcome.

But the issue had finally become very clear to Axworthy: the Stratford Board, contrary to their claims, had not really undertaken a thorough search for a qualified Canadian, as the law required, before offering the job to a foreigner. If there were to be dire economic consequences in Stratford, if the 1981 season were jeopardized, well, that really wasn't his responsibility. The Stratford Board would have to face the consequences of its own actions.

The stunning news was announced at the end of the afternoon

session in the House of Commons on Thursday, November 27. "It is my responsibility to ensure that Canadians get a reasonable chance at work opportunities," Axworthy said, "and I have regretfully concluded that the Board of Governors at Stratford did not carry out a thorough, comprehensive, and responsible search for a qualified Canadian artistic director." The search the Festival had carried out had been done months earlier, he noted, and there should have been a new search at the time the job was offered to Dexter. Axworthy was careful to say that he had decided to deny the application for Dexter's work permit "at this time."

One reason for the shock was that despite the law this was the first time the government had blocked the entry of an internationally recognized artist. Among those recently admitted had been Andrew Davis, conductor of the Toronto Symphony, and Alexander Grant, artistic director of the National Ballet of Canada, both British; and Lotfi Mansouri, director of the Canadian Opera Company, an Iranian-born U.S. citizen living in Geneva.

A frustrated Robert Hicks told the press he was mystified and baffled by the decision. "Frankly, we're at our wits' end to know what to do now. I'd like to know what his intentions are by those words 'at this time.' We're running out of time."

Axworthy told a CBC interviewer, "I'm confident the Board will find a candidate. It's just a matter of being more thorough....This has been bubbling away for almost eighteen months, and they knew what the law and regulations were. I think they just thought they could treat it with some degree of indifference. I think it's time we recognized there's a lot of Canadian talent available, and Canadians shouldn't be treated as second-class."

A jubilant Dan MacDonald noted that Axworthy had used the very words Equity had asked him to use, "It is my hope that the Festival will now undertake an immediate and comprehensive search [for a Canadian artistic director]."

Within the cultural world, the most common reaction was elated surprise on the part of people who didn't think Lloyd Axworthy had the guts to make the decision he did. The mail and phone calls pouring in to his office were running nine to one in favour of his ruling. But the press reaction was almost uniformly negative. Editorial writers who never concerned themselves with the theatre unless it became a front-page political issue were indignant that a Cabinet minister dared to meddle with artistic freedom. A cartoon on the editorial page of the *Ottawa Citizen*, which would later find a place of honour, framed, on the wall of Axworthy's office, showed the minister, clad in a toga and wielding a bloodied knife, while Robert Hicks, mortally wounded and also toga-clad, echoed the famous death line of Julius Caesar in Shakespeare's version, "Et tu, Lloyde? Then die, Stratford."

No one was more scornful and angry than the *Toronto Star*'s Gina Mallet, who was also so persistent that she alone among the journalists actually got Axworthy on the phone and told him off. In the next day's *Star*, Mallet wrote, "The Board may feel it is better to close down the Festival than allow it to be turned into a political football and see the standards it has achieved over twenty-eight years collapse." She also reported that Robin Phillips had let friends know he would be willing to come back if coaxed. In a survey of potential Canadian candidates for the job, Mallet included Mavor Moore, remarking that he had been fired as an actor by Tyrone Guthrie and that some said he had been waiting ever since for a chance to get back to Stratford. Moore threatened legal action, denying that he had been fired by Guthrie, pointing out that he had over the years turned down numerous offers from Stratford, and stating that he was emphatically not a candidate for the job of artistic director at Stratford. The *Star* printed a retraction the next day, apologizing for any embarrassment the errors may have caused.

The night Axworthy made his announcement, John Dexter, sitting in his Manhattan apartment across Lincoln Plaza from his office at the Metropolitan Opera, surrounded by stage mock-ups and precious old books, made an entry in his personal diary: "Axworthy is a cunt."

Hicks was, of course, furious. He had understood that everyone from the Stratford Manpower office on up was behind the Board. Now suddenly Axworthy had done them in. He demanded an appointment with the minister to find out what happened. But Axworthy, in Winnipeg at a Liberal convention, didn't want to talk to the Stratford Board. No one was getting through to him, not even a Liberal bagman who was asked by some friends on the Board to get them an appointment. Hicks, a Conservative whose friends were also mostly Conservatives, did have a few friends who were prominent Liberals, and he sought advice from one of them, "What do we do? He's shut his phone off." The Liberal friend said, "Leave it with me, I'll talk to Donald Macdonald about it." But even Macdonald, a former finance minister, couldn't get through. Finally, Hicks got word that Axworthy wouldn't see the Board but Joseph Stern, his executive assistant, would; Hicks was also told that Axworthy wasn't going to change his mind. The heat was on. John Turner, who once employed Axworthy as his executive assistant, called Axworthy to say he hoped the minister was giving this matter his personal attention, not leaving it to staff.

John Heney, Hicks' predecessor as president of the Stratford Board and a member of Hicks' inner circle, was determined to see Axworthy, and he went to Ottawa with William Somerville, a strong Liberal supporter and president of the Stratford-based Victoria and Grey Trust Company. They had a very fast greeting from Axworthy on the night of their arrival. The next day they were joined by John Lawson, and Joseph Stern spent the day with them.

Axworthy joined them when the House of Commons adjourned about five in the afternoon, and spent three hours with the group. But the more he was subjected to pressure on points other than what he considered the merits of the case, the more he was determined to resist: the Stratford group, for example, wanted a commitment from Axworthy that if the Board went through a search and then came back without finding someone, Axworthy would let Dexter in. Axworthy, however, kept insisting it would have to be a genuine search, not a *pro forma* exercise. The condition Stern and Axworthy emphasized was that the search would have to be led by someone with a reputation for playing fair. Heney knew that the Board would have to move fast: the very next day, December 6, the Board would face its most severe test – the annual general meeting, set for 12:30 P.M. on the stage of the Festival Theatre.

* * *

For twenty-eight years the Stratford Festival's annual meeting had been a dreary ritual attracting little or no attention from the general public. But this time it was threatening to turn into a circus. Opponents had been alerted to the fact that by turning up on the day of the meeting with twenty-five dollars, anyone could become a member of the Festival Foundation, which carried the right to speak and vote. There was just one catch: there were rumoured to be thousands of proxy votes controlled by the Board, and outsiders who tried to get the membership list in an attempt to woo some of the proxies were told that it wasn't available.

This year only three of the thirty faces on the Board would be changing. Those retiring were Barbara Ivey, Hume Cronyn, and W.H. Young of Hamilton. The Board had nominated its choices to fill those spots, and the election was being contested by several candidates who did not have the Board's endorsement.

Traditionally, the outgoing Board meets before the general meeting, and the new Board meets after. Ivey told Hicks she wanted to make a speech to the outgoing Board but the proceedings dragged on and on. A few minutes before the general meeting was scheduled to begin, Hicks turned to her and said, "Barb, you had a few words you wanted to say, didn't you?" She had more than a few words, and now there wasn't time for her to say them. Back into her Stratford files went the speech she never gave:

We have all been present at a strange time in Festival history. It is the end of an era and a time of great difficulty. You are all going to be part of a new period, which I hope will be a strong and valuable one. As this is my last meeting after thirteen years, I would like to leave you some words of advice and encouragement. Before that I must clarify my position. I'm not comfortable discussing myself but I have been urged by friends and especially my family to do so.

Contrary to some expressed opinion, I have not turned my back on the Festival because things have gone somewhat sour, nor did I decide not to stand for re-election because Robin Phillips was leaving.

Although I had been a vice-president for two years, I was never asked by the nominating commitee to become chairman at any time in any year until October, 1980. I had made it clear both to the president and to the chairman of the nominating committee that I had a personal deadline of the end of June, 1980, when I would have to make some decisions. I also told each of them that Stratford was closest to my heart. When mid-August came and I heard nothing, and my repeated requests to have the nominating committee convened had not been answered, I felt I had no choice but to make other plans for my time.

And now for the advice and encouragement. There is a cardinal rule in the entertainment business that if an actor or a personality begins believing his own publicity, he's heading for trouble. I suggest that the Board is now in that danger. It is very easy when

174

trying to justify a position to begin to believe it completely. One's ability to make an open and honest assessment of a point or position becomes difficult, without realizing it. Again, I suggest the Board is in that danger. As a new year begins, I beg you to look inwards and make an honest assessment of the way the Board is functioning and your position in it. At the present moment, the credibility of the Board is deeply suspect. Never mind whether that is fair. It is fact. It is suspect with some of the individual contributing members of the Festival, some corporate members, the arts councils, the ministries, the Stratford company. Our credibility has been questioned in Parliament. Because of all this, the autonomy of our Board is at risk. And that is very dangerous indeed.

The time has come for a return to a basic but solid method of Board function. There should be an immediate return to the system of regularly scheduled meetings of all committees. For additional non-scheduled meetings, every member of that committee should be notified regardless of the length of notice possible. Telephone conversations to keep one informed while necessary on occasion can never equal the give and take of opinion at a meeting. They deprive one of the opportunity of making one's own decisions based on all available information. For without regular meetings, one can only get the information and opinion given. Assuming that of course the information is accurate, it is still subject to the natural bias of the person transmitting it. I urge each Board member to remember you are not here to rubberstamp the decisions or actions of the executive or any other committee. Each of you has a responsibility to make your decisions based on all the information you can get.

I believe in the principle of self-perpetuating boards, but with that comes enormous responsibility for the nominating committee. Prospective members should be considered for what strength they can bring to the Board. They should be clearly informed of the responsibilities one assumes when joining the Board – the commitment required, the importance of Board confidentiality. The Stratford Board deserves nothing less than the best qualified people for its Board, and the best members for its officers. Its record over the years shows it can attract them. I have said many times during the past year that this is a good Board with some of the most able people I've ever worked with. I will continue to say it because it's true. But the sad fact about boards is that in ten years, few but those of us here at the time will remember who we were.

What is remembered and will be remembered is what this place is, and what it stands for, what it has contributed to the quality of life in this country, to the standards of theatre in this country, what has happened on its stages. This theatre has a heart and soul, which come from all the people who have worked in it – their triumphs and disappointments, their giving of individual talents to make this wonderful whole. The Board's job is to protect this place, its heart, its soul. Our reward is to be associated with its glory. My time with the Stratford Festival has been very special. I'll always do anything I can to help. With all my heart I wish you well. Please take care of our theatre.

CHAPTER FOURTEEN

Darkness at Noon

By the usual standards of Stratford's annual general meeting, the turnout was terrific. About 800 people filed into the Festival Theatre on a wintry Saturday afternoon. Later on, it would become a cliché to say that this was a more dramatic show than any Shakespeare play ever produced on that famous stage. Robert Hicks, bad back and all, was marching on toward what he must have known would be his darkest hour. He took his place at the official table on the stage, flanked by Gary Thomas, John Lawson, John Heney, Donald MacLeod (chairman of the Board's finance committee), and Dr. Reva Gerstein, a member of the Board chosen to be honorary secretary for the day's proceedings.

The meeting started on a low-key, humdrum note, with a series of routine procedural points and a statement about the year's financial operations: grants had offset an operating loss, and the box-office had been so good that the Festival had wiped out its worrisome deficit of the previous year and now had a surplus. Hicks presented himself as flexible and open-minded. He kept saying he wasn't "hung up" on rules or regulations. The strategy was to let people have their say, weather the storm, and carry the votes with the help of the proxies.

Greg Wanless, a member of the acting company, read into the record an open letter to the Board from Urjo Kareda, Martha Henry, Pam Brighton, and Peter Moss:

This will be the last public statement made by the Canadian artistic directorate of the Stratford Festival – empowered September 13, 1980, dissolved November 10, 1980, both actions executed by the 1980 Stratford Festival Board of Governors.

If it had been possible for people to look at us as we looked at ourselves, as a single organism, then it would be clear that the qualifications, the expertise and the experience of this organism were varied and powerful indeed. This artistic directorate, a unit implemented by the 1980 Board for the purpose of supplying artistic leadership, was Canadian-born, a naturalized citizen, and had landed-immigrant status. It had roots in Canada, in the United States, in Europe and in England. It received education and obtained degrees at the University of Toronto, Cambridge University, London University, Michigan State University, Carnegie-Mellon and the National Theatre School. It has run two theatres and has helped to run the administration of the Stratford Festival for a collective ten years, including four years on the Board's own planning committee. It has directed and co-directed fifteen productions at the Stratford Festival. It has worked on new plays by James Reaney, Timothy Findley, Sheldon Rosen, Larry Fineberg, Suzanne Grossman, Tom Cone, Steve Petch, Susan Cooper and Hume Cronyn, Edna O'Brien, Edward Bond and David Edgar. It has worked at the Shaw Festival, Lincoln Center, the Royal Court Theatre, the Manitoba Theatre Centre, the Centaur Theatre (Montreal), Theatre London, the Globe Theatre (Regina), the Phoenix, the Half Moon Theatre, the Leatherhead Theatre, the Arena Stage in Washington, the Leicester Haymarket, Theatre Plus, Toronto Workshop Productions, the Adelaide Court, the Young Vic, the Adelaide Theatre Festival in Australia, the New Play Centre, the Crest Theatre, the Canadian Players, the Crewe Theatre, the Leicester Phoenix, Young People's Theatre and in the West End. It has worked for the BBC and the CBC. It has acted in thirty-two productions on the Stratford Festival stage, giving approximately fifteen hundred performances. It has worked under the artistic direction of Robin Phillips, John Hirsch, Jules Irving, Jean Gascon, Jean Roberts, Marigold Charlesworth, Oscar Lewenstein, Murray Davis, Vivian Matalon, William Hutt, Eddie Gilbert, Anthony Page, William Gaskill, Lindsay Anderson, Zelda Fichandler, Michael Bogdanov, Paxton Whitehead, Marion André, Robin Midgley, George Luscombe and Michael Langham. It has worked for five years as a drama critic for a leading Canadian newspaper. It has taught at the University of Toronto, Michigan State University and the National Theatre School. It has won awards from both the *Toronto Star* and the *Globe and Mail* as "director of the year." It has won grants and fellowships from the Canada Council, a British Arts Council associate director's award, a Theatre World award and a Genie. It has worked in the theatre for a combined total of sixty-three years. It has been married six times and has five children. It has never – until November 10, 1980 – been fired.

On November 10, 1980, the Stratford Festival Board of Governors chose to dissolve this artistic directorate.

We have stood by until now without a formal public statement because we knew perfectly well that not every member of the Board was responsible for this decision. However, they continue to present themselves as a complete entity with the right to slander our professional reputations. The continual and constant media coverage since November 10 has summarized the events leading up to that date in a misleading and often totally inaccurate fashion. Not one member of the 1980 Board has spoken on our behalf. We can no longer allow this situation to continue.

On the CBC on November 11, John Lawson of the Board said, "It comes back to maintaining a financially viable theatre. If the artistic directorate could have done that, then fine. Unfortunately, they were not able to, in the Board's opinion."

Peter Trueman on the Global TV news on November 27 said, "The Stratford Board hired Dexter two weeks after the firing of its four-person artistic directorate for coming up with a financially unviable season."

These statements are false.

We were given the go-ahead by the Board, in a letter of intent signed by R.V. Hicks at 3 P.M. on Saturday, September 13, 1980. We were fired at 8:15 P.M. on Monday, November 10, 1980. Between these two dates, working swiftly and with the total support of a highly efficient and gifted production staff, we were able to plan a 1981 season.

We had made commitments to five Canadian directors, not counting Pam Brighton herself; seven of these eleven productions were to have been directed by Canadians, and three directors were invited from England. We had made actual verbal offers to seventeen leading actors, and on Monday afternoon, November 10, we had drawn up the basic construction of the rest of the company, which would have reached a total of approximately seventy-five actors. We had scheduled auditions in Vancouver. We were in the process of constructing a workshop and teaching situation which would have involved permanent movement, voice, fencing and Alexander technique instructors working within the company, as well as text, improvisation and music sessions taught by senior members of the acting company and the artistic staff. We had begun discussions with Michael Ondaatje (working with Paul Thompson) and Erika Ritter about new scripts for the 1982 season, following workshop explorations in 1981. We had a meeting scheduled for November 14, 1980, with Nielsen-Ferns to discuss a forthcoming link in film production. And we had asked Len Cariou to do a solo concert on a Monday night in August during the 1981 season.

Although we had within the building *no person empowered to draw up any contracts* for the actors, directors and playwrights we had contacted, no person other than the executive director, Peter Stevens, and *therefore we have not one signed contract for the 1981 season,* we do have documented proof of our work. This is documentation of commitments in the form of notes, memos, letters, telegrams, and verifiable telephone conversations to prove that every word of the above is true and factual. We have not included the names of artists from whom we had not yet heard, nor of artists who turned down our invitation. We have not included the many thoughts and plans which were only in our heads or in private notes. Everything stated above was actually in the works.

On October 21, 1980, this season was presented to the planning committee of the Board, and was received with acceptance and, indeed, enthusiasm. (Arnold Edinborough, who was at the meeting, wrote a laudatory paragraph about our plans in his column in the *Financial Post* appearing November 1, 1980.)

On October 31, 1980, a balanced budget based on this same season was submitted to the Canada Council in a detailed application signed by R.V. Hicks, the Board president; Peter Stevens, the executive director; and Gary Thomas, the general manager. On that same date the Board executive – by its own account – "unanimously agreed to recommend to the Board that the program should not be proceeded with and the artistic directorate be disbanded." Also on October 31, the Board states – in its own account – that they learned John Dexter was available.

On November 2, members of the Board met with John Dexter. By November 5, this same season had acquired a deficit of $1.3

million, and in the same breath we were told that we were being replaced by John Dexter as a *fait accompli.*

At a press conference on November 17, the Board was asked by what manner they had arrived at this deficit figure. Gary Thomas, Stratford's newly appointed (October 15) general manager, stated that using attendance data collected over twenty-eight years, they had decided that our proposed season would not come in at the eighty percent attendance in the Festival Theatre they had set down in the Canada Council application, but only sixty-five percent, and that the Avon would draw only sixty percent rather than the budgeted seventy-five percent. (The figure of $1.3 million can be culled only by taking fifteen percent off a total projected revenue, a total which includes corporate funding and council grants as well as box-office revenue.)

Yet we used some figures from these past twenty-eight seasons in helping us plan our 1981 season, and they may be interesting here: In 1977, *Ghosts* at the Avon Theatre (an Ibsen play like *The Wild Duck* we planned for 1981) drew 87.2 percent of capacity. In 1980, *The Gin Game* – a famous American play with Kate Reid and Douglas Rain, who were both to appear in another famous American play, *Who's Afraid of Virginia Woolf?* – achieved 89.7 percent attendance. In 1977, when Maggie Smith opened in *As You Like It* at the latter end of the season, as she would have done with *Madame Sans Gêne* in 1981, the production achieved 92.9 percent attendance. In 1976, *The Merchant of Venice* achieved 87.5 percent regular attendance and 96.2 percent at school performances; in 1970 *The Merchant of Venice* achieved 96.6 percent. In 1969, *Hamlet* on the Festival stage, without an international star, achieved ninety-three percent. In 1976 *the Way of the World,* in 1970 *The School for Scandal* and in 1972 *She Stoops to Conquer* – all examples of non-Shakespearean classic comedies on the Festival stage, as *The Rivals* would have been in 1981 – achieved over ninety percent attendance. *Eve,* a new Canadian work at the Avon, achieved 99.4 percent attendance in 1976; John Murrell's *Waiting for the Parade,* its popularity already established in this country, could reasonably be expected, given its cast, to attract a large audience. In 1968, John Hirsch's production of *The Three Musketeers,* a French popular classic as *Madame Sans Gêne* would have been in 1981, achieved 95.2 percent.

If the Board of Governors wished to fire us because they were more impressed with someone else's biography, then fine: let them do it. But let them do it cleanly and let them have the courage to say that's why they are doing it. We might be angry or wish to jump on a nationalist bandwagon, but basically we would have had no recourse. The Board runs the theatre and has the final say, as much as we might disagree with their decision.

But for the Board to try to discredit us artistically and financially in order to justify their decision is intolerable. For a building contractor, the vice-president of a furniture company and an insurance man to sit in front of us (as Oliver Gaffney, John Heney, and John Lawson did on November 23, 1980), and tell us that our season was not *artistically* viable is a ludicrous, craven and intolerable insult.

We would demand from this Board of Governors some evidence of its honesty and good faith. The Board has created this crisis, and only the Board can resolve it. Nothing can happen until confidence and good faith are restored. Not until that faith is restored can the Stratford Festival represent Canada or Canadians. Let them quickly empower a Canadian or Canadians as artistic directors so that Actors Equity can lift its boycott, and so that the Stratford Festival can proceed with a 1981 season which we could call upon the entire artistic community of this country to support.

There was wild applause when Wanless sat down, signalling that the Board was in for an even rougher afternoon than it had realized. Among those applauding most enthusiastically was Barbara Ivey, seated discreetly to one side of the theatre, next to Robin Phillips.

Hicks began his reply with a back-handed compliment: never had he worked with people who displayed greater credibility or acted in more good faith as a unit. Then came the buts. "There wasn't any question at any time of being out to get anyone. We applied ourselves with the best advice possible, advice we have drawn on over a period of many years, from highly qualified people, credible people in our organization. This was not a capricious decision. It was unrelated to the possibility of Mr. Dexter or anyone else. It was entirely done independently. When we came to file a *pro-forma* budget we did not have enough information to make even a draft budget, and the Canada Council extended the deadline for us to October 31. When we met to review the budget and started to relate it to 1979 – when we lost over $600,000 – and we compared the nature of the program that was then very tentatively in place, we were concerned we were going to be in a situation similar to 1979, if not worse. We were pressed by the Canada Council to file something, having already missed their deadline once. We filed on the understanding that there would be a later submission which would be considered at their March meeting, which again is an understood practice and procedure.

"Some of the information that you have provided us now is not exactly what we were told then. We also learned that some of those deemed to be committed were very conditional. They depended on certain directors being available, and if those directors weren't available, the whole complexion of the program would be changed. There were very few of the plays in place. This is not without saying we knew they had a difficult job ahead of them, and we knew they were applying themselves as assiduously as possible. Because of that it was a very difficult decision to take in good faith.

"You say: why the change? Because the evaluation that our people made, the judgement that was applied, indicated there was not a secure program shaping up, nor was it a program that was as attractive as we have had in the past. You can quarrel with our judgement, ladies and gentlemen, and that's fair enough, but you have got to understand that we were acting in all honesty and in all integrity, and in the best interests, long term, short term, of this marvellous Festival.

"We had not heard about John Dexter and his availability until after this decision was taken. Mr. Dexter had been considered [earlier] by Mr. Phillips on the recommendation of Mr. Cronyn, conveyed by me, to be part of next year's artistic directorate team and maybe to direct one or two of next season's productions, back in February. Robin Phillips spoke to John Dexter about guest directing; these discussions took place late winter or early spring. Otherwise no one had spoken to John Dexter. It so happened Mr. Dexter had been collaborating with Canadian artists trying to design a season for another company elsewhere. He already had an offer outstanding from Stratford, Connecticut. He had other offers pending. He had been working with Christopher Plummer, one of our finest Canadians. It was very easy in a fashion simply for Mr. Dexter to convert that into a season here in Stratford. When we met with Mr. Dexter, we checked for his interest, his availability. We then learned increasingly of this package he had been putting together. Before we asked him how he would convert it to a Canadian season, he volunteered first that it would be Canadian and second that he would bring along and develop as much as he could our Canadians.

"I would like to remind our audience that it wasn't until November 2 that we considered an approach to a non-Canadian anywhere in the world. There can't be I don't think surely any doubt in anybody's mind as to our commitment to that objective. We have a broader commitment as well and that is to the perpetuation of the Festival as a viable financial operation. Without being financially successful we won't be here with any production or any director.

"It's interesting that since the directorate was dissolved we have learned the names of some of the people who were approached that were not mentioned to us earlier in the presence of the Board. Using the best judgement of many, many collective years of experience in this theatre and theatre generally, we were driven to a single simple conclusion – that it wasn't going to work. Now this was a heart-rending decision. This was not a flip of the coin or a simple decision. It was a most difficult decision. It was one we had to sleep on – one we had to work with to satisfy ourselves that we were doing what was proper. None of us was out to damage the reputation of any of our people. I feel quite frankly they haven't helped their reputation by the publicity and notoriety they have given their situation. We have refrained, and I refrain today, from being critical of them. They were most co-operative. They applied themselves most conscientiously. We had a decision to make and it was made with substantial input from people who have been here and have been in theatre both in management and on the Board, who made a conscientious, well-thought-out analysis, presented it to the committee, then presented it five days later to the Board as a whole. On both these occasions and in between there was substantial reconsideration and re-evaluation. I would like to mention that no one stood up [to object]; all those attending voted unanimously for this result.

"I can understand the sympathies that prevail, and I would be the first to have compassionate understanding. I have experienced this over the years with my own career and with others. This was not a simple decision. It was one that your Board with the best of conscience, with the best of faith, felt had to be reached."

The thin, rasping quality of Hicks' voice made a startling contrast to the booming bass of the next speaker – the veteran actor Douglas Campbell, who had come to Canada to act at Stratford in its early days, and had stayed on. "I don't think any of us doubts the Board's sincerity in its desire to serve the community," Campbell allowed. "Some of us very strongly doubt its capability to do so. Hume Cronyn has been known to be wrong. Speaking as a member of Canadian Actors' Equity Association, we find your actions objectionable and ill-advised, whether sincere or not. The boycott will not be lifted until you either resign or make it possible for us to move in another direction."

Eleanor Kane, the co-owner of the Old Prune restaurant in Stratford, raised the matter of the cancelled *King Lear* tour. Hicks replied, "It was conditional on Robin Phillips being identified as director and being present. We are not responsible as a Board for the casting of our artists. That was the responsibility of the artistic director. He was not successful at putting together a company for London to meet these requirements. The concern he had which we shared was that it would not have the same quality because of the recasting. That decision was out of our hands. The contract required that Mr. Phillips agree to the recasting and that it be satisfactory to him as to its quality. Those conditions were not satisfied. We had no option, given Mr. Phillips' report that he could not recast to his satisfaction. Believe me, we were not responsible for the cancellation of the *Lear* tour."

At this point Robin Phillips, looking like a schoolboy dressed up for graduation day, scurried over to a microphone, explaining that he wanted to clear up two things. "I hadn't intended to speak at all today," he apologized. "I just came to find out how this last season went financially. First of all I have to make it clear that the first time I heard John Dexter's name mentioned was back in February when I heard about his presence from Mr. Hicks through an intercom at his office. He was in Florida and I was in his office with Mr. Bedford, Mr. Bryden, and Mrs. Ivey. The mention of his name and his proposed visit was apparently news to all of us. Later in the year, I was asked by Mr. Hicks to try to arrange for Mr. Dexter to come to Stratford as guest director for the '81 season. I thought this was difficult for me as at that point it was unlikely I was going to be present for the '81 season. Nevertheless I was prevailed upon and I went through to Mr. Dexter. We agreed on a play, the date the production would take place, and his staff. Later on a phone call went through to England at the National Theatre – to ask if he would like to settle a designer. At that point he refused to talk to me any more and said, 'I do not want to come to Stratford to give an audition piece. I will only talk further when I know what my ongoing commitment to the Stratford Festival is going to be.' From that point he refused my calls, and I only had contact with his agent, who asked would I please stop telling people he was going to be the next artistic director of Stratford. A similar case happened to the directorate when they were in place. They also had discussions with Mr. Dexter about coming as a guest director. Their discussions were stopped because he was now being talked to about being artistic director.

"As far as the *King Lear* tour is concerned, I on five separate occasions cancelled the tour to London of *Lear*. I did it at times when I thought we could save any financial problems for the Festival before the box-office opened; the only bookings received had come in by mail, and therefore we had addresses, telephone numbers and names. I did it throughout the year at times when I thought we were never going to get a contract settled with Mr. Ustinov or the Haymarket Theatre, and that the only responsible thing to do was cancel. I had given my personal word to Mr. Ustinov that he need not play at Stratford unless he also appeared in the West End. Two weeks before the production was about to open, I again cancelled the performance at Stratford because I was not sure Stratford was able to take the tour to London. I gave Mr. Ustinov the opportunity to leave Stratford and I would take the responsibility of coping with the public and refunding money. All these decisions were overturned, and when the decision finally came about over the opening day and subsequent days, I refused any further to make the decision because I could no longer protect Mr. Ustinov, and at no point from that final decision by the Board would I ever have made the decision. It was in their hands. Just those two points."

Jeffrey Macdonald, one of the candidates for the new Board from the general membership, rose to say, "I have been associated as physician with the Stratford Festival since 1957. It is a sad afternoon for me, sir, when I have to move a motion of non-confidence in this Board." The motion was seconded by Douglas Campbell.

Speaking to the motion, an unidentified woman addressed herself directly to Hicks: "You have accused the directorate of being vague and unspecfic in their programming, yet you ask me to have faith in you – you who ask someone to come to Stratford as artistic director before getting any kind of commitment from the federal government, which is capricious at best, that that person would be allowed into the country. Mr. Hicks, you have asked me to put money on a horse that isn't even being allowed into the ring, and you ask me to have faith in your integrity."

Attempting to answer her, Hicks commented, "We had the green light all the way until it came to the minister's desk. I am not going to take issue with him now. He may have his reasons and he's entitled to them, but we weren't proceeding without some indication that Mr. Dexter's work permit would be granted."

Martha Henry then rose and read from the little black book in which she kept all the dates and facts about the 1981 season, "To clarify what Robin said. Wednesday October 15: I talked to Mr. Plummer about wanting myself to come to New York to speak to Mr. Dexter. Mr. Plummer had talked to Mr. Dexter and Mr. Dexter thought it was not worth my while because a member of the Board had said to him they would be back to him within two weeks. According to Chris, Dexter will not come unless it's as artistic director."

Hicks interjected, "I know nothing of that conversation. The first occasion we talked to him was November 2."

Martha Henry continued, "I asked Mr. Plummer if he knew who the Board member was. I asked if it was Mr. Hicks, and he said no. I didn't mention it at the time because I assumed Mr. Plummer was mistaken. Now I'm not so sure."

Hicks insisted, "I can't understand, I can't imagine why anyone would be talking with Mr. Dexter at that time."

Clearly, Hicks wasn't giving much consideration to Peter Stevens, who was keeping a remarkably low profile during this meeting.

Betty Jane Wylie, the widow of William Wylie, took her turn at the microphone: "Bill used to say if he could merchandise a voodoo doll of the Stratford Festival he wouldn't sell the doll for much but he could make a fortune on the pins. I think if you people had been selling pins today you might have solved some of your problems. Bill had a theory about the care and feeding of Board members.

They should be treated gently and guided, because they're from the business community. They can read a balance sheet quite well, but they're bemused by the mystique of creation. Somewhere along the way you lost your guide. I figured you were in trouble when Bruce Swerdfager left, and I've watched you with some concern. I know you went a little rudderless for a while."

Before the vote was taken on the non-confidence motion, there was a fight about the use of proxy votes. The Board insisted the proxy votes would have to be used. Then there was a break while people went out to the lobby to cast their votes. There was some confusion about the fact that to vote *for* the motion was to vote *against* the Board. The Board survived the motion by a vote of 874 to 305 – saved by the 633 proxy votes.

It was soon time to vote for the new Board members. After John Heney gave the report from the nominating committee, Leon Major – one of the rebel directors who issued the nationalist manifesto in 1973 – suggested that given the feeling in the room, Hicks should withdraw his name from the list of nominees for re-election. (Several Board members who were not planning to retire had to be re-elected; this was considered a formality. Hicks, though stepping down as president after the general meeting, with Lawson expected to succeed him, *was* running for another term on the Board. Traditionally, the Board's immediate past president serves on the executive as an adviser to his successor. Excluding incumbents who were expected to be re-elected, there were three vacancies for new Board members. Once the new Board had been elected by the membership, the executive would be chosen at the first meeting of the new Board.) Major's point was that although Hicks could carry the vote with the help of the proxies, the feeling of those present at the meeting was clearly against him. But Hicks was determined to fight right to the end. "Mr. Major," he announced, "I have no intention of withdrawing. This is open to a free ballot."

There was another break as members voted. With the help of the proxies, the slate proposed by the Board's nominating committee was elected without exception. None of the challengers – Dr. Peter Basher, John Hayes, Jeffrey Macdonald, Betty Macmillan, Bruce Swerdfager, or Gordon P. Wilkinson – was successful. The three new Board members were Julian Porter of Toronto and Murrey Dubinsky of Calgary – both prominent lawyers – and Dr. Thomas Brzustowski, an engineering professor from Waterloo. Announcing the new Board, Hicks remarked, "Thank you for your patience. We've had quite a full discussion."

Before he could adjourn the meeting, Beverly Nye, owner of a local art gallery, rose to say, "I do have some business....It is evident to everyone here that things haven't been fair." She wanted to propose that the next time proxy names be made available to everyone. There hadn't, after all, been as many proxy votes in the Board's pocket as people had thought. Had the opposition been organized, it wouldn't have been impossible to get enough opponents of the Board to become new members and defeat the Board at the ballot box.

At this point, someone asked whether there was a plan to make any statement to the press. At the final meeting of the old Board that morning, a motion had been passed to set up a search committee in accordance with Lloyd Axworthy's demands, but this had not been announced at the public meeting. The chairman of the search committee had yet to be named.

Now Hicks was saying in answer to the question from the floor that there was going to be a closed meeting of the new Board, and that afterward there might or might not be an announcement to the press.

At that moment, Richard Monette, one of the company's leading actors, jumped to his feet and shouted at Hicks, "You pig!"

Monette was an unlikely ally for the Gang of Four, since he had made no secret of being irritated with them for offering him only one small part in their proposed 1981 season. But he had been outraged by the Board's behaviour in firing them. He had been critical of the Board in a television interview a few days earlier, but several times during the general meeting he had said no to friends who suggested he make a speech. During the second voting break, he got some of the anger out of his system by grabbing John Heney in the lobby and saying, "How can you *do* this, John?" During the break there were rumours that there was going to be an announcement to the press after the meeting was over, and someone asked Monette to question Hicks about this when the meeting resumed. Monette declined, and the question was raised by Rod Beattie, another company actor.

Despite his decision not to speak, Monette lost control when he heard Hicks' reply to Beattie's question. Even he was surprised and frightened by the violence within himself as he jumped to his feet and began shouting at Hicks. Later, Gina Mallet would suggest in the *Star* that the outburst had been prepared, and Monette would serve notice on Mallet and the *Star* under the Libel and Slander Act (though later he decided not to proceed with legal action). What was true was that in his fury he repeated some of the things he had said earlier in the TV interview and to Heney in the lobby.

People were stunned. The meeting was dissolving into chaos. Hicks called back at his assailant, "What is your name, sir?" The remark would be held against him. His enemies would say it summed up what was wrong: the president of the Board couldn't recognize one of Stratford's most familiar actors. But defenders of Hicks would point out that the lights made it impossible for anyone on the stage to recognize any faces in the audience.

Monette, who was already being approached by two of the security guards hired by the Festival to ensure order, continued his outburst: "We have all spent our lives in this theatre, we have given of our time and art. You talk about money all the time. You have no morals. I don't know how you can sleep. I care deeply and passionately about this place, and you must address yourselves to your consciences and to your hearts."

Hicks was obviously rattled by the outburst. "This meeting is adjourned," he sputtered.

But Amelia Hall, an actress who had been at Stratford a long time, caught the crowd's attention, "I want to say something to you this afternoon and my subject is theatre, not this theatre but theatre. Back before 1952 when there were no arts councils and no corporations giving money to theatres, I happened to belong to a non-profit professional theatre, and I remember one day meeting on the street a businessman who was the president of our board of directors, and he said to me, 'Well, Amelia, we dropped a thousand dollars on that production last week but by God we can be proud of ourselves.' I'll tell you something: it isn't the building, it isn't the foundation, it isn't property, it isn't the balance sheet, it's heart and spirit. And in 1953 when this theatre went up like a great rocket it was heart and spirit that did it."

Leon Major and his wife, Judith, helped Monette out of the auditorium. Robert Hicks had handed down his last ruling as president of the Stratford Board. The afternoon of the long knives was over.

CHAPTER FIFTEEN

Waiting for the Messiah

John Lawson, who on December 6 succeeded Robert Hicks as president of the Festival's Board of Governors, wasn't a man who had been groomed for the limelight. As one of two vice-presidents, Lawson had been in the shadow not only of Hicks but also of Barbara Ivey, the other vice-president, who had been expected to succeed Hicks. Lawson's involvement in the Festival had begun almost by osmosis. His father-in-law had been on the original Board in 1953, and John Killer, Lawson's partner in a Stratford insurance business, had been the president of the Board when Robin Phillips was recruited.

Lawson was the first to point out that he knew very little about Shakespeare or the theatre in general. It was his wife, Ruth, who always followed the Festival's productions closely. But Lawson, known for his earnestness, was always willing to work in community service. When he assumed office, one of his strongest credentials was that he was a resident of Stratford. Some people felt very keenly that the trouble with Bob Hicks was that he lived in Toronto, in the sophisticated world of corporate boardrooms. The Stratford contingent on the Board needed a demonstration that the Festival still belonged to them. Barbara Ivey, who lived forty miles away in London, was no more one of them than Bob Hicks was. John Lawson might not set the world on fire, but Stratford people would never have to look twice at him and wonder who he was. He was an old army man, a family man, a businessman. He had the common touch.

But on the evening of December 6, as he faced the press in the rehearsal hall of the Festival Theatre, Lawson was visibly shaken. Journalists had not only stayed through the dramatic revelations of the afternoon, they'd been kept waiting while the new Board held its first meeting and plotted its strategy. They'd sent out for food, and now they were tired of waiting. It was Saturday night, and they wanted to get out of Stratford. Lawson stood before them and promised that the lessons of this day would not be lost on him. He announced that the Board had decided to set up a search committee to find a Canadian artistic director for Stratford. This was the mysterious announcement Hicks had hinted at just before the end of the general meeting, provoking Richard Monette's tirade.

Actually the search had been authorized by the retiring Board earlier in the day. It had been moved by Donald MacLeod and seconded by Robert Heneault "that the 1980 Board of Governors recommend to the 1981 Board of Governors that a search committee be established immediately in accordance with Lloyd Axworthy's request that a new search be undertaken by the Board to ascertain the availability or otherwise of a suitable Canadian to fill the position of Artistic Director, and to make recommendations to the Board."

At the first meeting of the new Board, another motion was passed, though Lawson reported only part of it to the press. A fuller version appeared in the minutes:

Further to the recommendation of the just retired Board, a search committee was set up consisting of the President, John Lawson, who was ex-officio; Arnold Edinborough; John Heney; Ronald Bryden; with Julian Porter as chairman. The committee was given power to add other people (one suggestion was John Hayes), and Peter Stevens was to be available for consultation to the committee as required. The committee was asked to approach John Hirsch, Jean Gascon, Hume Cronyn, Robert Whitehead and John Neville to ascertain an interest and availability from each before reporting back to the Board with their findings and recommendations.

Axworthy had made it clear that the head of the search committee must be someone with credibility, and Julian Porter was made to order. As a high-powered Toronto lawyer specializing in litigation and an influential member of the Conservative Party, Porter was a member in good standing of Upper Canada's WASP establishment. His father, Dana Porter, had been the chief justice of Ontario and, before that, the province's attorney-general. But Julian Porter wasn't one of those little grey men in the back rooms; he had enough charisma to be a Tory version of John Turner. He was handsome, charming, and gregarious. His wife, Anna, of Seal Books, was a glamorous and powerful media executive. Porter moved in cosmopolitan, sophisticated circles; he could drink with the best of them, and late into the night he had been known to burst into operatic arias. Porter was also a friend of Bob Hicks, a fellow Tory. They had come to know each other on the board of Gray Coach Lines, and Hicks had invited Porter to stand for the Stratford Board. Porter was a new boy on the Board, but he knew his way around the arts bureaucracy better than some who had been on the Stratford Board for years. Porter had been secretary to the Canadian Conference of the Arts in the days when Jean-Louis Roux was running it, and he'd put in his time watching potters fight with painters and Quebec delegates arguing theoretical points of a constitution.

On the morning of the general meeting, Porter's car was the second one parked on the Festival lot (Hicks' was the first). As a nominee, he had been invited to observe the final meeting of the old Board. Though much of the meeting dealt with matters of housekeeping, Porter found it a valuable preparation exercise. He learned who was who; he had time to size up the situation, to consider what role he could play later in the day.

At the general meeting in the Festival Theatre, he experienced a sense of déjà vu: the squabbling reminded him of his days with the Canadian Conference of the Arts. Porter was appalled at how bad the Board was looking in public. Had he stumbled into an alliance with the bad guys in the great public morality play of Canadian culture? If so, it was too late to bail out, though that wouldn't have been Porter's style. Among the people he spoke to during the afternoon were Gina Mallet and Leon and Judith Major. Porter could see that Hicks' strategy was to let people have their pound of flesh and then carry the vote with the proxies, but he could also see what this was costing in terms of the Festival's image. Already Porter was being placed on the defensive in his conversations with people about the course of the meeting. The most he would say was that this wasn't necessarily the way he would run a meeting.

Porter knew why he had been chosen to lead the search: the Board needed a new face, untainted by the mud-slinging of the preceding month. He accepted the challenge with breath-taking naïvete. He knew almost nothing about what had happened at

193

Stratford to precipitate this crisis, but to him *not* knowing about the past was one of his greatest assets. He could refuse to make judgements about it; he could be above all that.

During the new Board's discussion about the mandate of the search committee, Peter Stevens kept talking about the "availability" of a prospective artistic director, and Porter didn't pick up the nuances. The way he understood it, the search committee's job was to find a Canadian artistic director in five days. It didn't occur to him that this might be an impossible mandate. And it didn't occur to him that there might be powerful forces within the Board with strong reasons for wanting the search to fail, allowing the Board to go back to Axworthy and say, "The search has been completed, and unfortunately it has failed. Now can we please have John Dexter?"

Porter told his new colleagues on the Board that it wouldn't do to go back to Axworthy saying no one in Canada was available. Lloyd Axworthy was from Winnipeg and so was John Hirsch, Porter said, so the likelihood was that Axworthy knew Hirsch well enough to know he was available. Axworthy's assistants had done enough scouting to be able to say that there were qualified Canadians available; they weren't saying who. Porter asked his colleagues for an assessment of Hirsch, and Hope Abelson, a respected Board member from Chicago long associated with the Lyric Opera, spoke eloquently on Hirsch's behalf, saying he was absolutely first class and of international repute. Porter knew that there had been some trouble between Hirsch and the Board years earlier, but at that moment he sensed that John Hirsch was going to be Stratford's next artistic director.

Julian Porter was unnerved after the meeting when he and Lawson faced the press; he could see that the journalists were sceptical of almost everything coming from the mouths of Stratford Board spokesmen. The idea that the search might be a sham came as a shock to him. His private reaction was: well, busters, you don't know me. But Lawson, who was presenting a humble, chastened face to the press, was stuck for an answer when he was asked whether the Board had withdrawn its offer to Dexter in light of this dramatic new development. In fact, Peter Stevens had asked Lawson to give Dexter an undertaking that the Board was not withdrawing its offer, and that Axworthy would be approached again with the results of the search – a search that Stevens for one fully expected to fail.

Porter decided to stay the night in Stratford. After the press conference he went to Lawson's house, and from there to a party at the home of Dr. Ian Lindsay, a former Stratford Board president who was famous for having fought with Hirsch at the time of Hirsch's departure from Stratford in 1969. There were scores of people at the party, including Robin Phillips, whom Porter had never met before, and Hope Abelson. Porter spent much of the evening with Dr. Lindsay, drinking with him, listening to opera music on his stereo, swearing eternal friendship, and avoiding any mention of John Hirsch. The party went on into the small hours, and Porter stayed until about 4 A.M. and then went to Peter Stevens' house (once the residence of Tom Patterson), where he slept in the spare room. By 8 A.M. Porter was up, listening to music and making coffee. Then he went to Lawson's insurance office for a meeting with Lawson and Heney.

At 11 A.M. Porter phoned John Hirsch at Hirsch's Toronto home and arranged a meeting for 4:30 that afternoon. It so happened that Hirsch had just returned to Toronto (where he was directing a production of *A Funny Thing Happened on the Way to the Forum* at the St. Lawrence Centre) after months of being away. Though Porter had never met him, Hirsch's house on a Moore Park ravine was within walking distance of Porter's house at the other end of the ravine. Porter drove back to Toronto, stopping at home only long enough to change his clothes.

Before the meeting with Hirsch, Porter had a preliminary meeting at a midtown Toronto hotel with Lawson and Stevens. There were five names on the search committee's list, but Porter had decided that since the smart people seemed to think Hirsch was the best of them, he would start there. If they could get Hirsch, fine; in Porter's view, there would be no need to look further. He was already getting worried by the suspicion of others that the search was a set-up, and he was determined to make it work. At the hotel he said to Stevens and Lawson, "I'm running this. Neither of you guys say anything at the meeting with Hirsch."

"What are you talking about?" Stevens demanded.

"If he's available," said Porter, "that's it."

"That is not it at all," Stevens objected. "Your job is to make a search and report back to the Board. That's all you can do. If you start making any offers, you're going way beyond your brief. All we should do is establish Hirsch's availability or unavailability or whatever. The moment we've done that, we withdraw."

"Okay," said Porter, "but I'll start off. Now first, tell me, what does an artistic director do?"

Peter Stevens was chagrined. He couldn't believe the search was being led by a man who didn't know what an artistic director was.

"Availability" turned out to be a loaded word. Stevens seemed to be using it to mean someone who could start immediately, though even Dexter wasn't fully available in this sense. (Dexter was going to give Stratford a few weeks around the end of December and beginning of January, then be tied up on other projects until late March.) Porter could see there was going to be a showdown on this point, and he said to Stevens, "Look, you think I'm an asshole, and that's all right. You and I are going to wind up having a brawl over this, and that's okay, too. Let's just both be sure we understand clearly what we're doing." As a litigation lawyer and a compulsive tennis player, Porter respected a strong opponent, and he had a certain grudging fondness for Stevens. He even enjoyed mimicking the way Stevens, with his broad north-of-England accent, pronounced the word "available" – ah-vile-ah-bill.

Stevens took another turn when the three men arrived at Hirsch's house and Porter said, "I've come here to offer you the job," and immediately started talking terms.

John Hirsch, after years of being outraged at never being offered the job, was taken aback by the pressure now being put on him. His attitude was: not so fast. He would need time to think it over carefully. He had other commitments: he was consulting artistic director to the Seattle Repertory Theater: he had promised to develop and direct a play for the Mark Taper Forum in Los Angeles, and so on. He would need to know what the Stratford Board really wanted, and whether it was compatible with what Hirsch might be prepared to do. Porter didn't seem to understand that world-class directors plan their commitments years ahead; they don't decide in ten minutes on a Sunday afternoon to tie up the next three years of their lives, starting immediately.

All this was music to the ears of Peter Stevens. "So you're not available," he said to Hirsch. "That's all we need to know."

Hirsch knew he had to think fast. At the age of fifty, he had reached the point where he had decided to put big institutional jobs behind him and concentrate on what he loved doing – directing plays. He had finally left after four years as head of CBC television drama because he couldn't go on facing the frustration of having to work with inadequate budgets, and the brass at the CBC had tired of his exhausting demands. He had taken the Seattle position on a part-time basis, after being chosen over John Dexter, among other candidates. He had wanted to run Stratford earlier in his career, had been passionately offended when he wasn't even given the courtesy of an interview in 1973 or earlier in 1980, and had been an outspoken critic. Now he wondered whether it was too late for him to take on Stratford. At this point in his career, it might be just a giant headache that he didn't need.

Yet Hirsch understood that he was in an extremely ticklish position. As one of the ringleaders of the 1973 nationalist manifesto, he might put himself in an indefensible position if he turned down the top job in the Festival's hour of need. Hirsch had suddenly been cast in the role of the great hope of the Canadian nationalists, the Messiah that Stratford had been waiting for. He knew that if he said no, he would be saying no not just for himself but for everybody in the Canadian theatre community. The Board would be able to use his reluctance as an excuse for getting Dexter in, and it might be a very long time before the Board offered the job to a Canadian again.

With all this in mind, Hirsch proceeded with the greatest of caution. The most important thing that happened that Sunday afternoon was that Hirsch made a fantastic impression on Porter. In effect Hirsch said, "Back off, let's get to know each other; we'd better both think it over carefully before we rush into anything." Hirsch played the reluctant sage, and Porter began to perceive Hirsch the way Hirsch liked people to perceive him – as an internationally respected figure who was wanted all over the world but who was for some reason not as well treated on his home ground as he ought to be. Hirsch let Porter know that he had good reason to be wary: he had had bad experiences at Stratford before, he had been snubbed and treated discourteously and ignored. When he left in 1969 he had been given the impression that he was going to be invited back under better conditions very soon. Eleven years had gone by, and this was the first approach that had been made to him about becoming artistic director of the Festival.

In the meantime, he had carved out an international reputation, though Stratford seemed unimpressed. Now suddenly the Festival was beating a path to his door. Well, he needed time. Porter was so impressed by Hirsch, and so persuaded that Hirsch had been badly treated by Stratford before, that he made a personal commitment: no matter what happened, this time the Stratford Festival was damn well going to show John Hirsch every possible courtesy. That meant they were not going to use Hirsch as leverage to get somebody else. Porter undertook that while he was negotiating with Hirsch, he would not approach any of the other four people on the list he had been given by the Board.

Hirsch's next step was to seek advice. Almost immediately he began nosing about to assess how difficult the situation would be, and what actors and directors would be available on short notice to help salvage the 1981 season. Two days after his first session with Porter, Hirsch held a meeting at his house, trying to get a sampling of opinion from his friends in the theatre community. Among those who attended were several people who had been active in the month since the firing of the Gang of Four in an *ad hoc* committee that had been holding regular meetings at the Tarragon Theatre: Timothy Bond, freelance director and member of the Equity executive; Tom Hendry, executive producer of the Toronto Free Theatre, and Hirsch's original partner at the Manitoba Theatre Centre; and Bill Glassco, artistic director of the Tarragon. Originally the group's purpose was to protest the firing of the Gang of Four, and do what it could to get the directorate back into power, but now it was ready to rally behind a Canadian who had a chance to get the appointment. Robert Sherrin, a CBC producer and husband of Muriel Sherrin, Hirsch's second-in-command at CBC drama, came to the meeting, and so did Hirsch's old friend Martha Henry, who made it clear that in the circumstances she did not feel she could work at Stratford in 1981.

A serious fear on Hirsch's part was that the Stratford offer was going to disappear while he and Porter were negotiating. At least one of Hirsch's advisers who attended the meeting at his house suggested that Hirsch make his position public to prevent the Board from misusing it. There were a couple of possible ploys: a leak to the press, or direct communication with Axworthy's office. Hirsch rejected these alternatives, but he wrote a very carefully worded memorandum to Porter, confirming that he was available and interested, but explaining that he had other commitments and could be only partially available for 1981. Hirsch wanted to be available enough to get the job, but he wanted some protective distance between himself and the 1981 season. When he phoned his colleagues in Seattle, he explained that he was protecting not only their right to have him complete the job he had agreed to do there, but also his own interests.

Meanwhile, another alternative to Dexter had emerged. A group of citizens, calling themselves the Festival Action Committee of Stratford, had been organized by Eleanor Kane, a co-owner of the Old Prune restaurant. FACS was appalled by what was happening and wanted to create a liaison between the Board and the community, so as to make the Board more responsive to the wishes of the community. Eighty people had come to the first FACS meeting, and the group was initially very supportive of the Gang of Four. A week after the annual meeting, William Hutt was put forward by FACS as a possible artistic director. Hutt had been a candidate for the job before Robin Phillips was appointed, and he had been a member of the two-tier directorate that collapsed at the end of the summer. Hutt's response to the FACS proposal was that while he wasn't running for the job, he would certainly consider it if it were offered by the Board. Hutt asked Robin Phillips whether he would lend a hand.

Both Hutt and Phillips had been approached by Julian Porter, who had asked Hirsch for clearance to speak to them to determine whether they would be willing to help get the 1981 season on if Hirsch accepted the artistic directorship. Phillips had said earlier he was willing to do anything to assist the Festival, but he let Porter know he was less than thrilled to be asked to help Hirsch; he suggested that his other commitments – especially to direct the film *The Wars* – would preclude his participation in the 1981 season. In a phone conversation with Peter Stevens, Phillips asked whether he would be correct in thinking that if he agreed to put together a consortium, he would be shutting the door on Dexter. "Yes," said Stevens, "I think you would be shutting the door on Dexter." In that case, Phillips said, he would do nothing. He didn't want to be used that way. He would discuss his own participation in 1981 only after the Dexter question had been resolved.

It was essential for Hirsch and Porter to come to an agreement and to take it to the Board quickly, before they were undermined by public debate about it. They had both agreed not to talk to the press, but the media, not surprisingly, were hot on the trail. When Hirsch failed to answer his home phone, a CBC journalist reached an elderly neighbour and had the neighbour trek through the snow to take a message to him. On Saturday, December 13, exactly a week after the stormy annual meeting, the papers were full of speculation about an impending deal with Hirsch.

In Montreal, the *Gazette* broke the story: Hirsch had conditionally agreed to take the job. Hirsch was quoted as saying "I have said yes, depending on certain negotiations." And Porter was quoted as saying, "We've been negotiating with Hirsch since Sunday, and we hope to come to a mutually satisfactory agreement by Monday or Tuesday." Peter Stevens was quoted as saying that no appointment could be made without the approval of the Board of Governors, and that the Board had not withdrawn its offer to Dexter.

The *Globe and Mail* quoted Hirsch as saying, "They asked me to start straight away, and I said sorry, I can't. I'm committed to July and even beyond. I told them the best I can do is to supervise the '81 season or act as a consultant, and then I would be fully available for the '82 season....I am not doing a saviour act. I've always said you can't walk on water at Stratford unless you have a hundred people standing under the water for you to walk on." Hirsch went on to say that the real problem at Stratford was "not Robin Phillips or John Dexter or Lloyd Axworthy or John Hirsch but simply the failure to seek out and train talented people, and spend the money necessary." He pledged to undertake such a training program if he took the job, because, as he put it, "The judgement on an artistic director is how well an institution goes on after he leaves. To judge him only on what he does while he is there is Broadway thinking."

Peter Stevens was enraged, and he wasn't alone in his view. In a boat-rocking, red-line story at the top of the front page of the *Star*'s Saturday editions, Gina Mallet announced, "If, as John Hirsch says, he was offered the artistic directorate of the Stratford Festival, the search committee had no authorization to do so." It was becoming all too clear why Porter and Hirsch should have stuck to their agreement not to talk to the press. The *Star*, having badgered Hirsch into saying something, was now attacking him for not keeping quiet.

Porter told the *Star*, "We are negotiating with Hirsch to find out if we can come to a mutually negotiable agreement. I wanted to go through all the negotiations without anyone knowing. I only talked when Hirsch had talked."

Hirsch told the *Star*, "I was approached by Stevens, Porter and

Lawson on Sunday to see whether I would be interested in doing the job. According to Porter, it was a direct offer. According to Stevens, it was an availability check. Porter said he would like me to do the job. I said to them I have commitments in Seattle until July 1. I have a commitment to the Mark Taper Forum in Los Angeles to do a project with Gordon Davidson [the artistic director]. I said I'd like to find out what kind of season could be put together without taking any responsibility for it."

According to Mallet, Hirsch's "premature announcement" had caught the Board by surprise. She quoted Board minutes which showed the search committee's mandate was to ascertain the availability and interest from each of five candidates before reporting back to the Board with their findings and recommendations. What she didn't mention was that it would not be possible to get a firm commitment on the availability of any senior artist without a detailed discussion of what the offer would be, and without assurances that a commitment would not be misused. She also didn't mention that Julian Porter had good reason to suspect that his own reputation was on the line, or that to follow Stevens' interpretation of the mandate might well be to assure the failure of the search.

In another article in the same day's *Star*, Mallet asked a series of rhetorical questions: "Would it be better to have a Canadian artistic director who hires foreigners or a British director who wants to use Christopher Plummer, potentially Canada's finest classical actor? Will Immigration Minister Lloyd Axworthy bar Joan Sutherland from singing Norma with the Canadian Opera Company, saying 'No, we've got Anne Murray'? If a Canadian is made artistic director in lieu of Dexter, should political reporters rather than theatre critics attend next season's openings? It will, after all, be art dictated by government."

Porter wasn't fazed by the criticism of his conduct, but he was worried that Board members might be irritated enough with Hirsch for letting the cat out of the bag that they'd vote against him. Porter felt he understood why Hirsch had talked: he was worried that the offer would disappear before there was anything on the record about it.

CHAPTER SIXTEEN

The Divided Kingdom

John Lawson, the new president of the Stratford Board, was conspicuously absent when the Board met on Thursday, December 18, at the Bristol Place Hotel – site of the secret interview with Dexter on November 2 – to consider the search committee's report. Lawson was finding the pressure hard to take; the stress was getting to him. Exhausted, he had gone on holiday with his wife to calm his nerves. Julian Porter knew what he was up against. He realized there could be an attempt to reject his work on the grounds that he had violated his mandate. But he also knew that if he resigned, the Board would be in trouble again; there would be reason to suspect that the Board had wanted a sham search, and that Porter had failed to provide it. Porter now found himself in a peculiar position. A strong Conservative, he was challenging the Tory element on the Board that wanted to force a Liberal minister to back down. And he was doing exactly what Lloyd Axworthy would have wanted him to do.

Porter's chief obstacle was Peter Stevens, who was making a last stand. Stevens didn't seem to realize how completely the tide had turned against him. He was still carrying on like a man who thought the Board was under his control, as it had been six weeks earlier when it followed his advice and dumped the Gang of Four in favour of Dexter.

After the search committee report, Stevens presented the Board with an extraordinary four-page memorandum. Stevens reminded the Board that Axworthy had used the words "at this time" when he refused a work permit for Dexter. "The minister was not '*at this time*' satisfied that an adequate search had been undertaken to find a qualified Canadian who might be available to fill the post. It was clearly understood that the Board could reapply for Dexter's clearance should a renewed search for a qualified Canadian of equivalent availability prove fruitless." After quoting the minutes from both the old Board meeting and the new Board meeting on December 6, Stevens continued:

The new president on the Board's behalf gave John Dexter an undertaking that the Minister of Immigration would be reapproached with the results of the search, and confirmed to Dexter that the Board was not withdrawing its offer. On this understanding, Dexter continued to maintain his availability.

The Board has now received a report from the search committee. Of the five people it was asked by the Board to approach, only one has officially been contacted, and there have been discussions with others not on the short list. Of the five shortlisted by the Board, only John Hirsch is showing interest. He offers limited availability for 1981, and is prepared to negotiate, with no guarantee of agreement, full availability with effect from 1982.

The Board is thus considering three courses: 1. To pursue its right to appoint its first choice and commitment, John Dexter. 2. To accept a bridging season leading to the fully effective appointment of Hirsch in 1982, a situation which would put Hirsch in a very strong negotiating position. 3. To appoint at this level secondary talent who may now be disposed to accept the substantive as opposed to temporary appointment of artistic director.

My advice to the Board is that in the circumstances it is bound, under its agreement with Dexter, in the public's interest, and in the Festival's own legitimate commercial interests, to make a vigorous and thorough reapplication to the minister for Dexter's work permit.

An immediate start on preparatory work for the 1981 season is crucial. At the present time, with a fully committed Artistic Director immediately in place and designers appointed by the New Year, the earliest possible date for previews prior to the formal opening of the Festival is estimated to be the last week in June. Were the season to close at the end of October, each 5 percent of attendance represents about $330,000. Each day of delay represents a loss in gross income potential of $50,000.

Dexter, the Board's first choice, is immediately available and has done considerable preparatory work in consultation with me and the Festival technical staff. He has star talent on call. He is therefore in the most favourable position to achieve the earliest possible start date and produce the most attractive and coherent program with a more integrated (if smaller) company. A Dexter season performing to 75 percent in the Festival and 70 percent in the Avon would produce some $660,000 more in box-office receipts than a less attractive scratch season playing to 65 percent and 60 percent respectively. A Dexter integrated company would comprise sixty actors. A less integrated company or two separate companies, which are the probable alternatives in a badly planned or poorly supervised season, might comprise an average of seventy-five actors. The difference in cost between the two is some $200,000. Thus the net cost of a non-Dexter season could be some $860,000 greater than a Dexter season. It is still just possible, given an immediate start, the prospect of a late June opening, and the achievement of a 75/70 percent box office, for the Festival to avoid a deficit in 1981.

Those are the practical and commercial considerations for which the Board must take responsibility. Other factors which I urge the Board to consider are as follows: 1. The Stratford community interest, which is heavily dependent on a successful Festival and which has expressed itself overwhelmingly in favour of the Board's right to hire the best man available in the job. 2. The national and international media support (which will be reflected in box-office receipts, particularly the 40 percent which originate in the U.S.A.) for talent rather than nationality to be the main criterion when making senior appointments in the arts. 3. The manoeuvres of the Council of Canadian Equity, which is using threats to intimidate and coerce the Board in this matter. Should the Board allow itself to be seen to be influenced by such threats, it will seriously and permanently compromise its negotiating strength with the union, and at the same time set a precedent for successful union action of this kind for which the Board will not be thanked by other Canadian arts organizations. I therefore urge the Board to deal with the union in the context of its actions, rather than its threats. I am not convinced that a boycott, if legal, would be applied, but I am convinced that were it to be applied in the face of a government clearance for Dexter it would not be long lasting or effective, particularly where senior and important talent is concerned.

Should the Board concede on the Dexter issue, it will have condoned rather than challenged government intervention. This again would not only establish a precedent which would cause other arts organizations great unease, but would admit a greater influence on the Board's decision-making by the Canada Council and the Ontario Arts Council than is politically desirable or financially justifiable.

The alternative to the appointment of John Dexter, a world-class director, is indubitably a financially and practically suspect 1981 season, the result of which could do lasting damage to the Festival's reputation for high quality. In effect, it could be something akin or even inferior to that in which the Board expressed emphatic and unanimous no-confidence on November 5, a result which would leave the Board (not the new director, and not, if he has not been asked for a review, the Minister) open to criticism and ridicule.

There is no Canadian of both equivalent quality and equivalent availability. Senior representatives of the Board must therefore approach the Minister for a review in the light of its latest and properly documented search (as invited by the Minister) and most cogent arguments. If such an approach fails again, it will be deeply regrettable but it will represent the political will of this government and will have to be accepted.

If, however, the Board lacks the will to secure Dexter, is afraid of the consequences of his appointment threatened by certain sectional interests, and a rationale is sought for not going back to Ottawa, the Board will in my view be in breach of a verbal contract and will not have kept faith with a distinguished director who has kept faith with the Board. It will have volunteered a move towards a nationalistic closed shop in the arts which would be a recipe *in any country* for the compromise of standards and at some point the denial of talent. It will also have rejected the most considered recommendation of its Executive Director on a matter of the greatest operational and policy importance. On all three counts the implications for my future working relationship with the Board are fundamental.

Ironically, Stevens, who had been unimpressed by arguments about the Board's moral obligations to the Gang of Four, was now arguing that the Board had to stick to Dexter to show it was acting in good faith. By now, however, the Board was aware of the more pressing need to demonstrate it was dealing in good faith with Axworthy, Hirsch, Porter, and the angry people who had come to the December 6 meeting.

A motion to go back to Axworthy again and ask him to approve Dexter's work permit was defeated by a vote of ten to four. Once the Board had given up on Dexter, there was only one alternative to Hirsch – Hutt on a temporary basis, with help from Phillips – and there was little enthusiasm for it. The Board voted unanimously to offer the job to Hirsch.

But this was only the beginning of negotiations with Hirsch. Once the public was aware of the Board's commitment to Hirsch and of the Festival's desperate bid to save the 1981 season, Hirsch was – as Stevens had seen – in a very powerful position. If the Festival's terms proved unacceptable, and Hirsch decided to walk away from it all, the Board would be in even worse trouble than before. And there were some highly troublesome points to be worked out.

Hirsch knew it was very late to be planning a season, but he thought it would be far more damaging to cancel the 1981 season than to mount a shaky, thrown-together-at-the-last-minute one. It was only partly because of his other commitments that he decided to keep his distance from the 1981 season. He realized that 1981 was a no-win situation. And he felt that given the traumatic events of the past five months, he would need some time to survey the damage, do some political fence-mending, attempt to fix the structural and administrative problems, and create an atmosphere in which he could function by 1982.

The solution, in his mind, was to bring in Muriel Sherrin, who had been his chief lieutenant at CBC drama, and who had a track record as an independent producer. Sherrin, in consultation with Hirsch, could put together the 1981 season. But all the details remained to be worked out. Would Sherrin be willing to take this hot seat? What kind of contract demands would she make? And would she and Hirsch be able to work out some sort of peaceful co-existence with Peter Stevens?

The day after the Board voted to offer him the job, Hirsch called Stevens to ask, "How do you feel about it?"

Stevens told him, "Go round to Julian Porter and get a copy of my memo to the Board, and you'll know how I feel."

Hirsch was shocked when he read the memo. Why would Stevens

want him to see it? Was this an announcement that there was no way they could work together? Or was Stevens just being aggressively up-front, as if to say, "We both have to be completely honest if we're going to find a way of getting on together"? In Stevens' mind, the message he was sending Hirsch was, "You've been very open with me, and I want to be very open with you. As far as I'm concerned, you are not available to do this job on a proper basis, and that is why I'm unhappy. And if you want to know why, read this. That memo says it."

Temperamentally, Hirsch and Stevens were not made for each other. Hirsch's reaction to Stevens' memo was, "This guy is firing cannons across my bow. How can I ever trust him?" That wasn't the only problem: Hirsch could see there were going to be conflicts over jurisdiction. He didn't like the fact that Stevens' contract gave him the right to talk directly to the Board. He could see that Stevens' contract would prevent him from restructuring the Festival's chain of command. Hirsch, who was going to rehearsals every day for *A Funny Thing Happened on the Way to the Forum*, asked Stevens to come to see him on December 24 in Toronto, and Stevens replied, "That's not how I'm going to spend Christmas Eve."

It may have been genuinely hard for the two of them to find a mutually convenient time to get together, but Hirsch assumed that Stevens was being less than fully co-operative. Stevens went to New York to see Dexter, and he spent Christmas in New York with friends. When he finally got together with Hirsch, it was on the afternoon of New Year's Eve. Hirsch's show was opening that night at the St. Lawrence Centre.

Hirsch advised Stevens, in effect, to keep his head down and sit very still. Stevens would have to realize, Hirsch told him, that he was seen as the manipulator of a discredited Board, and an advocate of a policy that had been rejected. It would be impossible for Stevens to have a good relationship with the Canada Council – which had suggested in a public statement that the Board had not made an adequate search for a qualified Canadian before hiring Stevens. Hirsch said he needed someone who could give him that, someone who knew Canadian theatre, someone Hirsch knew intimately, someone Hirsch trusted. It was very clear that Peter Stevens was not that person. Yet Stevens got the impression that Hirsch was really saying, "If you want to sit around for six or eight months, maybe it will be all right."

While waiting for contractual matters to be sorted out, Hirsch was in a ticklish position. He couldn't afford any further delay in pulling together the 1981 season. But after spending days on the phone trying to find out who would be available to work at Stratford in 1981, he realized he was putting himself in the same untenable position as the Gang of Four: working without a contract. And the contract was becoming so problematic that on some days there were real doubts whether it would ever be signed. But Hirsch enjoyed negotiating, and he did it skilfully.

As a result of his probing, Hirsch received a letter from John Dexter, dated December 24:

Milton Goldman has conveyed to me your enquiry as to the possibility of my doing two productions at Stratford. This seems to me an inopportune suggestion, much as I understand the thought behind it. As neither I nor my agent has received any communication from the Stratford Board as to what compensation they propose to offer, it seems inevitable that I shall be in litigation à la Ustinov with them. You will, I know, understand that this action casts no reflection on you personally but reflects my disgust with the Board's handling of the matter. Since Nov. 5, when the Board decided to offer me the post, they have asked me a) not to speak to the press, and b) to maintain myself in readiness. It is my understanding that they had reached an agreement with you by Dec. 9. I was still at that time in my view under verbal contract and continued to be so until Dec. 18 when Mr. Heney telephoned and told me that they had decided to engage you.

To put it more bluntly, we were both being negotiated with and manipulated at the same time. I'm sure your diary and mine contain records of all the meetings. I asked Mr. Heney to contact my agent with a view to resolving the situation quietly. As we have so far heard nothing, the intervention of a lawyer seems inevitable, and in my view, does preclude the possibility of my working for you, much as I appreciate the difficulty of the situation in which you are placed. Please accept my good wishes for your appointment and your future.

Another New York correspondent, Hume Cronyn, had written to John Heney a few days before the stormy annual meeting:

I'd like to confirm for the record that my decision to withdraw from the Board was made on Sunday, November 9, and was motivated solely by the Board's action of November 5. I do not wish to have seemed to withdraw simply because the going got rough, or shall I say rougher....It's all very sad.

Cronyn had sent a copy of the letter to Robert Hicks, and Hicks followed up with a letter to Cronyn that Cronyn regarded as an act of generosity from a man who was bleeding badly:

I would like you to know that out of respect and affection for you, I've deliberately avoided in the media contacts any drawing upon your name in terms of any decisions made by the Board. While there was great curiosity of how we learned about Peter Stevens and how we first talked to John Dexter back in February of last year, fortunately there was no need to draw you into the controversy surrounding their involvement with us.

Cronyn replied:

I'm grateful for your consideration in avoiding the use of my name throughout what must have been very trying inquiries by the press. However, it's really not necessary. I'm pleased to have it known that I introduced Stevens and Dexter, and there's nothing in my involvement in the sad events of the last six months that I feel is particularly sensitive or confidential.

John Hirsch signed his contract at a meeting of the executive committee on Monday, January 5. It was a three-year agreement, at an annual salary of $75,000. Earlier Hirsch had told the Board that he wouldn't direct more than one or two plays in 1981; now he was adamant that he wouldn't direct any. He would be away until July 1, and in the meantime he would be consulting regularly with Muriel Sherrin, who was being brought in as executive producer.

Muriel Sherrin started work officially on January 15, and the 1981 season had to be fully planned by the end of January. Early that month, Oliver Gaffney and Peter Stevens met Sherrin in her downtown Toronto office to discuss her contract and her mandate. She said, "Listen, I'm here for several months and out the other end. I'm not after anybody's job. I'm here to produce a season, period. I think John and I can do it. If we all work together it will be fine. Do you have any problems with that?"

Stevens said, "No, as long as your role is the artistic one, I can understand that."

When Sherrin arrived in Stratford, though, she felt like a lonely stranger. Hirsch had been there before. Michal Schonberg, his new literary manager, seemed to know his way around the building.

But Sherrin not only had to produce immediately, she had to discover how the system worked, get to know the staff, find out where the washrooms were. She was living in a rented house, having left her husband and two teen-age children to fend for themselves in Toronto.

By the time she came to work, Sherrin and Hirsch had already had a fair idea of how the season was going to shape up. Jean Gascon had agreed to direct Molière's *The Misanthrope* and one other play. He had put aside his other plans to come to Stratford; he loved the place, and, after an absence of seven years, he was delighted to be asked back. Hirsch wanted to do a Gilbert and Sullivan operetta, and Sherrin wanted to invite Leon Major to direct it. (They chose HMS *Pinafore.*) They had talked to Peter Dews, and they knew Dews would direct *The Taming of the Shrew* and one other show.

There were a number of people Hirsch and Sherrin wanted and couldn't get. Martha Henry and Douglas Rain refused on principle to work at Stratford in 1981. Christopher Plummer said no out of loyalty to Dexter. Hume Cronyn and Jessica Tandy said thanks, but no thanks. Roberta Maxwell said, "Not this year, Muriel." Peggy Ashcroft declined to make the trip from England to play the mother in *Coriolanus.* Frank Langella wasn't available. Hirsch was interested in producing Gordon Pinsent's *John and the Missus* only if Pinsent would star in it, and Pinsent didn't want to commit himself. R.H. Thomson, who was invited to play Hamlet, said he would rather wait a year.

One breakthrough was getting Brian Bedford to change his mind. Bedford had decided he definitely wasn't coming back to Stratford in 1981. He had spent four seasons there (1975, 1977, 1978, 1980), and he felt he had acted himself out. Working with Robin Phillips and Maggie Smith, he had done some of the most satisfying work of his life, and he had even made a creditable debut as a director, but it was a taxing experience, for relatively little money, and he was ready for something else.

The Stratford crisis changed his mind. He knew if Stratford stopped functioning, he would feel bereaved. It would be a great loss for North America and a particular loss for Brian Bedford, who might never find another such showcase for his talent. Bedford was in Toronto starring in the touring version of *Whose Life Is It Anyway?* when he got the call from Hirsch. They had serious talks even before Hirsch signed his contract. It was very late to be approaching an actor as heavily in demand as Bedford. Other people were hanging back; they'd gone ahead with other commitments, or were nervous about appearing to choose sides in what had become a bitter dispute. The situation was politically risky and emotionally strained.

Boston had just been dropped from the touring schedule of *Whose Life Is It Anyway?* (in which Bedford played a quadriplegic arguing with the hospital administration for his right to put an end to his suffering), so it turned out he would have some free time in the spring. There were a number of other possibilities, in general more lucrative than a season at Stratford, though Hirsch and Sherrin were offering a far better deal than Bedford had ever had at Stratford. Bedford decided to make a commitment to Stratford in its hour of need. As a star player who had been closely associated with Robin Phillips, he thought he might even be able to contribute some continuity.

Bedford was interested in directing *Coriolanus,* and Len Cariou was interested in starring in it, so that production was set. Bedford was perfect to play the title role in Gascon's *Misanthrope,* so that was settled, too. The other two shows for the opening week in June would be Major's production of *Pinafore,* which was to run eight times a week at the Avon throughout June and July, and *The Taming of the Shrew,* which Dews would direct, with Len Cariou starring. The question of who would play the shrew became one of Sherrin's major problems. Among those who turned it down was Lally Cadeau, who chose to accept a film offer instead. It wasn't until late February that Sharry Flett was cast. She would also play opposite Bedford in *The Misanthrope.*

Later on in the summer there would be four additional productions. The three midsummer openings would be *The Comedy of Errors,* directed by Dews, which would introduce Fiona Reid, the Toronto TV and stage actress, to Stratford audiences; Durenmatt's *The Visit,* directed by Gascon; and *The Rivals,* directed by Bedford, with a cast including Nicholas Pennell, Pat Galloway, and Richard Monette. The late-season opening would be *Wild Oats,* a nineteenth-century farce rediscovered by Ronald Bryden in his days as literary manager for the Royal Shakespeare Company and produced in 1977 by the RSC with considerable success. It would be months before a director was announced for *Wild Oats* – Derek Goldby, the

Englishman who had staged several farces for the Shaw Festival.

The first catastrophe of the season was the withdrawal of Danielle Darrieux. William Hutt had been asked to star in *The Visit* and *The Rivals*, and he had come to Sherrin's office and had a long chat with her about Stratford history. Sherrin knew how important it was to land Hutt. He was one of the veterans of the company, and one of its most distinguished actors. (Martha Henry and Douglas Rain had already been lost.) Hutt said he had a film to do – Robin Phillips' *The Wars* – and he didn't want to kill himself. He didn't want to do *The Rivals*, but he would do *The Visit* under certain conditions. One was that there be an actress of international stature as his co-star.

Everyone thought it was a great coup when the Festival landed Danielle Darrieux. Muriel Sherrin personally negotiated the deal. She phoned Darrieux' agent in Paris and said, "We have to print this brochure. Can you send me a telegram giving me the right to release her name?" The agent sent a letter, agreeing to the deal, saying they would be delighted, and so forth. No contract had been signed, but as far as Sherrin was concerned, the letter of agreement was binding. When Darrieux pulled out, reports began to circulate that the Festival had failed to settle her contract.

Muriel Sherrin was furious. She called Darrieux' agent, who seemed extremely embarrassed. "Look," she told him, "if she wants to get out because she has an offer to do something else for more money, just tell me and I'll release her. But don't tell me it's because you didn't get the contract."

The agent replied, "Oh, *je m'excuse*, I'll speak to Madame Darrieux and call you next week." But he didn't call back, and Sherrin couldn't get him to answer her calls after that. The Festival sent a letter, but it was never answered.

Now came the rush to replace her. Sherrin knew that Hutt might pull out if she didn't find a name actress. After a few false starts, she landed one: Alexis Smith. Canadian-born, she had been a movie star of an earlier era and had had a come-back of sorts in the Broadway show *Follies* and the movie version of Jacqueline Susann's *Once Is Not Enough*, in which she played the third-richest woman in the world, a role not unlike the one in *The Visit*. But did she have any credibility as a classical stage actress? That remained to be seen.

Budgets for the 1981 shows were higher than had been usual

under Robin Phillips. Sherrin believed in paying actors well, and in the circumstances she didn't have a lot of choice. Given the late start, Stratford was in a poor negotiating position. Very early on, rumours began circulating that Stratford was going to lose a bundle in 1981, perhaps more than the $1.3 million projected deficit over which the Gang of Four had been fired. Everything was late, and that increased the costs. The season had to be shorter than usual. The brochures didn't go out until February. And there were the payoffs: a year's salary to the Gang of Four, Ustinov's lawsuit over the King Lear fiasco, John Dexter. By March there was the matter of Peter Stevens, who wanted to settle his contract and go.

Peter Stevens wasn't at work the day Muriel Sherrin arrived. He had an intestinal infection, and the illness proved to be serious and long lasting. He was away from work for several weeks, and when he did come back, it was only for a few hours a day. Stevens and Sherrin did not develop a real relationship, and he never took her up on an offer she had made him. "Look, Peter," she told him, "I'll share everything I know with you. I'll introduce you to the people you need to know in this country. I'm having casting sessions, I'm having producing sessions. I have all these people coming to see me. You're welcome at every meeting. I'm happy to do it. You get along in this business on longevity, and I've been doing it a long time. I know everybody – actors, directors, producers, the Canada Council people, government people, CBC people."

Sherrin could see that Stevens was no fool, but he was new to Canada, and he didn't have the contacts she had. However, Peter Stevens had no intention of taking instruction from Muriel Sherrin. At the beginning of January, he had let the executive committee know that he thought Hirsch's contract was in conflict with his. The gist of Stevens' message to the Board was, "Come on, let me go." The gist of the Board's response at this point was, "Stick around for a while, we'll see what happens." Stevens decided to let it ride for a while. Then he got sick. Then he learned that his mother was dying in England. Stevens thought the matter was close to being resolved at an executive committee on March 11. He said he didn't want to leave the Festival in the lurch, and he would stay until the end of the season. After that he wanted to be let off the hook. To his surprise, the Board decided on March 14 to ask Stevens to leave sooner rather than later. He was told he would be offered a settlement. In the midst of all this, he had to go to England to see his mother before she died. John Lawson told him, "Don't worry about it now, we'll discuss it when you get back."

While Stevens was in England, news of his imminent departure found its way into the newspapers. Through his wife, Stevens issued a statement, "The Canadianization of the control and direction of the performing arts in this country renders my position as executive director of the Stratford Festival untenable." Stevens was interviewed by the *Times* of London, which ran the item on April 2 under a headline that revealed something about the growing animosity of the British to Canadian nationalism: "Another Briton falls victim to Canadian narrow-mindedness." Stevens was quoted as saying his position had become untenable in Canada because the Canada Council had told the Festival "they could not be sympathetic to any grant application while I was still there."

Mavor Moore, the chairman of the Canada Council, immediately issued a denial. "Any suggestion that the Canada Council's grant was dependent on Mr. Stevens' leaving is entirely mistaken," he said. Two years earlier the Council had published its Guidelines for Theatre Companies, which stated that Canadian talent should be given first and due consideration for appropriate openings within publicly funded theatres, and that any publicly funded theatre which filled such openings from outside the Canadian theatrical community should be able to demonstrate that all reasonable efforts had been made to fill them from within.

At the Canada Council's December, 1980, meeting, in response to inquiries about the funding of the Stratford Festival, the Council had reaffirmed the Guidelines and stated that Council "could not accept that in the appointments of their executive director [Stevens] and artistic director designate [Dexter], the Board complied with either the letter or the spirit of the policy." According to Moore, the Festival had been aware of the Canada Council's position throughout, and what the Festival decided to do about it was entirely up to the Festival.

After the appointment of Hirsch, the Festival had appealed to the Canada Council for additional funding, on the grounds that the Festival was now acting in the ways prescribed by the Canada Council, at great cost and risk, and it was up to the Council to bail out the Festival.

Council staff, including Walter Learning, the theatre officer, argued that given the freeze the government had put on its funds, the Council couldn't increase Stratford's grant while other theatres were suffering. No one suggested that Stratford's grant would be cancelled if Stevens remained in his job, or that the Festival could look forward to an increased grant if Stevens left. The Council was merely reprimanding Stratford for violating the Guidelines, and by implication warning the Festival not to do so again. In effect the Canada Council was telling Stratford, "You got yourself into this mess without paying any attention to our conditions, so don't tell us it's our responsibility to bail you out."

While Stevens was away in England, his wife, Rochelle, was feeling very isolated in Stratford. What had become of all the people who had been supportive a few months earlier? Suddenly the phone had gone very, very quiet.

When Stevens came back from England in April, he and his wife began getting ready to pack up and leave. By now Stevens was trying to be philosophical about his experience in Canada. He hadn't really understood the political and psychological forces at work within the country. He thought he had been "underadvised" about the Canadian situation at the time of his appointment. He would shrug and smile, showing the large teeth that had led his detractors to call him "Jaws 3," and remark, "Sometimes in life you just dial a wrong number."

Stevens left Canada for England on May 1, 1981. A day or two before that, clearing out the answering machine on his telephone, he came across an old message. He heard the voice of Robert Hicks, phoning from Ottawa on November 7, to say that things were going very well indeed with Axworthy's office. Suddenly Stevens was struck by the comedy of it all. Alone in the study of his Stratford house, he began to roar with laughter.

CHAPTER SEVENTEEN

The Hollow Crown

John Hirsch returned to Stratford two months ahead of schedule, at the beginning of May, and immediately plunged into what he considered his main task—healing the wounds and repairing the damage. To him the most frustrating aspect of the whole mess was that everyone wanted to talk about the trouble and what had *really* gone on, and nobody seemed terribly interested in getting on with the future. Hirsch is a great orator and *animateur*, and he began pouring his energy into rallying people to the Stratford cause. In his mind, it was far more important to take on this political role than it was to sit in Stratford and direct plays or be a glorified bureaucrat. Hirsch could see that he had some major problems ahead of him, and his way of dealing with them was to try to coax and prod people into seeing the situation his way so they would accept his solutions.

One of his biggest problems was the Board itself. During his contract negotiations he had strongly suggested that some resignations within the Board would be necessary, but in the end nobody resigned. Because there had been no public admission that the Board had accepted the blame for what had gone wrong, many people felt that Stratford under Hirsch could not start with a clean slate. Martha Henry and Douglas Rain, for example, had made it clear they would not act at Stratford until there was some demonstration of a major change in the Board's attitude.

Another big problem for Hirsch was the deficit looming over the 1981 season. The only question was how large it was going to be. As far as Hirsch was concerned, he couldn't be blamed for it, given the circumstances: a preposterously late start, large payoffs and legal costs, a shorter season, and the worst publicity imaginable.

But what if the Board tried to curb the Festival's operations as a consequence of the deficit? Then Hirsch's hands would be tied. He wouldn't be able to do any of the things he deemed necessary to restore Stratford to a state of health. The answer was simple in Hirsch's view. Stratford would have to be perceived by the whole country as a national treasure, and the government would have to accept more responsibility for it. Stratford businessmen would have to realize that there was a price to be paid for the goose that lays the golden egg. The Festival spent about $7 million annually and stimulated $35 million in tourist dollars spent in Stratford.

Hirsch knew that he was going to have to fight for every penny. When he spoke to John Lawson about what would be done about replacing Peter Stevens, Lawson suggested it might not be necessary. The Festival couldn't afford a lot of high-priced people, and Lawson suggested that since Hirsch was planning to direct only one or two plays each season himself, he would be able to take over a lot of the administrative work. This notion enraged Hirsch, "That's not what you hire an artistic director to do," he ranted at Lawson. "Do you know what you're paying the artistic director to do? I'll tell you. To go around giving speeches and have a presence in the right places, and take long walks in the park and figure out what should be done here." Hirsch couldn't believe the mentality of the town and the Board. It was, he remarked, as if the Metropolitan Opera were being run by a few grocers from the Bronx. But later he came to perceive Lawson as an ally and benefactor.

Hirsch was determined to build a strong administrative organization that would function well no matter who the artistic director was. Stratford, he insisted, could not be a one-man band. The Festival was not only a national resource, he kept saying, but a continental resource – the only great classical repertory company left in North America. If there wasn't enough money to nurture it, that was because the right people hadn't been prodded into helping. Specifically, he wanted to develop a much more sophisticated approach to marketing, and to this end he commissioned a report from Hugh Southern of the Theater Development Fund in New York. He thought the arts councils should be asked to fund Stratford as a special case – a unique institution of national importance. He felt that links with schools and universities would need to be strengthened. The way Hirsch told the story, nothing less than the survival of western civilization was at stake. Stratford represented a standard of culture and literacy that was in danger of disappearing from the world.

Hirsch was in splendid form when he spoke on Tuesday, May 19, at a discussion program organized for the Toronto Theatre Festival. He began by telling the story of his life, from his earliest memories of Hungary through his wanderings as an orphan of the Holocaust, through his rebirth in Winnipeg to the creation of the Manitoba Theatre Centre, through his years at Stratford and the CBC, to his perception of how he had changed in recent years. When asked why he had taken the job, he said that he felt a great responsibility to Stratford. Guthrie, Langham, and Douglas Campbell had helped him establish a professional theatre in Winnipeg. Now Stratford was in trouble, and it had to be nurtured. It must have a vital connection with all the other theatres in Canada. As a responsible theatrical professional of a certain age, Hirsch felt he ought to give his time to this place and to the country. He saw the job as a service, a calling. He wanted to have a training school. It would be necessary to train young directors, designers, lighting people, costume people.

When Herbert Whittaker, the critic emeritus of the *Globe and Mail,* asked Hirsch for his version of the great upset at Stratford, Hirsch's voice became even more intense, as if some great store of anger had been tapped, and he could barely keep it under control. Again, this obsession with the trouble of the past was getting in his way. Hirsch began by saying he hadn't been there, but he would give his perception of what had happened:

"For the past seven years, in my opinion, the Festival became more and more dependent on stars until last season we had Maggie Smith, Brian Bedford, Peter Ustinov, Jessica Tandy, Hume Cronyn, Kate Reid and Roberta Maxwell sitting like a crown on the company. The reputation of Stratford was gained by the existence of a strong company. People went to see *this company* doing Shakespeare. Over the last seven years there was a slight shift, and in my opinion to some extent the shift really has proven to be disastrous. I don't know why this happened, whether it was necessitated by economic demands and needs. The Festival got longer and longer; it was a way for the town to get a lot of income as fallout. Times have changed. It's more difficult to get people to Stratford. Somehow the mandate of that place got diluted or slightly corrupted, and that was one of the reasons why the place collapsed.

"I also feel that over a period of time the Board was not in as close contact with the artistic director as desirable. The Festival wasn't in as close contact with the arts councils and educational institutes as it should have been. There were some tremendous mistakes made when the directorate was appointed and when they were fired. Then we went into the Dexter phase.

"I only know we must somehow correct the mistakes of the past and we must somehow stop hugging all those troubles and difficulties close to our breasts and begin to think positively of what can happen there and what *must* happen there. I think in spite of the trouble the institution is still extraordinarily strong. It is a unique place, a continental resource, and it is a national responsibility to see to it that the place survives, flourishes and develops."

Hirsch was warmed up now, and the exasperation and the impatience were no longer concealed. "This country, the media, unions, can go on for ten years talking about the troubles [at Stratford], and they'll do nothing but further weaken the place. Whatever mistakes were made must be closely examined, and remedies must be found, but at this point in time what the place needs is the support, the love, the care, the concern of every single person who cares about theatre in this country. Institutions are incredibly precious, and as weak as human beings. They can get weak, die, disappear. We must stop in this country rejoicing in troubles and difficulties. Generations of young people went to Stratford and were exposed to theatre, and they became actors, directors, writers, cutters, wigmakers, critics, whatever. Do you want to deny that to the next generation?"

He was spitting out the words now, like a preacher threatening eternal damnation for unrepentant sinners. "There were periods when we didn't like what was going on there. This director was lousy. But the thing went on, and there were always people who benefitted from its existence. We cannot be so cavalier as to kill the place because we enjoy negative things more than positive things. We can't afford it, because we ain't got that many things around. So what the hell is going on?

"The essential thing is to ensure that good things go on. All things are in trouble all the time. *I* am in trouble all the time. It takes me two hours in the morning to pull myself together because of what happened the night before. I have to tell myself, 'Come on Hirsch, get up, shave, make a speech, get something going.' Not to sit and moan and nitpick and analyze and put everything down, which is so much fun, because then you don't have to be good, you get off the hook, you just say, 'This is shit, it's terrible.'

"The place was in trouble and it collapsed. A was guilty, B fucked up. But all that is gone. What can we do about what happened? What are we going to do now and who is going to come and help? This is why I told you the story of my life. If anybody has a reason to sit and moan, it's me – a Jewish orphan left alone to starve at thirteen, wandering around.... What more terrible thing can happen to anybody?"

With this passionate outburst, Hirsch brought back into focus not just his concern for the future of the Festival, but also a matter of some delicacy – his highly critical view of Robin Phillips. Hirsch tried to be diplomatic, to avoid saying anything directly critical of Phillips in public. But it would be stretching things to say he kept his view of Phillips to himself. Sid Adilman of the Toronto Star played up Hirsch's reference to the "disastrous" emphasis on stars during the preceding six years and wrote that Hirsch had been harshly critical of Phillips. The item upset Hirsch. To him, it was another example of the press taking things out of context, twisting his words, emphasizing the negative. Why pick that out of an hour-long session in which so many positive things were said? Hirsch even called Phillips to explain that he had no bones to pick with him.

But the battle lines were drawn. The deep rivalry between Hirsch and Phillips festered throughout the 1981 season. Those loyal to Phillips complained that Hirsch was trying to change everything, as if to erase the Phillips era from public memory. Hirsch felt inhibited by the presence of Phillips, who still lived in Stratford, and could be seen regularly at The Church restaurant, often surrounded by an entourage of people who were known to be sharply critical of Hirsch. Phillips was directing his first movie, based on Timothy Findley's novel The Wars, and featuring many of his favourite Stratford players – Martha Henry, Brent Carver, William Hutt. Among the extras were Barbara Ivey, sitting in a pew in a red fox coat; eight-year-old Emma Rain (daughter of Martha Henry and Douglas Rain); Marion Isherwood, co-owner of the Old Prune restaurant; and Joe Mandel, owner of The Church. Referring to the controversy at the Festival, Phillips told Gina Mallet in an interview, "It'll take a long time to get over it. I feel very much as if it's a separation or divorce and somebody else has custody of the children."

Phillips had been negotiating with Duncan Weldon of Triumph Productions to direct a series of plays with the projected resident company at the Theatre Royal in the Haymarket in London, and Weldon believed they had reached an agreement. However, in August 1981, when it was time to start rehearsing the first show – *Cyrano de Bergerac,* starring Derek Jacobi – Weldon discovered that Phillips wasn't satisfied with the arrangements and had decided not to go ahead with the project. Many people involved in the project found themselves out of work on short notice, and the Birmingham Repertory Theatre, which had been offering a pre-London engagement of *Cyrano* as the first production of its subscription series, had to find a last-minute substitution.

Mallet kept up her role as leader of the opposition. Having been persuaded of the genius of John Dexter, she refused to get off the Dexter bandwagon when the Board changed its mind about hiring him. She went to England, hailed Dexter's work at the National Theatre, and published an interview with Sir Peter Hall, head of the National, which included some astonishing remarks about Stratford.

"It's difficult for me to comment on another country's business," Mallet quoted Sir Peter as saying, "but I find it absolutely appalling – and I don't mean this to sound just anti-Canadian – when a person's nationality bars him from exercising his talent. I think this is very wrong. If John Dexter was the man to do the job – and if he wasn't, then why was he asked? – the fact that he had the unfortunate fate to be British should not have been used against him....I think it's racial prejudice. If we'd been talking about colours of skins, it would have been a different matter. People would have been out in the streets."

Sir Peter didn't say what would have happened in England if for three decades the top job at the National Theatre or the Royal Shakespeare Company had gone almost every time it was open to someone outside Britain.

Gina Mallet also made it clear she wasn't impressed by John Hirsch's rhetoric. "Hirsch has proclaimed himself saviour of the

Canadian theatre," she wrote in the *Star,* "implying that all those who do not give him 100 per cent support are not only against him, but even un-Canadian."

Muriel Sherrin invited Mallet to lunch and had a long, frank discussion with her. Mallet talked about what she felt was happening at Stratford and told Sherrin what she thought was wrong with the casting. Sherrin took the position that 1981 was an extraordinary season and everyone should give the new management a chance. She wondered how some of her critics would like to try putting together a list of plays and do all the casting in six weeks. Her plea was, "Just help us get through. Let's not harp on the past. There's nothing I can do about it. I wasn't here." Sherrin was as impatient as Hirsch about the extraordinary amount of valuable time being taken up arguing about the past. She wanted to say to everybody, "Give me a break. I know you don't agree with certain things, that's your prerogative. My concern is to get those shows on stage."

Sherrin was sticking to her guns about leaving after the 1981 season, but she wanted to have an input into the 1982 season, which she felt should be announced in July, 1981. It wasn't until later that she understood that once she had announced she was leaving on Labour Day, people stopped paying attention to her ideas about the future.

She had not only been invited to stay on, she had been almost harassed into staying. Hirsch and Lawson kept coaxing her: "What can we give you? What do you want?" They knew her range of experience made her valuable: she could do casting; she knew how to talk to governments; she could go over a budget; she could organize tours and deals with the CBC. (Early on, in 1981, Sherrin had arranged for the Festival's production of *Wild Oats* to go to the National Arts Centre at the end of the season, and for CBC television to tape two Festival shows – *The Taming of the Shrew* and HMS *Pinafore.*)

Sherrin kept saying, "I'm fulfilling the terms of my contract. I'm happy to do it. But this is not for me. I'm not going to change my mind. I want out at the end of the season."

Board executives assumed she would change her mind. They told her to take her time and give the matter some thought. From time to time she would say to someone, "Do you want to know today?" And the answer would be, "No, we don't want to know today. You think it over." Finally she said, "Look I have to tell you, I absolutely do not want to stay beyond the terms of my contract."

One of Sherrin's most important tasks was to write a description of how the Festival as an institution should work. She spent a long time explaining to various Board members why the Festival needed someone to replace Stevens. Eventually they accepted her views. Then she took part in the search for a new executive director. She was enthusiastic about Gerald Eldred, then with the National Ballet School, who was eventually chosen for the job. He was, in Sherrin's view, tough, solid, honourable. Eldred would have working under him Gary Thomas and John Uren, whom Hirsch had brought in as head of marketing.

As the opening of the 1981 season approached, Sherrin was presiding in an atmosphere of crisis. Advance ticket sales were down, and Hirsch was saying that the deficit might be as high as $2 million. And there were some troubling reports coming out of rehearsals. Brian Bedford was less than thrilled with Barbara Chilcott, who was playing the mother in his production of *Coriolanus*, and with Sharry Flett, who was playing opposite him in *The Misanthrope*. At one point, Bedford threatened to quit unless he could have 100 extras for *Coriolanus*. Sherrin, who had no patience with threats of resignation (even when they came from John Hirsch), told Bedford, "Let me know by ten o'clock tomorrow morning, because I'll replace you." Bedford saw her later, much calmer, and said of course he was staying. Sherrin promised to do the best she could with extras, and in the end there were forty-two.

The day before the season opened, the Board held its annual garden party, and that night the guest speaker at the annual Stratford Festival Senate dinner was Pauline McGibbon, the former lieutenant-governor of Ontario. A woman of unquestioned integrity, she was a walking model of what the Board aspired to be – a patrician emblem of Upper Canada's most honourable tradition. Unlike many political figures, she didn't have to fake an interest in the theatre; her commitment was genuine. And she had no enemies; she was as untouchable as the Queen Mother. McGibbon recalled attending Stratford's legendary first night in the tent in 1953, when Alec Guinness spoke the Festival's first words:

Now is the winter of our discontent
Made glorious summer....

Then Mrs. McGibbon had some soothing words for Stratford

Board members past and present. "In a sense one can say that the Board – and I know you will deny it, but I'll say it anyway – is the 'genius' of Stratford, at least in one meaning which the Romans gave to the word 'genius.' For the Romans, every man has his personal spirit – his genius – a kind of cultural Guardian Angel. On behalf of all Canadians for whom the Festival is so profoundly important, the Stratford Board is its Guardian Angel.

"Stratford will always be a target. And since coming to my new role as chairman of the board of the National Arts Centre, I have achieved a heightened awareness of the extent to which Canadians enjoy target practice. As that well-known English playwright, William Shakespeare, has said, 'Greatest scandal waits on greatest state.'

"It is not long before anyone who serves on the board of an arts organization comes to feel like a member of the Flying Wallendas – those miraculous artists of the high wire. High above the comforts of solid ground, balanced precariously on next-to-nothing, and burdened with all manner of impedimenta, human as well as inanimate, they succeed in proceeding from height to height.

"Those who dare greatly should refuse discouragement if, on occasion, achievement falls short of aspiration. High wire artists fall; they never give up. No particular intelligence is required to comment from the sidelines, or with hindsight. Unburdened by fact, and excused from complexity, urgency and responsibility, decisions come rapidly and are never wrong.

"It was an expatriate Canadian playwright, Bernie Slade, who noted that in the States one is judged by one's last performance, in Europe by one's best, and in Canada by one's worst. Canadian artists would no doubt encourage us all to follow the European model. Can these artists refuse to apply the same standard in judging the performance of a Board of Governors? I think not."

McGibbon's apologia for the Board was greeted with roars of approval. Some Board members were very bitter about the public criticisms to which they had been subjected. They had only been trying to do their best. They had contributed their time and energy to an institution they believed in, and what did they get for it? Abuse and contempt. What right did journalists think they had to question the motives and integrity of Board members, to write those insulting things about them? It was about time that somebody spoke out against the slurs on the Board's reputation. Yet, outside this little gathering of Board members and former Board members, there would be few who could entirely agree with Pauline McGibbon's defence.

The next night the trumpets blared, and once again men in tuxedoes and women in formal gowns filed into the Festival Theatre. It was a fine June evening, and John Hirsch, in an off-white suit, spent a great deal of time hovering around Pauline McGibbon, who was wearing a pale blue gown and had her grey hair done up in ringlets. The surprise was somehow not whether this or that play was good or bad, but that finally after all was said and done, the Stratford Festival was going on.

On opening night, Brian Bedford in the title role of *The Misanthrope* provided a desperately needed touch of star presence. True, Jean Gascon's production was old-fashioned to the point of being static, and true, Sharry Flett wasn't able to give the role of Celimène more than a gallant stab. But the role of Alceste, that witty crank who imagines himself the only honest man in the world, is not only one of Molière's most satisfying creations but also a part he might have written in the hope that one day Brian Bedford would be born to play it.

On the second night, Bedford's own production of *Coriolanus*, starring Len Cariou in the title role, drew the most enthusiastic ovations and the most respectful press notices of the week. This despite the fact that Cariou was almost as charmless as usual, that the first act made it quite clear why this play is so rarely staged, and that Barbara Chilcott's rhetorical affectation was an embarrassment. Still, with the help of wonderful supporting performances by Scott Hylands and Max Helpmann, Bedford and his assistant director, Robert Beard, did manage to give the proceedings an undeniable zing.

At the Avon, Leon Major's production of HMS *Pinafore* had settled in for a two-month run. Apart from Eric Donkin's amusing performance, it couldn't be called a triumph, but it was a fail-safe production of a Gilbert and Sullivan show that would keep the crowds coming.

At the end of opening week, the Stratford *Beacon-Herald* published a lead editorial headlined "Congratulations!" "Stratford has done it again!" crowed the newspaper. "In spite of all the gloom and doom that has been cast on the Stratford scene in the past year (mostly, but not all, from Toronto), the Stratford Festival has successfully launched its twenty-ninth season.... John Lawson and the Board had to carry the heaviest burden of criticism when the Festival was in trouble. It would have been awfully easy for some of them to quit but they nearly all stayed on and stuck it out. If they hadn't, there might be no Festival today...."

Later in the season there were four more shows. *The Visit* revealed in the person of Alexis Smith that it takes more than a familiar name to provide star chemistry, especially in a schematic Swiss parable whose Brechtian social lessons are all too clearly marked off. *The Comedy of Errors,* clunkily directed by Peter Dews, returned to the mug-them-until-they-respond style of Stratford's bad old days, and gave Fiona Reid, the charming Toronto actress, her classical debut in less than ideal circumstances. Brian Bedford's production of *The Rivals* was a bit of a muddle, though Pat Galloway was amusing as Mrs. Malaprop. At season's end, *Wild Oats,* directed by Derek Goldby with the desperation of a man whose life depended on squeezing out every laugh, demonstrated that not everybody can get away with what the Royal Shakespeare Company can.

It wasn't, all in all, one of Stratford's finer seasons, but it was a better season than anybody had a right to expect. If it lacked greatness, it was still respectable. Even the mediocrities were within the normal range of Stratford failures. Nobody had to feel ashamed or scandalized. That the season went on at all had to be counted a kind of miracle – for which Muriel Sherrin deserved a lot of credit. Amazingly, the machinery still worked: actors had costumes to wear, the sets got built in time, and the lights went on when they were supposed to. The apocalypse had come and gone, and the Stratford Festival survived.

The critics were generally restrained and charitable. As Robert Cushman remarked in the London *Observer,* after all the fuss, the season turned out better than people expected – or in some cases, hoped. At the end of the season, Gina Mallet wrote a scathing wrap-up article in the *Star,* characterizing Hirsch as man dominated by paranoia, painting a bleak picture of Stratford's future, and blaming the nationalists for what she saw as a disaster. By now the very mention of her name was enough to put Hirsch into a frenzy. At a company meeting, Hirsch had just launched into a tirade about Mallet, saying she wanted to destroy him, when Max Helpmann excused himself. A few minutes later Helpmann came back, and Hirsch was still talking about Mallet. Helpmann had gone to the bathroom, but pretending that he had been using the phone, he quipped, "Oh, by the way, John, Gina sends her regards." It broke up the room.

The annual general meeting on November 28 was subdued and orderly compared to the fiasco of December 6, 1980. John Hirsch wasn't there (he had gone to Victoria to receive an honorary doctorate) but he had just announced the 1982 season. Hirsch would be directing *The Tempest* on the Festival stage and *Mary Stuart* at the Avon. Brian Macdonald would be returning to Stratford to direct a production of *The Mikado* at the Avon. Michael Langham would be returning for the first time since 1970 to direct a production of Shaw's *Arms and the Man* on the Festival stage, starring Brian Bedford. Derek Goldby would be directing *Julius Caesar*, and the other Shakespeare production on the main stage would be *The Merry Wives of Windsor*. Brian Bedford would be directing a late-season production of *Blithe Spirit*, and the one new play in the line-up would be Brian Friel's *Translations*, a parable about the effect of British colonialism in Ireland, which Hirsch considered relevant to Canada. Hirsch had also announced the formation of the Shakespeare 3 Company at the Third Stage. The company was to include twelve young actors and four senior actors, who would go through a summer-long training period culminating in two productions, *A Midsummer Night's Dream* and *All's Well That Ends Well*.

The financial report at the annual meeting revealed that the loss for the season was a staggering $1,077,639, though this was not as much as had been feared a few months earlier. The payoffs included a $49,000 farewell to Peter Stevens and $152,000 to settle the *King Lear* fiasco, including a $45,000 out-of-court settlement with Ustinov.

The president's report was exceedingly careful to absolve John Hirsch of any responsibility for the loss. At Hirsch's request, Lawson stated, "By the time the season was set, no opportunity existed to arrive at a break-even position. Although there is a final shortfall, the Board is aware of the reasons for it and fully accepts its responsibility to find solutions to the financial problems we face."

He listed a number of reasons for the loss: the late start, the price of gas, the payoffs, the decreased fundraising, the ticket discounting that became necessary, the harsh attitude of the press, the cost of introducing credit-card ticket sales. Lawson was careful to single out for praise Hirsch and Sherrin. Referring to the troubles of a year earlier, Lawson commented, "It wasn't easy. We were very saddened by the resultant hurt." As for Martha Henry, he said, "Martha will make her own decision and when the time is right she will return to the Festival. And I hope it is soon." Henry sat calmly in the audience and did not comment.

The total box-office revenue for 1981 was $5,259,476, compared with $6,000,377 for 1980. (Hirsch had claimed the Festival was having its second-best season in history, but critics were quick to point out this wasn't really true. It had the second-highest revenue in history, but this represented fewer people paying higher ticket prices.) At the 1100-seat Avon Theatre, *Pinafore* played to 92 per cent capacity over 70 performances. *The Taming of the Shrew* played to 77 per cent capacity at the 2200-seat Festival Theatre. The weakest draws were *The Comedy of Errors,* with 69 percent, and *Coriolanus,* with 61 percent.

The changing of the guard within the Board was so low-key, it went almost unnoticed. Among those retiring from the Board were George A. Allan, Mona Bandeen, E.G. (Ted) Burton, Arnold Edinborough, Reva Gerstein, Robert Gordon, John Heney, Robert Hicks, and Judge J. Arthur Mullen. Another vacancy was created through the death of Derek Mitchell. Among the new Board members selected by Hirsch were Peter Herrndorf, vice-president of the CBC; Don Harron, the broadcaster, writer, and former Stratford actor; David MacDonald, the former secretary of state in Joe Clark's government; David Silcox, the ubiquitous cultural bureaucrat. They represented a new breed – heavily involved in the culture industry – whose presence was perceived as a way of preventing a recurrence of what had happened at Stratford a year earlier.

Also elected to the Board were Richard M. Clarke, a Montreal businessman; Edward Escaf of London, Ontario, long associated with the London and District Art Gallery; Kenneth W. Lemon, a London, Ontario, accountant; David Raitblat, a business consultant and former Toronto Symphony violinist, married to Reva Gerstein; William Somerville, of Victoria and Grey, Stratford; and

Dr. C. David Tamblyn, a Stratford physician.

Again, there were several nominations from the membership, none successful. With its proxy votes, the Board was assured of having its way. During the voting break, one cynical observer remarked, "So democracy takes its course again." As soon as the new Board convened, Peter Herrndorf complained about these tactics, saying he was embarrassed to have been elected this way.

Attending his last Stratford Board meeting, Robert Hicks kept a low profile. During the voting break midway through the general meeting he put on his coat. When others went back into the auditorium, Hicks wandered into the VIP lounge, the room where Urjo Kareda and Martha Henry had been fired. He chatted with a couple of the theatre staff while his wife waited for him in the lobby of the theatre. At the front door, he paused to tell a friend how disappointed he was that eight or nine Board members who should have made a point of turning out were't there. Then he climbed into his cream-coloured Ford Granada and began his last official journey down the long, winding road from Stratford to Toronto.

Two weeks later a form letter went out to everyone who had served on the Board with Hicks. It was signed by Donald MacLeod, a vice-president of the new Board. "The November 28, 1981 Stratford Festival Board meeting marked the retirement of Bob Hicks as a member of the Board after many years of diligent service to the Festival. At the meeting a number of Board members who served on the Board during Bob's presidency felt that some tribute 'over and above' the customary presentation should be made in recognition of the very great stress and strain to which he was subjected in circumstances that were extremely difficult. [The customary presentation to each retiring Board president was an original design sketch.]

"It was our conclusion that the best way for us to express our affection and admiration for him was to contribute to the endowment of a seat in the Festival Theatre in his honor. The fund was substantially subscribed at a meeting but it was felt all those present and former members who served with him should have the opportunity to contribute to the fund." (The cost of endowing a seat at the Festival is $1,000.)

Just before Christmas, Gary Thomas received a note from Peter Stevens in England, asking the outcome of a wager they had made eight months earlier. Stevens had bet that the Hirsch season would draw less than 75 per cent capacity. Thomas had bet it would draw more than 75 per cent. The final figure was 74.6 per cent. Gary Thomas, who had now emerged as the Festival's great survivor – one of the few who weathered the storm and kept his job – had lost the bet. Peter Stevens collected his last payoff from Stratford.

CHAPTER EIGHTEEN

Exeunt All

Urjo Kareda moved to Toronto, where he became the director of script development for CBC radio drama. In the fall of 1981, Bill Glassco announced that he had decided to step down after ten years as artistic director of the Tarragon Theatre, and that Kareda had been chosen to succeed him, starting in June 1982.

Martha Henry continued to act on stage, screen, and television, but not at the Stratford Festival. Among her stage projects was a production of *The Lion in Winter* in Hamilton and the first production of John Murrell's *Farther West*, presented by Theatre Calgary and directed by Robin Phillips.

Pam Brighton moved to England, where early in 1982 she became the artistic director of the Hull Truck Theatre Company.

Peter Moss carried on as artistic director of the Young People's Theatre in Toronto.

John Dexter continued to be one of the world's most acclaimed directors – one of his great successes was a production at the Mermaid Theatre in London of *The Portage to San Cristobal of A.H.*, based on George Steiner's book about Hitler – but he did not get his own company, and continued to work as a globetrotting freelance.

Peter Stevens worked for a time as a consultant to the Royal Opera, Covent Garden, and then accepted an executive job with the London Tourist Board.

Muriel Sherrin returned to Toronto as a freelance producer and entrepreneur.

Roberta Maxwell begged off again for 1982, though Hirsch was directing *Mary Stuart,* a play he might well have chosen with her in mind. Earlier, Hirsch had created a bit of a flap by jokingly remarking that he might want to do *Hamlet* with Maxwell in the title role.

The press took it seriously, and when Maxwell called Hirsch to ask what was going on, he told her that if she wanted to do it, he would give her the role – but in a workshop production. In the end, she let it go, and *Hamlet* was shelved.

Peter Ustinov came to Toronto in March for the North American premiere of *Evil Under the Sun*, accompanied by Maggie Smith, one of his co-stars in the film. The opening night was a $100-a-ticket benefit for UNICEF. Soon after arriving, Ustinov received a huge box of flowers from Leonard McHardy, who had become a personal assistant to Robin Phillips. When Gina Mallet asked Ustinov whether he would speak to Phillips if Phillips came to the UNICEF party, Ustinov said he would. But Phillips decided not to attend.

R.H. Thomson, making his Stratford debut in 1982, rented Urjo Kareda's house for the season.

Mary Jolliffe, whose job as Stratford's first publicist started her on a distinguished career, returned in May, 1982, to the newly created post of director of communications – which meant she would supervise and co-ordinate the marketing, publicity, and public-relations departments of the Festival.

With the help of a $200,000 grant from Imperial Oil, John Hirsch managed to establish the training program that he considered so essential for Stratford's future.

Robin Phillips became involved in plans to launch a new classical repertory company in Toronto, with a home at Harbourfront. After completing his movie *The Wars* and directing the play *Farther West* in Calgary, Phillips returned to London's West End in May, 1982, to direct *The Jeweller's Shop*, a play written by Pope John Paul II while he was still a priest in Poland. The opening of the play was planned to coincide with the Pope's visit to London. Then Phillips was to direct a production of *The School for Scandal* starring Donald Sinden and featuring Duncan Weldon's new resident company at the Theatre Royal in the Haymarket. (Weldon's partner, Louis Michaels, had died a few months earlier.)

Phillips was tempted to accept the title role in the Vancouver Playhouse production of *The Dresser*, opposite William Hutt, but the dates couldn't be worked out. Some people close to Phillips were betting that, before the end of 1982, he would return to England permanently.

Index

234